D0640074

FICTIONS OF GERMANY:
Images of the German Nation in the Modern Novel

OSMAN DURRANI

Published by Edinburgh University Press for
THE UNIVERSITY OF DURHAM

© Osman Durrani, 1994

Edinburgh University Press Ltd
22, George Square, Edinburgh

Typeset in Linotron Palatino
by Koinonia Ltd, Bury, and
printed in Great Britain by
The Alden Press, Oxford

A CIP record for this book is
available from the British Library

ISBN 0 7486 0491 X

Contents

Textual Note and Acknowledgements

Each of the main novels cited in this book is quoted in the original, followed by an English translation and page references to the German paperback editions, which have been given in the List of Abbreviations. In order to keep the footnotes down to a minimum, I have referred to works listed in the Bibliography by author and year of publication only, followed by a volume number, where appropriate, and a page number. The Bibliography itself contains only those works that have a direct bearing on the main body of my text, as well as a small number of other publications which I found exceptionally helpful.

German quotations are glossed, except where their meaning is self-explanatory or when they have been paraphrased in an adjoining portion of my text or in the notes. At the time of writing, all four novels were available in the United Kingdom, published by Penguin Books. I have consulted the translations by Eugene Jolas (Döblin), Richard and Clara Winston (Hesse), Helen Tracy Lowe-Porter (Mann) and Ralph Manheim (Grass), but have frequently deviated from them in my own versions. All other English renderings are my own.

Several sections of this book have appeared in literary journals, and I should like to take the opportunity to thank the editors of *Modern Language Review, German Life and Letters* and *Oxford German Studies* for their kind permission to reproduce the gist of these articles in the present volume.

I am happy to acknowledge the generous support of the Publications Board of the University of Durham, which helped to finance this book. Acknowledgements are also due to the University of Durham for several terms of research leave, which enabled me to work at home and abroad, to the Inter-Library Loans Service of the University for tracking down obscure material, to Professors Patrick Bridgwater and Alan Bance for advice and regular encouragement, and to my mother, Mrs Melanie Durrani, for tirelessly checking typescripts and proofs at all stages. The responsibility for any remaining errors rests entirely with myself.

effects; both must rely on rhetoric to formulate ideas about what was and what might have been. Eminent historians have claimed that ninety per cent of their work involves the cultivation of good style; in the words of one, writing in the *International Encyclopedia of the Social Sciences*, 'Rhetoric is ordinarily deemed the icing on the cake of history, but our investigation indicates that it is mixed right into the batter.'[1]

The rigorous demarcation between the story and the history, which many of us would accept without questioning, is a modern one. It derives in part from the views of Leibniz about the systematic collection of sources and the need to print them as they were, without 'corrections'. These ideas began to affect research at the beginning of the nineteenth century. In Germany, it was Leopold von Ranke who laid the foundations for a new approach to historical studies by demanding that the scholar's overriding concern should be *Nackte Wahrheit ohne allen Schmuck; gründliche Erforschung des Einzelnen ... ; nur kein Erdichten, auch nicht im Kleinsten, nur kein Hirngespinst*[2] ('the naked truth without adornment, thorough investigation of details ... ; no invention, not even in the most minor matters, and please: no fantasies'). Ranke set his face against invention and insisted that the historian had just one cardinal duty, to reveal *wie es eigentlich gewesen* ('what actually happened'). This would seem to place him firmly on the side of those who wished to excise all purely literary features from the history books; and in fact Ranke listed many devices which he considered to be detrimental to the work of the historian: to attempt, for example, to enter into a person's mind by means of reconstructed monologues or conversations.

But the very same authority that pressed for the acceptance of a rigorous discipline among scholars was acutely aware of the other dimension of his subject: 'History distinguishes itself from all other disciplines in that it is both a science and an art. It is a science when collecting, finding and investigating; it is an art when it reshapes and portrays what it has found and perceived.' Herein lies a paradox: the historian may conduct investigations by collecting and classifying data, but as soon as actual findings are made public, their presentation will depend on authorial rhetoric. Every historian pursues a purpose or is motivated by a desire to praise or condemn, to assess or reverse opinions about individuals and their cultures. The polemic drift displayed by the professional historian can be as great as, or greater than, that found in novels and dramas. Ranke was aware of this, but attempted to play down the significance of the rhetorical component in historical treatises, if only to allow his discipline to partake of the increasing prestige which the natural sciences were enjoying during the nineteenth century.[3] The creative writer has shown a tendency to move in the opposite direction, with the rise of Realism making its mark on nineteenth-century fiction, and social concern combining with documentary methods in more recent times. We often find that the modern narrator tries to appear objective and unbiased, mimicking the perceived role of the historian in this respect, seemingly intent on manoeuvring the reader into viewing him as a trustworthy chronicler of his age.

The argument of this study rests on an assumption that all novels are historical documents whose inherent literary qualities are enhanced by their necessary association with specific social circumstances. At a time when Germany's role in Europe is again under close scrutiny, it seems appropriate to evaluate the work of her major twentieth-century writers by analysing four representative novels not only as literature but also as landmarks in the evolution of her national identity. Sociologists have demonstrated that our images of nationhood derive from a wide variety of sources, among which artistic works are prominent.[4] The present study, however, differs markedly in its scope from the work of imagologists such as Koch-Hillebrecht and Trautmann. Its objective is not to underline the historical context and relevance of the texts at every step or at the expense of all other components, but rather to keep this context in sight as one important factor among many, and as an element that could be decisive for an understanding of the overall design of the texts. The novels selected for the purpose of this investigation were the work of prolific writers who have already been identified by the German public as speaking for their generation. Alfred Döblin penned what is universally recognised as the most enduring monument to the Berlin of the interwar years. Hesse was revered as a sage at home and abroad. Mann addressed himself to and spoke out on behalf of Germany during the Weimar Republic and the years of Fascism, and Grass has long cast off the garb of *enfant terrible* and assumed an important role as a campaigner and educator on the political stage of his country.

An examination of the methods employed by these writers will reveal further affinities with the endeavours of social scientists and historiographers. All of Alfred Döblin's fictions make substantial use of facts and sources. His first major novel, *Wang-lun's Three Leaps*, tells of an uprising in eighteenth-century China, and contains few apparent concessions to the modern Western reader. It assumes an intimate personal knowledge of the Chinese culture and wastes little time on explaining the traditions to which it refers or the technical terms which it applies. It won the coveted Fontane Award in 1915 and was later acclaimed as the first truly modern German novel.[5] While he was working on a subsequent novel about the seventeenth-century general Wallenstein, Döblin declared that he was 'enamoured' of the facts he was unearthing, and that he had a yearning to incorporate them into his text just as he had found them.[6] No-one could dispute that the fascination exerted by the unadulterated, 'raw' fact – viewed as a narrating entity in its own right – comes across with tremendous power in his maturest novel, *Berlin Alexanderplatz*.

Döblin was, after all, a scientist by training. He had elected to study medicine, for very specific reasons:

> *Weil ich Wahrheit wollte, die aber nicht durch Begriffe gelaufen und hierbei verdünnt und zerfasert war. Ich wollte keine bloße Philosophie und noch weniger den lieben Augenschein der Kunst. Ich hatte schon schwere Dinge erlebt und mochte den Spaß der gutsituierten Leute nicht und das Künstlertum, wenigstens das was ich sah, widerte mich an. Dagegen war ja mit Ernst und Energie das Leben geladen ...* [7]

(Because I wanted to get at the truth, but not the kind of truth that had been adulterated and fragmented by abstract concepts. I would have no truck with philosophy on its own, less still with the outwardly pleasing forms of art. I had experienced bitter things and had little time for the recreations of the well-to-do, and the world of art, such as I knew it, filled me with revulsion. By contrast, life was charged with a serious purpose and with energy ...)

Before he had properly embarked upon his career as a writer, Döblin had already begun to abhor the self-indulgence of the creative artist. He wished to do better, to approach life directly. He retained his medical practice in the eastern slums of Berlin long after achieving recognition as a writer. He was therefore in a unique position to monitor the health of the city through direct observation of a wide range of ordinary citizens. It is his intimate knowledge of people, especially the underprivileged, that gives *Berlin Alexanderplatz* its remarkable aura of authenticity. The language of that mythical creature, the 'man in the street', is reproduced in an astonishing variety of registers. The daily life of the city is a major – some would say, *the* major – theme of the book. *Berlin Alexanderplatz* is a valid source of information about the affairs of the capital's citizens in 1928. Tram-routes and cigar prices, pop songs and advertising slogans are quoted repeatedly to fashion an authentic picture of the urban environment. News items and passages from political speeches typify the data that continuously bombard the city-dwellers on their daily round of the streets. Much of this, inevitably, has only a very tenuous connection with the activities in which these people are engaged. It is part of the web of words, the web of significance, which constitutes their culture.

Yet it would be misleading to speak of Döblin as a committed realist. He is the author of a fiction so complex that it would be futile to explain it by reducing it to one single formula. There are certain strands which can be isolated, but the reader must decide how they relate to each other and which, if any, is the dominant one. The documentary layer builds up an authentic picture of Berlin, but this may not be where Döblin's main interests lie. The linguistic medium assumes importance for its own sake, as Döblin reproduces the thought patterns of major and minor characters; the language of twentieth-century Berlin in all its astounding variety is not the least of Döblin's subjects, and one that is in opposition to the outwardly factual layer, since it is here that the inventive powers of the imagination are being plumbed. The interplay of city life and individual careers, of order and chaos, of reason and emotion are dichotomies which Döblin exposes and explores in the novel by means of a narrative strategy that ranges from the use of non-verbal icons to impassioned inner monologues. Oscillations between extremes are suggestive of inner uncertainty, and the open ending of *Berlin Alexanderplatz* is no mere literary device, but the inevitable product of the political climate of the time, which saw the working populace divided between those supporting rightist and those supporting leftist causes: the impression of chaos which the novel generates serves not least as an indicator of the moral disorientation of its time. The reader will recognise that Döblin has created a compelling image of Germany in which it is possible to re-experience the climate of a generation more vividly than in an ostensibly non-fictional analysis.

Hermann Hesse became known throughout the world following his receipt of the Nobel Prize for Literature in 1946, and is remembered today for the influence he exerted on postwar youth in America and Japan, especially during the 1960s.[8] Many of his fictions, like those of Döblin, are set in the remote past or in exotic locations. He was more of a neo-Romantic visionary than a scientific observer of reality, and yet he managed, in several of his early novels, to give gripping accounts of the social pressures which prevented talented individuals from achieving their potential in present-day Europe (*Peter Camenzind, Under the Wheel,* and later in the more conciliatory *Steppenwolf*). A major concern of Hesse's was the education of the young, and he repeatedly returns to the harm that was being done by an ossified system to young people during their formative years. He did not depart from this theme when he came to write what was to be the final novel of his career, *The Glass Bead Game,* but expanded it in various directions, so that the resulting work can be viewed as a satirical account of a future republic of aesthetes under the shadow of a strife-torn present.

When this novel appeared during the Second World War, it was widely felt that Hesse had sublimated his frustrations about the present into a utopian dream of a better future in which the evils besetting his generation had finally been banished. It is only by subjecting the institutions of the republic of Castalia to close, critical scrutiny that one becomes aware of its many defects: its rigid authoritarianism, its axiomatic claim to know best, and the thirst for power which its elitist rulers display. By and by, the better future takes on the appearance of the all-too-familiar present: Hesse, like Döblin, has designed an appropriate fictional monument to the Germany he knew, the land whose intellectual potential was being destroyed by a totalitarian regime which paid lip-service to traditional values but cared little for the rights of the individual and quickly marginalised and disenfranchised those who showed the slightest sign of disloyalty towards an ostensibly common cause. Leading personalities are no less vulnerable in this respect than ordinary individuals, as Master Knecht's rise to fame and sudden disappearance will demonstrate.

Here, the historian will find no detailed descriptions of day-to-day life in the manner of *Berlin Alexanderplatz*; Hesse uses subtle, indirect means to portray the pressures that are brought to bear on people who are caught up in the system. One such 'victim' is the narrator. He is not the playful virtuoso of the type that Döblin had employed, but a hidebound bureaucrat struggling to compile a semi-official biography of a potentially uncomfortable subject: his position is that of an author working within the constraints of conventions which he dare not criticise openly. It is tempting to suggest that in the anonymous Castalian scribe who retells the story, Hesse has painted a frightening picture of an author working under a highly restrictive form of censorship, and by doing so has created a masque of all those authors who, in 'inner emigration' or otherwise in opposition to the state, have had to conceal their critical intentions behind a confusing array of dissembling devices. In this reading of the text, *The Glass Bead Game* will be construed as a fiction of an inward-looking, culturally isolated, rigidly regimented Germany devoted to the service of an ideal that is of questionable value, a nation that is governed by a clique of ruthless mandarins.

While Thomas Mann had left Germany in 1934, he continued to observe and comment on events there from his new home in California. Taking that most German of all myths, the story of Faustus and his pact with the devil, as his starting-point, Mann investigates the cultural heritage of the nation from the days of the Reformation onwards. The progress of the legendary magus, albeit in the modern garb of an avant-garde composer, becomes a cipher for the decline of modern Germany, goaded into the pursuit of the impossible, and incorrigibly blinkered in the conviction of its own superiority. This is a more direct and polemical history of the nation than the ones considered so far, written from the point of view of a man of letters who was striving to find an explanation for his country's tragic descent into self-destruction. While Brecht and others sought to argue that the German people had been led astray by a small minority of evil-doers who had captivated the rest of the populace with tempting promises, Mann reached a very different view of the developments, seeing them as the ultimate consequence of a tendency towards isolation that had its roots in the distant recesses of the nation's history. Only by exploring Germany's past progress, and its lingering legacy in the present, can one understand why the nation lapsed so readily into a kind of collective insanity.

Mann is much more specific than Döblin or Hesse were when it comes to naming individuals whom he sees as responsible for shaping the mentality of twentieth-century Germany. A number of historical figures are introduced into the narrative as examples of great masterminds whose influence on the intellectual evolution of modern Germany can be felt in the doctrines of National Socialism. They include internationally renowned figures such as Martin Luther and Friedrich Nietzsche. Details from the lives of these and several other individuals are woven into the narrative, where they appear as important influences on the composer Adrian Leverkühn. His personal downfall is equated with that of Germany. Even the dates and circumstances of Leverkühn's biography were chosen in such a way as to fit in with key events in the recent past.

The result is a complex web of motifs which represent the nation's cultural history. Whether a culture can be defined, be it as a map, a sieve or a matrix, remains a question which is still

debated by philosophers and anthropologists.[9] Mann's deliberations may not 'define' modern Germany in an academically
rigorous manner, but they give a good indication of reservations
about many national tendencies and characteristics which he saw
as being deeply ingrained in his compatriots. The image he
constructed is, inevitably, one-sided and open to criticism, but
a fiction can do no more than reflect a series of subjective impressions. The central figure of the novel is a composer whose
innovative, highly disciplined and uncompromising compositional technique is indicative of an intellectual rigour verging on
obsessiveness. It is an image which extends the scope of the
criticism that was latent in Hesse's work: the sterile, inflexible
devotion to abstract ideology, the papery aestheticism of the recluse, are at the heart of this modern life in which a disdainful
attitude to conventional morality and a private sexual infatuation
propel a highly talented individual ever closer to self-destruction.

Mann described *Doctor Faustus* as 'my Glass Bead Game with
black beads', and Grass has been called 'the Thomas Mann of the
1980s'.[10] There is a continuity in the modern novel which is also
emphasised by Grass himself in references to Döblin as his 'mentor'. More obviously, and within far wider temporal coordinates
than *Doctor Faustus*, the myth of *The Flounder* attempts to bridge
the gap between the story-book and the history-book. Its point of
departure is a pregnancy: the anonymous Author, both as 'himself' and in the guise of a host of episodic narrators, entertains and
instructs his wife over a period of nine months. The stories he
invents are 'histories', well-researched and yet at the same time
crammed with exuberant invention. Nowhere is the thin dividing
line between fact and fiction thinner and therefore harder to discern than in the eleven historic episodes of this novel. Grass leaves
his readers in no doubt as to his brief: to invent stories which are
more accurate than the so-called 'facts' that have come down to us
via those sources on which the professional historians rely. Thus
his Flounder, a flatfish from a folk-tale, functions as a professor of
history, explaining the stories invented by the Author to a panel of
disaffected feminists, the Feminists' Tribunal, or *Feminal*. He is
forever explaining, relating random events to theories, justifying
and covering up at the same time. His staunch commitment to the
male principle, to reason and to progress, awakens suspicions in
the audience, although some members of the tribunal are swayed
by what he says and come to side with him. In the end, his
conversion to the feminist cause is no less dubious than his earlier
paternalism.

There are many who would maintain that, because the German novel seems rooted in abstract ideas to a greater extent than its Anglo-American or French counterpart, it is essentially serious and closer in tone to a volume of intellectual history than to the kind of fiction that is normally seen as a purveyor of entertainment. As D. J. Enright put it in 1964, 'the most commonly-voiced English objection to German literature has it that this literature is wordy, philosophical, humourless, highly abstract, and crammed with details', an objection, he continues, that is advanced with equal vigour by those who have read some German books and by those who have not, because they already know them to be wordy, highly abstract, crammed with details, etc.[11] To suggest that the modern German novel be approached in relation to the social and political (mis)fortunes which the nation has undergone during the twentieth century, may be to agree, tacitly, with the claim that it resembles an academic thesis or a philosophic theory in disguise. It would be unfortunate if this view were to prevail, if for no other reason than that each of the authors considered in this study had deep reservations about the value of theory and speculation. Döblin's Franz Biberkopf very nearly comes to grief because he tries to implement a resolve to remain 'decent' in an indecent world; Hesse's Magister Ludi fails to find fulfilment in the republic of scholars dedicated to learning and opts for a simple but less sheltered existence outside its protective pale. Adrian Leverkühn would have been spared his personal misery had he not embraced the teachings of his theology professors with perverse and unquestioning enthusiasm, and the opinions and theories of Grass's Flounder prove to be misleading glosses on events in which the male principle is regularly shown up in a poor light. In any contest between ideas and reality, theory and practice, thinking and living, each of these novelists would put life first; each shows the disastrous consequences of attempting to live according to abstract notions of right and wrong while ignoring the empirical world. There is an irony here: the books warn against books, they rest on the idea that ideas mislead us. *Grau, teurer Freund, ist alle Theorie* ('Grey, dear friend, is the colour of all theory'), as Goethe had warned. The novelists of the present would undoubtedly concur. But then Goethe also opined, with consummate irony, for he was one of the most prolific writers the world has ever known: *Es bildet nur das Leben den Mann, und wenig bedeuten die Worte* ('Life alone is what shapes a man, and words are of little significance').[12]

For all the different levels, allegorical and otherwise, on which these novels are open to interpretation, it is certainly legitimate to view them, in the simplest terms, as portraits of individuals: Franz Biberkopf, Josef Knecht, Adrian Leverkühn and the unnamed Author in *The Flounder* are important persons whose development is examined in microscopic detail, and will provide an obvious and convenient point of departure. Two of the novels are formal biographies which record lives as lived from childhood to death; the other two focus on a crucial period in an individual's development over a period of approximately eighteen months. Three of the four characters are artists. Each text is therefore a Bildungsroman ('novel of education'); novels of this type have traditionally enjoyed favour in Germany, where they account for many of the nation's accepted classics.[13] Considerable space is devoted to the role of art and artistic accomplishment in novels such as Goethe's *Wilhelm Meister* and Keller's *Green Henry*; inevitably, they tend to concentrate on the frustrations rather than chronicle the successes of people with artistic temperaments, and such frustrations often stem from an unreceptive social environment and not from problems inherent in the media in which the artists are working.

The novels I have examined were chosen for their links with the past as well as with the twentieth century. Each of them explores the roots of the modern nation, going back hundreds, if not thousands of years to do so, to the age of the tribal witch-doctor, the Stone Age, and beyond. Each was written by a creative thinker in his maturity and is still surrounded by controversy. Although I have attempted to review them as literary and as cultural documents, I do not wish to lose sight of the fact that, within Germany itself, they have all achieved remarkably high sales figures and can thus be said to have popular appeal rather than mere academic or antiquarian interest. It is my view that this fact alone provides the most compelling incentive to investigate them in greater detail.

NOTES

1. J. H. Hexter, cited by Koselleck, Lutz and Rüsen, 1982, pp. 14–20.
2. Rüsen, p. 2.
3. Ibid., p. 5.
4. Koch-Hillebrecht, 1977, pp. 23–7.
5. Falk, 1970, pp. 510ff.
6. See p. 20f., n. 11, below.
7. *Schicksalsreise. Bericht und Bekenntnis*, in: *Autobiographische Schriften und letzte Aufzeichnungen*. Olten: Walter, 1977, p. 209f.
8. See Pfeifer, 1977, and Mileck (in GQ 15), 1978.
9. Geertz, 1975, p. 5.
10. See p. 130, n. 31, and p. 138, n. 6, below.
11. Enright, 1964, p. 93f.

12. *Faust*, line 2, 038; 'Erste Epistel', lines 38f.
13. For an introduction to the *Bildungsroman* tradition, see Swales, 1978. The origins of the term and the theories which it inspired are discussed by Martini, 1961; a full study of the genre is provided by Jacobs and Krause, 1989.

CHAPTER ONE

Alfred Döblin: *Berlin Alexanderplatz* (1929)

Er wird Sie beunruhigen; er wird Ihre Träume beschweren; Sie werden zu schlucken haben; er wird Ihnen nicht schmecken; unverdaulich ist er, auch unbekömmlich. Den Leser wird er ändern. Wer sich selbst genügt, sei vor Döblin gewarnt.

(Günter Grass: *On my Mentor, Döblin*)

You will find him unsettling; he will make your dreams weigh heavily upon you. There will be much for you to stomach; you will find him unpalatable: he is indigestible and at times unwholesome. His readers will find themselves changed by him. Whoever is self-sufficient is warned against reading Döblin.

1. FORMAT

On its simplest and most accessible level, *Berlin Alexanderplatz* (BA) tells the story of one man's attempts to find his feet in the German capital after his release from a long period in prison. In the space of approximately eighteen months, Franz Biberkopf, an outwardly nondescript, even ungainly, manual worker sustains three major and several minor setbacks, until he eventually reaches a state of equilibrium, having fought off the forces of evil, undergone a change of identity and resolved not to commit himself to any political ideologies without weighing up the consequences first. In German literary circles, the debate about the content of *Berlin Alexanderplatz* has tended to revolve around the issue of whether the text is concerned with the character of an individual rather than with the portrayal of the collective life of the city, a point to which we shall return. Whether we see the novel either as a *Bildungsroman* or as a *Großstadtroman* ('novel of character development' or 'urban novel'), it is clearly legitimate to give a preliminary account of it with reference to the activities of its main character, whose fortunes are highlighted in the preamble (BA 7) and in the *précis* sections which precede each of the nine books into which the text is subdivided.

The significance of the novel goes far beyond the events in which its hero (a term to be used sparingly and guardedly) is implicated. The unique texture of the book is determined in part by a relentless probing into the psychology of its major and minor characters, often in connection with their most mundane and trivial actions. Apparent digressions (news items, statistical data, stories and songs) help to bring the city to life with the help of a plethora of inconsequential *minutiae* culled from the day-to-day activities of its citizens. In addition, a fabric of recurring motifs, many of them biblical in their origin, is imposed on the novel, giving it what many critics have described as an 'epic' dimension.[1] The combination of a sweeping main title, *Berlin Alexanderplatz*, and a more mundane sub-title, 'The Story of Franz Biberkopf', may have added to the confusion as to whether the principal subject of the book is Berlin or Biberkopf. Further complications arise from Döblin's own remarks on the nature of the novel, which were published in the short essay *Bemerkungen zum Roman* ('Observations on the Novel') of 1917.

This essay contains the author's best-known theoretical pronouncement, in which he regrets that the reading public has come to expect heroes and to rely upon the creation of suspense and illusions. Invoking Homer, Cervantes, Dante and Dostoevski, Döblin arrives at a definition of a novel as an earthworm which retains its vitality even when cut up into ten separate pieces:

> '*Hier stehe ich, hier sterbe ich', spricht jede Seite. Wenn ein Roman nicht wie ein Regenwurm in zehn Stücke geschnitten werden kann und jeder Teil bewegt sich selbst, dann taugt er nichts.*[2]

> ('Here I stand, here I die', is what each page proclaims. If a novel cannot be cut up into ten separate pieces like an earthworm, and each piece goes on moving independently, it is worthless.)

The nineteenth-century Realists with their carefully constructed plots were, in this view, the exception rather than the rule in their literary practice. For Döblin, the emphasis should be on a loosely constructed plot in which the systematic development of a character is a less vital constituent than the cohesion of individual episodes or the realism produced by local accents and a verifiable ambience.

Whether one should attempt to apply the more radical aspects of this programme to a novel written eleven years later, after an avowed conversion to a more character-oriented approach (in

Manas, a verse epic written in 1927),[3] is doubtful. It is worth noting that *Berlin Alexanderplatz* consists, in effect, of ten sections (a preamble followed by nine books), yet each book begins with a summary in which the fortunes of the central character are invariably singled out for comment. Most of the chapters are interdependent, and the education of Franz Biberkopf within an accurately drawn environment appears to be the author's main concern. The novel has undeniable affinities with the tradition of the *Bildungsroman*, despite its factual topographical focus.

Franz Biberkopf is introduced on the first page, having emerged from the Tegel penitentiary in Berlin after serving his four-year sentence for the homicide of his woman friend, Ida. The moment of his release is an anti-climax; Biberkopf recognises that his real punishment is only just beginning. He is an outcast, born into an alien world. Just as his fears are about to get the better of him, he is befriended by two Jews who relate the cautionary tale of the arrogant Zannowich, in which the dangers of vainglorious arrogance are highlighted. This gives him the necessary impetus to face the world, but also illuminates an important factor in his character: his reckless self-confidence. Responding to a rudimentary physical urge, he seeks out prostitutes, only to discover that he is impotent. The drug 'Testifortan' does not improve matters, but when he visits Ida's sister, Minna, his potency is quickly restored to him. Such is his sense of relief that he now makes a resolution to remain *anständig* (BA 36)('respectable', 'decent') from this day on, come what may.

Book II opens with a kaleidoscopic collage conveying the various facets of urban life, outlining the world in which Franz must contend for a living. He acquires a girlfriend and peddles odds and ends in the street. Eventually he discovers that it is more lucrative to sell National Socialist newspapers than to deal in fancy goods, and his insensitivity to the new political climate which developed during his term in gaol leads to a brawl in Henschke's bar (BA 77–82). The first signs of violence are introduced, and political themes begin to assert themselves: there is a general atmosphere of foreboding, evident in the rhyming *précis*: *Ihr werdet sehen, wie er wochenlang anständig ist. Aber das ist gewissermaßen nur eine Gnadenfrist* (BA 37) ('You'll see him stay decent for many a week. But that's just a respite, so to speak'). Franz's first breakdown occurs in the third book, where he is seen doing the rounds as a door-to-door salesman. He meets a widow, whom he consoles in return for a present of twenty marks, and boasts about the conquest to his mate Otto Lüders, who promptly intimidates the woman and extorts money from her. Franz is devastated, loses faith in everything, and goes into hiding. Book IV finds him vegetating in a rented room, nurturing resentment at his misfortunes. Again, the life of the city is reviewed. It has become more sordid. Now attention focuses on the slaughter-houses, and a parallel is drawn between Franz Biberkopf and the long-suffering biblical figure of Job. Gradually, Franz begins to take an interest in his surroundings, and the first thing he notices is that large-scale thefts are being organised from a flat in the same house. The city seems full of little men like the carpenter, Herr Gerner, who are easily tempted into the criminal underworld.

In Book V, Franz goes back to selling newspapers and quickly drifts into bad company: Meck, Pums, Reinhold. Naively, Franz entrusts himself to them, believing them to be involved in the greengrocery trade since they claim to deal in *Obst* ('fruit': slang for 'stolen goods'). Reinhold is the least attractive member of the gang. He has a sickly yellowish face and a tendency to stammer, wears a military-style greatcoat combined with woollen socks, drinks coffee and lemonade, and is noted for his insatiable appe-tite for women. He becomes Franz's special friend, and the two of them are quick to arrive at the mutually advantageous 'white slavery' agreement (*Schwunghafter Mädchenhandel*, BA 156–63), un-der whose terms Reinhold, who quickly tires of his women, palms off unwanted lady loves onto Franz.

All goes well for a while, but after a few months of symbiotic woman-swapping, Franz refuses to abandon his current second-hand mate, Cilly, to make room for the next cast-off from his friend. He delivers a sermon on the virtues of fidelity, and is delighted when Reinhold appears to agree that orderly domestic arrangements are paramount in this world. But Reinhold is not a 'penitent sinner', and has no intention of letting Franz 'doctor him into becoming a hen-pecked husband' (*'Du möchtest mir wohl zu einem Ehekrüppel zurechtkurieren?'*, BA 174). Revenge comes when Franz is persuaded, very much against his will, to take part in a robbery. During the car-chase that follows, Reinhold opens a door and Franz tumbles out into the road, where he is run over by the vehicle behind.

Franz survives, but only just. The sixth book traces his slow re-covery. His arm is amputated, but two acquaintances, Herbert and Eva, take good care of him, although they fail to persuade him to expose Pums and his gang. He bears no grudge against Reinhold, makes contact with various crooks, finds another woman, Mieze, and lives contentedly off the proceeds of petty larceny, receiving stolen goods, and Mieze's immoral earnings. But a fatal attraction draws him back to Reinhold, who reacts initially with apprehension, and later with cold-blooded mockery to Franz's renewed overtures of friendship: *'Ick kann Krüppel nich leiden, Krüppel ist vor mir ein Mensch, der zu nischt taugt. Wenn ick nen Krüppel sehe, sag ich: denn mal lieber ganz weg damit'* (BA 266) (' "I can't stand cripples, cripple's jess no good for nothing in my book. I look at a cripple and say: better get rid of that thing completely"'). Amazingly, Franz ignores such outbursts and is blissfully happy to have rediscovered his former friend, whom he numbers among the two beings he loves best in this world (BA 269).

Book VII, 'Now the hammer crashes down, it crashes on Franz Biberkopf', narrates the third and final disaster. Franz has become an active member of Pums's gang, and now participates with enthusiasm in their nocturnal raids. Eager to win Reinhold's approval of Mieze, he hides his companion in his flat with the intention of showing her off to him without her knowledge. A violent quarrel erupts between Franz and Mieze at the crucial moment, which has the effect of inflaming Reinhold's passions. Later, he lures her into the country and murders her. In the eighth book, Franz learns what has happened and, in a last, defiant gesture, shoots a policeman while resisting arrest.

Reinhold is brought to justice in the ninth book. Franz has meantime been admitted to the mental hospital at Buch where he remains in a state of suspension. For a time it looks as though he has given up the will to live. But after an altercation with Death, in the guise of Reinhold, he is released from the hospital and acquitted of the murder on the grounds of his confusion. He acquires a new name and a new identity: Franz Karl Biberkopf. His new mentality is never investigated; Döblin observes that this part of his life is over and there is 'nothing further to report at this point' (BA 409).

The original cover of the 1929 edition bore a simple moral in the form of the statement *Man fängt nicht sein Leben mit guten Worten und Vorsätzen an, mit Erkennen und Verstehen fängt man es an und mit dem richtigen Nebenmann*[4] ('The way to a new life is not through good words and resolutions, but through insight and understanding, and the assistance of the right companion'). The sentiment is laudable, but it is difficult to see how Franz Biberkopf could put it into practice, given that no suitable companion presents himself for consideration within the text. A more specific political warning is to be perceived at the end:

> *Sie marschieren oft mit Fahnen und Musik und Gesang an seinem Fenster vorbei, Biberkopf sieht kühl zu seiner Türe raus und bleibt*

noch lange ruhig zu Haus. Halt das Maul und fasse Schritt,
marschiere mit uns andern mit. Wenn ich marschieren soll, muß
ich das nachher mit dem Kopf bezahlen, was andere sich
ausgedacht haben. Darum rechne ich erst alles nach, und wenn es
so weit ist und mir paßt, werde ich mich danach richten. Dem
Mensch ist gegeben die Vernunft, die Ochsen bilden statt dessen
eine Zunft. (BA 410)

(They often march past his window with their flags, their
music and singing. Biberkopf looks out calmly through his
door, he'll not join them any more. March in step, stop the
fuss, march along with the rest of us. But if I join in now, I'll
have to pay later with my life for what the others have
thought up. That's why I shall work everything out for
myself, and when everything is sorted out and the time is
right, then I shall act accordingly. Reason is given unto man;
beasts of burden form a clan.)

Embedded in these lines is an indication of Döblin's views on
Germany's uncertain prospects for the future. The precise terms
on which Franz Biberkopf's regeneration is effected remain elusive, but the concluding lines leave a clear impression of the
apprehension he feels at the sight of the menacing columns of
marching men who have become the latest feature of the urban
landscape. These sparse comments betray their author's reservations about what the future may hold in store for Franz and for his
country.

2. FRANZ BIBERKOPF

It is not easy to sympathise with the 'hero' of this novel; there can
be few central characters in works of fiction who come equipped
with as many unappealing traits as does Franz Biberkopf. He
emerges as ugly, weak, unstable, easily led, stubborn, violent,
amoral, stupid, sentimental, reactionary and possessive, to name
but a few of his most eye-catching qualities. The crimes he commits in the course of the narrative are legion. The womenfolk in
his life are treated especially badly. Ida dies of injuries she sustains at his hands, Minna is raped, the widow is robbed by a
'friend' of his, Reinhold's first cast-off – a drayman's wife – is
disposed of, Cilly is abandoned, Mieze is shown off to Reinhold
who then kills her, and Eva, who survives, is denied the child she
desires. His friends are either criminals or unremarkable non-
entities, even when presented positively, as Herbert and Eva are.

Most of the women in his entourage, from Ida to Mieze, survive by prostituting themselves. The references to Franz's appearance are not suggestive of an attractive exterior. Franz is presented as a 'raw-boned, big fellow' who is 'as fat as a pig' (*Dick wie ein Schwein, BA* 265). His ugliness is stressed on several occasions. At the end of Book I, the narrator calls him *ein grober, ungeschlachter Mann von abstoßendem Äußern* (*BA* 36) ('a rough, uncouth man, repulsive of aspect'). The most telling indication of how he looks comes as Franz inspects his own reflection in the mirror. The following interior monologue gives his observations an aura of vividly naturalistic authenticity:

> *Hat der Kerl eine Visage. Striemen auf der Stirn, wovon bloß rote Striemen, von der Mütze, und die Gurke, Mensch, sone dicke, rote Neese, das braucht aber nicht vom Schnaps zu sein, das ist kalt heute; bloß die gräßlichen ollen Glotzaugen, wie ne Kuh, woher ich bloß sone Kalbsaugen habe und so stiere, als wenn ich nicht mit wackeln kann. Als wenn mir einer Sirup rübergegossen hat.* (*BA* 140)

(What a mug this 'ere fellow has; red lines on 'is forehead, wonder where the red lines come from, from the cap, and that nose like a gherkin, man, what a fat red smeller, not necessarily the fault of the brandy though, it's cold today ... but those ghastly old goggle-eyes jess like a cow, where the 'eck did I get such calf's eyes and that way of staring with them, as if I couldn't blink 'em prop'ly. Like someone'd poured gooey stuff all over me.)

Nor do his intellectual properties hold out much promise. He is stubborn and clings rigidly to fixed ideas and principles in a way which his friends often find hard to accept. Whenever misfortune strikes, he reacts by retreating into a world of his own and refuses to come out of his shell until he is ready to do so on his own terms. This is especially evident when Herbert and Eva advise him to pursue the people responsible for the incident in which he lost his arm. All he does is to shrug off their well-meant suggestions. His friends are astounded by his sheer gullibility.

> '*Na und was wolltest du denn am Sonntag, wie du mit dem gegangen bist.*' '*Wir wollten Obst abholen für die Markthalle.*' *Franz liegt ganz ruhig. Herbert bückt sich über ihn, um seine Miene zu sehen.* '*Und das hast du geglaubt?*' (*BA* 200)

('Well then what were you up to that Sunday when you went off with him?' 'We went to fetch fruit for the covered market.' Franz lies there without moving. Herbert bends down over him to look at his face. 'And you believed that?')

Eva may love him to the extent of wanting to bear his child, but she refers to him as *ein gutmütiges Schaf* (BA 249) ('a good-natured simpleton'), warning Mieze to keep a close watch over him and make sure that he doesn't do something really stupid. His acquaintances regularly take him to task for his faults and misdemeanours: for drinking too much, mixing with bad company and dabbling in politics. Mieze's devotion to him does not blind her to the negative side of his character:

> *aber der Franz, der ist ein bißchen dumm, der läßt sich zu alles benutzen. Darum haben sie ihn ausm Auto geschmissen. Sone Brüder sind det. In son Verein geht der.* (BA 295)

(but Franz, why he's a little bit stupid, he lets them do as they please with him. That's why they chucked him out of the car. That's the kinda chaps them is. That's the kinda club he's in.)

If his closest associates have their well-founded reservations about him, it is hardly surprising that the underworld should see him as little more than a willing tool in their hands. The first brawl in Henschke's bar occurs when Franz readily allows himself to be provoked into singing patriotic songs, an activity which gives the militants the cue for which they have been waiting. When he starts to brag, selfishly and carelessly, about his experiences with the young widow, Lüders takes the initiative to visit her and humiliate her. Reinhold views Franz as little more than a welcome means of disposing of unwanted girlfriends. Clearly, his self-centredness and passivity prevent him from recognising both Reinhold's depraved character and his antipathy towards him: *Is een Hornochs, der Biberkopf ... das Schwein mit seine großen Glubschoogen, der Ludewig, das Vieh* (BA 279) ('What a bloody fool, this Biberkopf ... the swine with the big slimy goggle-eyes, that double-dealing pimp, the beast'. There is little indication as to why, in view of this animosity, Biberkopf is so strongly attracted to Reinhold as to 'love' (BA 269) him; a malignant fate appears to propel him towards the exponent of evil.

Yet Döblin goes to considerable lengths to counterbalance the ugly exterior and limited intellect of Franz Biberkopf, supplying many redeeming features which balance and outweigh his faults. Many of these reveal the kind of simplicity that may be related to ideals of meekness and Christian humility. His quest is for

Anständigkeit, for decency in an indecent world. He is repeatedly affronted by the uncaring or deceitful attitude of others. For a long time, he refuses to believe that Reinhold and Pums are members of a criminal fraternity. Swapping girlfriends seems, initially, an exciting new ruse, but before long the novelty wears off and a desire for stability takes over. At this point Franz does not simply disown his friend – he is moved to 'convert' him to a more humane attitude to women. The Christian motif of the repentant sinner is deliberately alluded to in the context of Franz's moral endeavours (*BA* 173). This motif may be inappropriate to Reinhold, but it serves to identify a paradoxical aspect of Franz's role. He reacts to each successive humiliation by turning the other cheek; he is a 'respectable' murderer, a sinner endowed with a streak of saintliness.

Passivity may be viewed as a virtue or a vice, but the passivity displayed by Franz always stands in sharp contrast to the evil of the world. The *précis* sections which introduce each chapter tend to portray him as sinned against rather than as sinning, as a victim rather than an active perpetrator of evil. The problem on which the narrator focuses is that Franz does not learn from his experience of wickedness in the world around him. It is perhaps less obvious that he is also a victim of bad luck, not intending, it would seem, to murder his mistress Ida, and after his release from gaol falling in with unsuitable comrades (Lüders, Meck, Reinhold). It is hard to agree with Müller-Salget and others who see in him an example of arrogance,[5] when one considers the detailed manner in which the social background is sketched in by Döblin. The *minutiae* of which Döblin is so keen an observer point towards a world in which the state assumes an indifferent stance towards the individual. The novel begins and ends with this theme. The prison sentence cuts him off from society for four years in a manner that mirrors the four-year period of military service which he discharged in the First World War. Then the system releases him, without adequate preparation, into the bustling city again. The two failed attempts to restore his self-respect through visits to prostitutes show how unready he is for social contacts. His prison sentence has rendered him less able to cope with other people and less aware of the changing political situation than he needs to be if he is to survive. The provocation he receives in Henschke's bar reveals another aspect of his ignorance: Franz is naively unaware that the singing of German patriotic songs in working men's drinking places is no longer acceptable in 1928 – something he would have realised earlier had he not been locked away.

Döblin's critical stance towards the German authorities emerges again when Franz is arrested in the final chapter of Book VIII. Here we have clear evidence of the workings of a police state, when the popular café Alexanderquelle is raided for no obvious reason by a police squad. Everyone is taken into custody for identification. The chapter-heading *Am Alexanderplatz steht das Polizeipräsidium* (BA 364) ('The Police Headquarters are located on the Alexanderplatz') makes the connection between the novel's location and the police, who on this occasion are clearly guilty of excessive zeal, as the unfavourable comparisons with Manchester, London and New York indicate:

> *Die Alexanderquelle ist dickvoll, es ist Freitag, wer Lohn hat, geht mal einen heben, Musik, Radio, am Ausschank vorbei schieben sich die Bullen, der junge Kommissar spricht mit einem Herrn, die Kapelle hört auf: Aushebung, Kriminalpolizei ... An der Tür steht ein Mann, den haben zwei Schupos gefaßt, er brüllt: ich war in Manchester, in London, in New York, so was passiert nicht in keine Großstadt, so was gibts nicht in Manchester, in London. Sie bringen ihn auf den Trab.* (BA 365f.)

(The Alexanderquelle is chock-a-block, it's Friday, those who've had their wages come along for a jar, music, radio. The cops sidle along the bar, the young inspector talks to somebody, the band stops playing: it's a raid by the Special Branch ... A fellow is standing by the door, two cops have grabbed him, he's shouting: I've been to Manchester, London, New York, things like this don't go on in no other city, they don't do this sorta thing in Manchester or in London. They move him on.)

This episode is one of many references to the way in which the state fails to administer justice in an equitable manner; its function must be to pose questions about the basis of Biberkopf's quest for 'respectability'.

By contrast with the uncaring agents of law and order, Franz is open and trusting in his dealings with others. We often see him buying food and drink for his companions, so much so that he attracts habitual hangers-on. He insists on repaying every penny of his debt to Herbert, and takes a bunch of flowers to the widow on his disastrous second visit. His crimes are done on impulse; he is often violent when provoked into jealousy, but equally quick to seek reconciliation (BA 300–3). There is a marked contrast here with the actions of cold-blooded professionals like Pums, and especially with the calculating, unpredictable Reinhold.

Another factor which helps to build up a favourable view of Franz is provided by the investigations of his recurring bouts of depression. These are repeatedly recorded in graphic detail, especially in Book VIII, where conversations between various doctors treating him are reproduced. It is known that Döblin worked in the same clinic into which he places Franz Biberkopf, Buch near Berlin. Investigations into the medical motifs will, however, reveal a purpose other than the addition of yet another documentary layer to the work.

Having spent time showing Franz suffering from clinical depression, Döblin is able to propel his readers into a position where it becomes difficult to deny him their sympathy. Several times, Franz is shown capitulating before the evil that is latent in the world, until a process of recovery sets in. This development is gradual and organic. It is the healing process that seems to interest Döblin more than the disasters which befall Franz, however graphic their description when they occur. The novel begins with a new lease of life after the prison sentence, and ends on a note of promise, although specific information about how Franz's recovery is effected remains difficult to deduce from the novel as it stands.

In his attitudes, Franz does not reveal himself as extraordinary. In *La Chute*, Camus defines modern man in a single sentence as the creature who 'fornicated and read the papers'[6] – a definition that seems eminently applicable to Franz. He is forever picking up newspapers and surveying the news-stands, and the extracts from news items with which the reader is frequently deluged give a good indication of what may be passing through Franz's mind as he ambles from one kiosk to another, his mind failing to filter the information sufficiently for it to crystallise into coherent opinions. In this respect, the structure of the work reproduces the structure of its main character's mind.

Ironically, Franz learns little from the organs of mass communication which influence and dominate public opinion in his time. His political position remains vague. There are periods when he gives service to the Fascist cause, mainly, it would seem, because of the remuneration which it offers. He prides himself on his 'Aryan' descent when it is a question of winning over customers, but remains cautious about encouraging people to boycott shops owned by Jews (*BA* 56). In a typical gesture that sums up his half-hearted position, he removes his swastika armband before entering a bar (*BA* 69). He supports right-wing views on the 'law-and-order' issue, while attending Anarchist meetings and engaging in petty crime, unconcerned about any inconsistencies.

When Franz rejects all political groupings of whatever colour at the end of the novel, however, his position resembles one of critical detachment such as may result from an insight into the relativity of all ideologies. At this point, the author's interest shifts away from psychology towards a moral cause.

Clumsy and ungainly, well-intentioned but easily misled, sentimental and brutal at the same time, Franz Biberkopf comes close to typifying the moral disorientation of a weakened and tormented Germany, attempting to preserve its dignity by decent means but vulnerable to the stimulus of evil. His responses are conditioned by his environment, as his language is by clichés. Yet despite his feckless passivity, there is another stratum in Franz that makes him rise above the generation whose characteristic dilemmas are so often evidenced in his behaviour.

3. LANGUAGE

The most pervasive stylistic feature of *Berlin Alexanderplatz* is the Berlin dialect in which many parts of it are written, not only the thoughts and speeches of the main participating characters, but narrative passages as well. Walter Benjamin speaks of the novel as 'a monument to the Berlin patois' (*ein Monument des Berlinerischen*).[7] Obviously, it follows that characters who speak in dialect must also think in dialect, and Döblin constructs his interior monologues accordingly. But just as he blurs the borderlines between conversations and inner thought-processes, he includes maɪ y passages in which dialect forms jostle with standard German, a technique which further complicates the question as to whose voice is heard at a given moment. Often, the narrative voice cannot be positively attributed to a specific character or narrator.

While it is thus true that the author seems to slide in and out of the idiom of his characters at random, close inspection will show that this process is controlled more carefully than a cursory inspection would suggest. Reading through a passage in which standard German and vernacular intertwine with one another, it is tempting to assume that the objective voice of the narrator avails itself of *Hochdeutsch*, while the figures from the story lapse into colloquial and regional forms of self-expression. This relatively neat separation between the narrated and the narrating voices contributes to the tension which patently exists between the impersonal, panoramic sections of the novel and the more narrowly character-oriented passages, a tension which has ultimately led to the twofold reception of *Berlin Alexanderplatz* as either an 'urban novel' or a 'novel of character development', an issue which will receive further consideration in due course (see section 10, below). The reader's attention is divided between two subjects, the city itself and its individual inhabitants, and in this sense the coexistence of two levels of language, private and official, seems appropriate to its twin themes.

The linguistic stratification of the novel can also be viewed in the context of Franz Biberkopf's personal dilemma. Torn between the ethos of 'respectability' and the pull of the instinct, he is a prey to the antithetical lure of the spirit and the senses, and these two realms are represented by a competition between the language of the mind (a standardised form of German) and the language of the emotions (a dialect enriched with many personal touches). While Franz oscillates between conflicting values, the narrator cannot be pinned down to either 'proper' or 'idiosyncratic' German, but seems to hover somewhere between the two idioms.

A more rigorous inspection of the text will show that the explanation given above simplifies a highly complex procedure of employing different linguistic registers at different times. The vernacular used, not merely by Franz but by most of the other figures as well, is in constant flux, as characters increase or reduce their colloquialisms in different situations, partly as a result of the subject they are discussing, the people they address, or for other less obvious reasons. The effect of this is difficult enough to assess in the original, and virtually impossible in translation. It should be remembered that there is a more pronounced tradition of writing in regional dialects in Germany than there has ever been in the English-speaking world, and that the German Naturalists who were active at the end of the nineteenth century did much to publicise the potential of dialects, including *Berlinerisch*, as vehicles of genuine and profound emotions. The basic constituents of the Berlin idiom, *Berliner Schnauze*, include a predilection for humour and the creation of odd metaphors, and its speakers are noted for their quick-wittedness. The sources of the idiom are too complex to delve into here: they include common north German slang, Yiddish and French.[8]

A sample of Döblin's narrative style will help to convey the unique linguistic texture of the novel, in which perspectives frequently change in mid-sentence. The following passage shows Franz setting off reluctantly to find Pums and deliver a message. He is plainly annoyed at having agreed to take on this chore and would prefer to go home to Cilly.

> *Flucht Franz, geht los, ein Wetter, immer machen, Mensch, ich will nach Hause, ich kann doch schließlich die Cilly ooch nicht*

warten lassen. So ein Affe, ich hab doch nicht meine Zeit gestohlen. Er rennt. An einer Laterne steht ein kleiner Mann, liest in einem Heft. Wer ist das eigentlich, den kenn ich doch. Da blickt der her, sofort auf Franz zu: 'Ach Sie, Herr Nachbar. Sie sind doch der aus dem Haus, wo die Wringmaschine und der Eisschrank waren. Ja. Hier geben Sie die Karte ab, nachher, wenn Sie nach Haus gehen, sparen wir Porto.' Drückt Franz die Postkarte in die Hand, infolge widriger Umstände zurücktreten. Darauf wandert Franz Biberkopf ruhig weiter, die Postkarte wird er Cilly zeigen, ist ja gar nicht so eilig. Er freut sich über den verrückten Kerl, den kleinen Postfritzen, der immer rumlooft und kooft und hat keen Geld, aber ein Vogel hat er, das ist schon kein gewöhnlicher Piepmatz, das ist ein ausgewachsenes Huhn, wovon ne Familie leben kann. (BA 182f.)

(Franz swears, trots off (*facts, telegraphic*), awful weather, always doing things (*Franz's thoughts, telegraphic*), for Pete's sake, I want to go home, I can't keep Cilly waiting all day either (*his thoughts become more specific*). What an idiot, my time is just as precious (*reflections on the man who sent him on this errand*). He starts to run (*fact*). A small man is standing by a lamp-post, reading a little booklet (*Franz's observation*). Who's this chap, I think I know him (*Franz's thoughts*). Now he looks in this direction (*from Franz's point of view*), addressing himself directly to Franz (*fact, observed by the narrator*): 'Hey, you there, aren't you from the house where the mangle and fridge were (*the other man asks a question*). Yes (*Franz answers, or maybe the other man supplies the answer himself*). Here, take this card, deliver it when you get back, save us the postage' (*the other man's words*). Thrusts the postcard into Franz's hands (*fact*), cancel on account of untoward circumstances (*bureaucratic-sounding message on the card*). Thereupon Franz Biberkopf proceeds calmly on his way (*narrator, leisurely*), he'll show the card to Cilly, it's not all that urgent (*gradual shift from narrator to Franz*). He's amused by that crank, the little postcard-wally (*Franz invents a nickname*), chasing 'is guts out buyin' stuff and ain't got no money (*dialect becomes broader*), but he's as nutty as a fruitcake (*popular cliché*), and that ain't no ordinary fruitcake but a giant-size one what a whole family could live off for a week (*Franz embellishes the cliché.*)

The panoramic content of the novel is matched by the wide range and variety of its language. Variations in diction are used to reflect changes in perspective; as the above passage shows, these are liable to take place anywhere, even in mid-sentence. In a single short paragraph we may have a description of the present, an intimation of some future occurrence, and various unattributed quotations, not all of which can be traced to an identifiable source:

> *Franz sitzt mit dem Langen in der Prenzlauer Straße … nur zwei Nummern weiter ist das Haus, wo nach circa 4 Stunden ein Dicker ohne Hut raustreten wird und Cilly anquatschen wird; sie geht weiter, den nächsten wird sie bestimmt nehmen, son Schuft, der Franz, Gemeinheit.* (BA 182)

> (Franz is sitting with the tall chap in Prenzlau Street … just two doors away is the house from which some four hours later a fat bloke without a hat will emerge to chat Cilly up; she walks past him, she's bound to take the next guy, what a bastard Franz is, what cheek.)

A wider range of techniques is used in those sections of the novel in which straightforward descriptions lead on into symbolism and the montage of seemingly unrelated material. The episode in which Franz and Mieze get drunk together is followed by an interior monologue, when Franz wakes up the following morning and struggles to remember how he got into this situation. Quickly, his thoughts move away from the present to memories of the accident: *Von wo tut mir die Schulter so weh, mir haben sie den Arm abgehauen* (BA 261) ('Why does this shoulder hurt so much, they've chopped off me arm'). What began as a monologue soon degenerates into expressions of inarticulate rage: *Au, au weih, au, auh, auh.* At this point it seems that Döblin cannot push his linguistic virtuosity to further extremes; but a new register is opened with the introduction of a symbolic fly, which climbs up a potted plant in a manner suggestive of a new desire that may now be stirring within Franz:

> *Die Fliege krabbelt und krabbelt, sie sitzt im Blumentopf, der Sand rieselt von ihr ab, der macht ihr nichts aus, sie schüttelt ihn weg, sie streckt den schwarzen Kopf vor, sie kriecht heraus.* (loc cit.)

> (The fly in the flower-pot creeps around endlessly, sand trickles off it, yet it doesn't mind, it shakes the sand off, sticks out its black head and crawls into the open.)

The symbols quickly become more ominous: after the black fly comes the Whore of Babylon, the biblical incarnation of evil, a fitting herald to Franz's desire to rekindle his relationship with Reinhold.

Variety of styles is matched by variety of subject matter. The title of the novel suggests that the author's concern is with a depiction of life in the city, and urban life is evoked in numerous different ways. There is the stratum of factual topographical information which entails frequent references to public places, to streets and buildings, and to bus and tram routes. The complexity of the city's transportation system, reflecting as it does the complexity of mass communication in a modern, urbanised society, receives prominence. Lists of tram stops and interchanges are printed on the 'mysterious long tickets' like meaningful runes: *Linie 12 Siemensstraße DA Gotzkowskistraße C, B, Oranienburger Tor C, C, Kottbuser Tor A* (BA 147f.). Joyce and Dos Passos produce similar lists in their novels *Ulysses* and *Manhattan Transfer*. The pictorial emblems at the beginning of Book II are another instance of the author's attempt to summarise the plethora of institutions at work in the city, cleverly breaking new ground and correctly foreseeing the increasing use of icons in communicating information of this type by visual means during the present century.

The modern factory and the telephone directory both reflect the sprawling quality of our institutions; Döblin refers to the former via the latter, and ends up with a concise evocation of an electricity works:

> Die AEG. *ist ein ungeheures Unternehmen, welches nach Telefonbuch von 1928 umfaßt: Elektrische Licht- und Kraftanlagen, Zentralverwaltung, NW 40, Friedrich-Karl-Ufer 2-4, Ortsverkehr, Fernverkehr Amt Norden 4488, Direktion, Pförtner ...* (BA 41)

> (The AEG is an immense corporation, embracing, according to the 1928 telephone directory: Electric Light and Power generation, Central Administration NW 40, Friedrich-Karl-Ufer 2–4, Local and Long Distance operations, North 4488, General Manager, Porter's Office ...)

Here again the syntax is accretive, the text becomes a list of locations, and these disjointed lexical units reproduce the seemingly endless ramifications of an impersonal but vital modern industry. Lists of cigar prices and information about the animals killed in the city's abattoirs (BA 145, 198) have a similar function.

4. COLLAGE, MONTAGE AND FILMIC DEVICES

Much of the material examined so far is of a random and ephemeral nature. Cigar prices can be expected to change, and the weather reports and day-to-day news items certainly will. Large sections of the novel appear to be given over to an apparently unstructured hotchpotch of unrelated, often inconsequential 'facts': stock-exchange quotations (*BA* 167), sporting fixtures (*BA* 150), extracts from political speeches (*BA* 105) and a host of minor news reports, some of which are tragic ('Russian student shoots fiancée', *BA* 167), curious ('What is the price of a woman , between friends?' *BA* 30) or just plain boring ('Meeting organised by allotment holders from Treptow-Neukölln and Britz', *BA* 150f.). The state of the manuscript has been cited in support of the view that press-cuttings were inserted more or less at random,[9] but in fact the version in the *Deutsches Literaturarchiv* at Marbach contains very few newspaper clippings and does not invite comparison with the illogical, accretive methodology of Dadaists such as Kurt Schwitters. The mounting of news reports onto the texts seems, more often than not, to serve a specific purpose within the overall narrative design.

Book v ends with the account of Franz Biberkopf's 'accident' after his reluctant participation in a robbery. We learn that he is seriously injured and wonder if and how he will ever recover. The narrative is interrupted by a casual reference to a famous film diva by the name of Raquil, who is pictured emerging from an overnight express train from Paris: *Mit den Worten: 'Ich bin wahnsinnig neugierig auf Berlin' besteigt die berühmte Frau ihren Wagen und entschwindet der nachwinkenden Menschenmenge in der morgendlichen Stadt (BA* 190) ('With the words: "I'm just crazy to see Berlin", the celebrated lady enters her car and is spirited away from the crowds who have gathered to wave at her in the city this morning'). Coming as it does immediately after the attempt on Biberkopf's life, which culminated in a car-chase in the best cinematographic tradition, this paragraph invites us to compare what we have just read with the artificiality of the cinema. Ironically, in so doing, we are comparing the artificiality of one medium with that of another, in such a way that the divisions between fact and fiction are blurred: the real film-star enters a work of fiction where she is quoted as saying that she wishes to see the real Berlin; but within the terms of the novel, the real Berlin is the world of its fictional hero, whom she will not (and cannot) meet. At this point, the novel reveals – perhaps more strikingly than anywhere else – its own textuality.

Not that this is the only intrusion by an author who delights in using 'extraneous' factual material to alert his readers to the illusory nature of what they are reading. The weather report preceding the robbery in Book VII (*BA* 282) is another such item of information which the narrator supplies for the seemingly benign purpose of producing a rounded picture of events. In so doing, he also slows down the pace of the narrative, heightens the suspense and draws attention to his own role.

In addition to verifiable interpolations such as extracts from the telephone directory or mortality statistics, events of a more private nature are often alluded to. They help to flesh out the picture of life in the big city, but often seem to have a particular relevance to Franz Biberkopf as well. An elderly man in horn-rimmed spectacles is involved in a questionable assignation with a schoolgirl; their conversations are reported in detail. It emerges that they are both from 'respectable' backgrounds (he has a telephone at work, she has been practising Chopin). Theirs is a sordid affair: '*Aber heut nicht lange, ich hab so wenig Zeit, ich muß nach Hause, ich zieh mich nicht aus, Sie tun mir nicht weh*' (BA 47) ('But not for long today, I'm in such a hurry, I've got to get home, I'm not undressing, you'd better not hurt me'). This is more than a slice of raw life in the late nineteenth-century Naturalist tradition: it has the effect of exposing the flaw in the pursuit of respectability, the cause which Franz has recently decided to espouse. If respectable people aren't respectable, how can there be hope for him? The same point is made in an excursus concerning a married man who commits an indiscretion with a young boy in a hotel (BA 62f.).

This is not to say that every fleeting episode has a significance for the development of character or the import of the work as a whole. Soft-focusing takes place with little apparent concern for the narrative line, especially at the beginning of Books II, IV, V, and VII, where the scene is set by a kaleidoscopic parade of visual impressions. Sometimes the author imitates the effect of a camera zooming in on the action. At the beginning of Book IV, for example, a general survey of the neighbourhood gives way to a floor-by-floor examination of the house to which Franz has withdrawn after his betrayal by Lüders.

It is no coincidence that one is tempted to speak of cameras and filmic devices when talking about this novel: the film as a genre had a powerful influence on Döblin. Walter Ruttmann's documentary *Berlin – Die Symphonie einer Großstadt* ('Berlin. The Symphony of a Big City'), released in 1927, used the technique of combining clashing visual images to record one day in the life of the German capital. It is beyond doubt that the atmospheric quality of this film had a major impact on the form of *Berlin Alexanderplatz*. In Ruttmann's film, sarcastic comments on society are commonplace. Shots of cows at the abattoir are blended into the surge of workers at suburban stations; the lunchtime bustle at fashionable restaurants gives way to feeding time at the zoo. The collage principle is employed by Döblin to produce the same effect: seemingly disjointed images are juxtaposed to reveal the thin dividing line between civilisation and anarchy. It is no coincidence that several excellent films have been made of this novel.[10] Musical motifs are incorporated into the text in various ways. When Franz eventually decides to make contact with Reinhold again after losing his arm, we see him making his way through the streets to the dingy room where his former friend is reading the paper. The expedition is treated as a military venture, hence the chapter-heading *Vorwärts, Schritt gefaßt, Trommelgerassel und Bataillone* (BA 262) ('Quick march, in step, roll of drums and battalions'). The words of a folk-song keep recurring, supplying martial imagery which underscores the dangers to which Franz is exposing himself:

> *Wenn die Soldaten durch die Stadt marschieren,*
> *Schauen die Mädchen aus Fenstern und Türen,*
> *Ei warum, ei darum ...* (loc. cit.)

> (When all the soldiers come marching through town,
> Then from their windows the young girls look down,
> Why, tell me why ...)

The words recall the catchy tune of this song, which is 'heard' by the reader at various stages during this chapter, e.g. while Reinhold is sitting on his own in his room, and later, when Franz is in conversation with him. By evoking a tune in the reader's mind, Döblin is able to supply the equivalent to film music within the text of his novel.

The terms *collage* and *montage* derive from the visual arts, and their significance in *Berlin Alexanderplatz* shows the extent of the non-literary influences on twentieth-century fiction. The musical term *leitmotif* is another example of an important structural principle that has its roots outside the genre of prose fiction. Of course, these terms acquire new facets when applied to different artistic media. In the visual arts, the principle of collage is employed in the still-life, a composition in which elements from various walks of life are depicted side by side and thus put into new, unexpected relationships with one another. The opening pages of Book IV, *Eine Handvoll Menschen um den Alex* ('A Bunch of People around the Alex'), could be described as a literary still-life, in which people at work, shoppers, newfangled fire-extinguishers, a political manifesto, drainage equipment, an advert for beer, are picked out one

by one like museum pieces in an exhibition devoted to the twentieth-century urban environment.

Montage denotes something more specific, usually a deliberate
contrasting of two essentially different media: bus tickets
mounted onto an oil painting. In the novel, this tends to occur in
the form of extraneous material that is divorced from its original
context and 'mounted' onto the narrative in order to allow the
author to make a specific point. Just as Franz is about to assault his
deceased friend's sister Minna, the narrative is interrupted by a
short paragraph in which we are asked to ponder the question
'What is the price of a woman, between friends?' The answer
comes straight out of the gossip columns of the press:

> *Das Londoner Ehescheidungsgericht sprach auf Antrag des*
> *Kapitäns Bacon die Scheidung wegen Ehebruchs seiner Frau mit*
> *seinem Kameraden, dem Kapitän Furber, aus und billigte ihm eine*
> *Entschädigung von 750 Pfund zu.* (BA 30)

> (The London divorce court agreed to the dissolution of
> Captain Bacon's marriage on the grounds of his wife's
> adultery with his associate Captain Furber, and granted him
> damages amounting to £750.)

This is the answer to the biblical question about the value of a
woman (cf. Proverbs XXXI:10). There follows a sarcastic comment
to the effect that 'The captain does not appear to have placed too
high a price on his unfaithful wife' (loc. cit.). This apparently
casual observation will not be wasted on the attentive reader of
Franz Biberkopf's story. Here the law courts themselves, as pillars
of the 'respectable' establishment, are seen pricing a woman as
though she were no more than a commodity; and this just after
Franz's failure with the two prostitutes whose love he had tried to
purchase, a failure presumably due to the impersonal, venal
nature of the transaction. Yet the example of Captain Bacon's
divorce settlement shows that the society which Franz is trying to
enter is itself organised entirely along mercantile lines.

The importance of devices such as these is evidenced by the fact
that, in relation to the length of the novel, interior monologues
account for approximately one tenth of the text, and factual or
otherwise extraneous material for a further tenth. But the term
'extraneous' is misleading in view of the many correspondences
between Franz Biberkopf's career and other events which at first
sight appear to have scant bearing on him. Döblin repeatedly
declares his love of facts for their own sake: *Ich war verliebt,*
begeistert von diesen Akten und Berichten. Am liebsten wollte ich sie roh

verwenden[11] ('I was thrilled by, enamoured of these documents and reports. I would have liked to use them neat'). By the time he came to write *Berlin Alexanderplatz*, both plot and excursus sections were grafted on to a stock of mythical references which overshadow the narrative and the documentary layers of the work.

5. RECURRENT MOTIFS

In a much-quoted passage from the autobiographical Epilog, Döblin answers the charge that *Berlin Alexanderplatz* was little more than an adaptation of Joyce's Ulysses to a German setting:

> *Aber blind, wie einmal Kritiker unserer Epoche sind, konnten sie bequem mit dem Buch fertig werden: 'Nachfolge von Joyce'. Wenn ich durchaus jemandem hörig sein und folgen soll (was ich gar nicht nötig habe, ich finde mich stofflich und stilistisch schon selbst zurecht), ... warum muß ich zu Joyce gehen, zu dem Irländer, wo ich die Art, die Methode, die er anwendet (famos, von mir bewundert), an der gleichen Stelle kennengelernt habe, wie er selbst, bei den Expressionisten, Dadaisten und so fort.*[12]

(But blind as the critics of our generation are, they were able to dismiss my book with the greatest of ease as an 'imitation of Joyce'. Now if I really had to obey and follow somebody else (not that I need to, I am quite capable of finding my own subjects and style), ... why pick on Joyce, an Irishman, when I had come upon the same approach, the same marvellous technique that he uses (which I greatly admire) in the same source: Expressionism, Dadaism and so forth?)

Much earlier in his career, Döblin had insisted that he was not acquainted with Joyce's work when he began his own novel:

> *Aber ich habe Joyce nicht gekannt, als ich das erste Viertel des Buches schrieb. Später hat mich ja sein Werk, wie ich auch öfter gesagt und geschrieben habe, entzückt, und es war ein guter Wind in meinen Segeln.*[13]

(I had not read any Joyce when I wrote the first quarter of this book. Later, as I have often stated in public and in print, I found his work enthralling, and it served as a favourable wind in my sails.)

There are many parallels to be drawn between the two novelists in areas such as linguistic experimentation, interior monologue and stream-of-consciousness techniques, the use of songs and music-hall lyrics, close attention to the urban environment, advertising slogans, and an interest in journalism. Both writers share an overriding preoccupation with seemingly trivial and insignificant, often sordid ephemera culled from the daily lives of 'typical' citizens of their nation's capital, the end result being an enduring snapshot of their country. But neither Joyce nor Döblin confront their readers with a mere potpourri of random thoughts and unstructured snippets. To give their works greater cohesion, structural elements are introduced, and these rely primarily on the principle of repetition.

Repetition is a vital constituent of all arts, most especially of those that depend on the passage of time: epic poetry, drama and music. It was music that supplied the term *Leitmotif* to literary criticism in order to describe a theme, a unit within a composition, which is repeated for the purpose of evoking an idea in the mind of the listener or reader. Of course, the technique of reusing set words or phrases is not peculiar to twentieth-century fiction: it is found in classical epics from Homer onwards. But recurring motifs play a major part in many modern novels; in *Berlin Alexanderplatz* they are a useful means of disentangling some of the novel's themes from the welter of unstructured incidents.

The number of minor motifs which proliferate within the book is very large. They include news items, weather reports, references to topical events and snatches from popular songs. These are slipped into the text at frequent intervals, giving it an instantly recognisable imprint and reflecting the author's intense interest in everything that was going on during the period in which the novel is set. The key importance of the newspaper has already been mentioned. Joyce saw it as a vital reflection of modern life and incorporated a history of the newspaper headline into the 'Aeolus' section of *Ulysses*. News features help to illustrate the characters' milieu and may even represent what is actually passing through their heads at a given moment.

Another documentary layer is the scientific/medical one. Franz turns to medical science at the beginning of the novel, seeking a cure for his impotence. The drug Testifortan, patent n. 365695, is accompanied by a leaflet which promises assistance and yet, in the end, seems to suggest that other methods might be just as effective: *Wann der Impotente die Versuche wieder aufnehmen soll, kann nur individuell aus dem Verlauf des Falls bestimmt werden. Eine Pause ist oft wertvoll* (BA 29)('The progress of each individual case must determine the precise point at which the impotent person may resume his activities. A period of abstention will often prove beneficial'). Here, medical science is shown to be less than helpful. The death of Ida is communicated, retrospectively, with reference to a number of physical laws which are introduced with mock sententiousness: *Was ... mit dem Brustkorb der Frauensperson geschehen war, hängt zusammen mit den Gesetzen von Starre und Elastizität, und Stoß und Widerstand. Es ist ohne Kenntnis dieser Gesetze überhaupt nicht verständlich* (BA 85) ('What happened to the female subject's chest ... involves the laws of density and elasticity, shock and resistance. It would be wholly incomprehensible without a knowledge of these laws'). Again, the laws of science themselves provide little information as to the real circumstances of the woman's death.

The medical theme finally comes into its own when Franz is admitted to the psychiatric clinic at Buch. The reader obtains an account of the patient's symptoms and the doctors' arguments, and is privy to an insider's view of the course taken by Franz's illness. Medical data of this sort provides a supplement to the narrative, not for its own sake, but again as part of an authorial view of Franz's condition. It can be inferred that the methods of science, the grape-sugar and camphor which the doctors agree to administer after much wrangling, are less effective in restoring him than the confrontation with evil that takes place in the recesses of his mind. References to science have the effect of exposing the inability of pure science to explain transformations within an individual.

Seemingly factual interpolations often function as ironic contrasts or foils. Characters are humorously contrasted with important historical personages; here again there are parallels with Joyce's use of mythology. Often, the overriding impression is one of incongruity:

Nein, es ist nicht der König von England, wie er in großem Gefolge zur Parlamentseröffnung fährt, ein Zeichen für den Unabhängigkeitssinn der englischen Nation. Dieser ist es nicht. Wer ist es denn? Sind es die Delegierten der Völker, die in Paris den Kelloggpakt unterzeichneten ... Es ist bloß, es latscht an, die grauen Wollstrümpfe hängen, Reinhold, eine sehr unscheinbare Gestalt, ein Junge mausgrau in mausgrau. (BA 172f.)

(No, it's not the King of England, driving in a huge convoy to the opening of Parliament, a symbol of the independence of the English nation. It is somebody else. Who can it be? Is it one of the signatories of the Kellogg Pact in Paris ... It's only – there he comes waddling in, his grey woollen socks

showing – that chap Reinhold, a quite insignificant fellow, a
mouse-grey lad dressed in mouse-grey.)

Here, the contrast between the solemnity of public occasions and
the triviality of private life is neatly brought out. A similar but
more specific point is made when Döblin mounts texts taken from
advertisements onto everyday situations and reveals the yawning
disparity between the ideal world created by the media men and
the real world in which their products are used. Eva and Mieze are
seen romping around in the flat in which Eva's wealthy lover has
set her up; their conversation is interrupted by slogans used to
promote the cigarettes and scent they are using:

> *Kann man hier roochen? Na ob. Ich bin erstaunt, wie Sie es*
> *vermögen, eine solche Qualitätszigarette in solcher Preislage*
> *schon Jahre hindurch auf den Markt zu bringen ... Der*
> *wundervolle Duft der weißen Rose, dezent, wie ihn die kultivierte*
> *deutsche Frau fordert ...* (BA 249)

(OK to have a fag here? Feel free. It amazes me that you are
able to offer this high-quality cigarette for sale at such an
affordable price over a period of many years ... The wonder-
fully delicate fragrance of the white rose is just what the
refined German lady demands ...)

High-flown eulogies of tobacco and perfume, combined with the
flattering reference to 'the refined German lady', contrast sharply
with the people we see enjoying these products. The real-life
predicament of the German lady is likely to be a far cry indeed
from the image which the media like to project. The sham ideal of
outward 'respectability' is again fleetingly touched upon.

6. THE NARRATOR

Behind these devices, it is occasionally possible to glimpse a narrator, who, like so much else in the book, is distinguished by
elusiveness and idiosyncrasy. Here as elsewhere, Döblin's resistance to classification is obvious. His narrator is neither omniscient, nor personal, nor impersonal, but seems to delight in appearing in a variety of (dis)guises. *Ich pflege meinen Döblinismus* ('I
shall cultivate my Döblinism', *Open Letter to F. T. Marinetti*,
1913),[14] seems an appropriate motto for an author intent on blaz-
ing new trails. For the most part, the narrator refrains from expressing personal opinions, contenting himself with a whimsical
aside every so often. '[... W]en erblicken meine Augäpfel? (BA 171)
('[... W]hom do the apples of my eyes behold?'), he asks with

rhetorical solemnity. Sometimes his comments are casual and derisive: *Was macht denn aber der Franz? Der? Na, was wird er machen?* (BA 290) ('But what, then, might Franz be up to? Him? Well, what do you think he's up to?'). The *précis* sections, on the other hand, convey the impression of a rigorous moralist determined to draw his readers' attention to the underlying issues of right and wrong.

On one occasion, however, the narrator steps out of his traditional role and confronts the reader with the doubly ironic observation that he might have told his story in a different way, had he wished to do so. This comes at the point when Franz has been pushed out of the car by Reinhold.

> *Ein anderer Erzähler hätte dem Reinhold wahrscheinlich jetzt eine Strafe zugedacht, aber ich kann nichts dafür, die erfolgte nicht. Reinhold war heiter ...* (BA 192)

> (A different narrator would probably have devised a punishment for Reinhold at this point, but it's not my fault that things didn't happen that way. Reinhold was in a cheerful mood ...)

Here, for a fleeting moment, the narrative conventions are suspended – and simultaneously strengthened. An unseen author identifies himself as a narrator who luxuriates in the theoretical freedom of inventing a story according to his own lights: and yet he immediately admits to being constrained by the 'facts' of the case. The distinction between reality and the imagination is deliberately blurred, which allows the author to project himself into the dual role of a story-teller and of a dispassionate chronicler of reality. A high degree of duplicity in the role of the narrating persona will recur in the novels of Hesse, Mann and Grass.

There are many other occasions when the narrator leaves his personal stamp on a character or an event. An individual may be mocked or ridiculed by means of some fancy nickname or derisive epithet (*Biberköpfchen*), though there may be an ulterior motive, such as when the variations on Franz Biberkopf's name reflect his disorientation. Here, he has been knocking his woman about, and his head is evidently spinning:

> *Der Franz Biberkopf aber, – Biberkopf, Lieberkopf, Zieberkopf, keinen Namen hat der –, die Stube dreht sich, die Betten stehen da, an einem Bett hält er sich fest ... Franz Biberkopf, Ziberkopf, Niberkopf, Wiedekopf hopst an das Bett.* (BA 301)

(But Franz Biberkopf – Beaverkopf, Sleeperkopf, Peeperkopf, he has no name – the room is rotating, beds are over there, he clings on to a bed ... Franz Biberkopf, Sleepikopf, Heepikopf, Zebrakopf hops up to a bed.)

The animal (*Biber*, a beaver) and the intellect (*Kopf*, a head) are themes to which we shall return; here, they are allowed to intertwine in a playful, apparently casual manner.

7. FOLK-SONGS AND POPULAR MUSIC

There comes a point in Döblin, as in Joyce, where linguistic virtuosity gives way to the creation of a modern myth. Neither novelist is content to dabble permanently in ephemera, however diverting the products of their experimentation may prove to be. There may be times when Döblin seems to be offering us little more than an attractively packaged catalogue of trivia, but in the long term he is no less concerned than Joyce to relate his work to older literature and mythology, notably to European and biblical traditions, in some intelligible fashion. His interest in recording the words of songs therefore extends beyond the transient strains of popular music, to a more systematic adaptation of the folk-song, the nursery rhyme, the hymn and the poetic books of the Bible.

Examples of these genres will be found in many areas of the text, often all but unrecognisable because submerged in the narrative proper. The diversity of the 'pop' song of 1920s Germany is brought out in many examples. *Mein Johannes, ach der kann es, mein Johannes ist der Inbegriff des Mannes* (BA 223) ('John's my guy, he makes me sigh, John's the apple of my eye') is a brash, fast-moving love-lyric; other songs are crude and comic (*Ich reiß mir eine Wimper aus, und stech dich damit tot* (BA 209), 'I'll pull an eyelash out and stab you dead with it'), slurpily sentimental (*Wenn das Mädchen einen Hörrn hat, den sie liebt und den sie görn hat* (BA 27), 'If a gi-irl knows a gent whom she lo-oves she'll relent'), or pseudo-rustic (*In der Schweiz und in Tirol, ja da fühlt man sich so wohl* (BA 306),' In Switzerland and in Tyrol, that's where I refresh my soul').

The contrast between innocence and sin is brought out in songs such as these, and also by the use of nursery rhymes, for example at the beginning of Book II, where a few words from Humperdinck's operetta Hänsel and Gretel are interpolated into the evocation of paradise, suggesting innocence and a new beginning (BA 37). The same words, *Mit den Händchen klapp, klapp, klapp* (BA 103) ('With our hands going clap, clap, clap') recur when Franz fails to remain in a state of innocence, after the affair with Lüders. There are many instances of folk-songs and nursery rhymes being used to underscore the idea of 'innocence lost' in the harsher world of reality; compare this linguistic accompaniment to Franz's first disastrous encounter with a prostitute:

> *Das schwammige Weib lachte aus vollem Hals. Sie knöpfte oben die Bluse auf. Es waren zwei Königskinder, die hatten einander so lieb. Wenn der Hund mit der Wurst übern Rinnstein springt. Sie griff ihn, drückte ihn an sich. Putt, putt, putt, mein Hühnchen, putt, putt, putt, mein Hahn. (BA 26)*

(The flabby wench uttered a great guffaw. She undid the top of her blouse. Once upon a time two royal children were very much in love. When the dog with the sausage jumps over the gutter. She grabbed him, pressed him close to her. Cluck, cluck, cluck, my little hen, cluck, cluck cluck, my cockerel.)

Here, snatches of nonsense verse with phallic overtones mingle with verse from an old anthology of folk-poetry, *Des Knaben Wunderhorn* ('The Boy's Cornucopia'), dating from the early nineteenth century. It is from this anthology that Döblin borrows the most striking of all the poems which he uses in *Berlin Alexanderplatz*, the hymn about Death the Reaper, *Es ist ein Schnitter, der heißt Tod*, which features in the anthology as 'A Harvest Song' and as 'A Catholic Hymn' (*Erntelied. Katholisches Kirchenlied*):

> *Es ist ein Schnitter, der heißt Tod,*
> *Hat Gewalt vom höchsten Gott;*
> *Heut wetzt er das Messer,*
> *Es schneidt schon viel besser,*
> *Bald wird er drein schneiden,*
> *Wir müssen's nur leiden.*
> *Hüte dich, schöns Blümelein!*[15]

(There is a Reaper, Death, abhorred,
Receives his powers from the Lord.
Today his blade he starts to whet,
Makes it sharper and sharper yet,
Soon his scythe will cut the corn,
And our losses we shall mourn,
Be wary, little blossom!)

In Book v, after Reinhold has been putting pressure on Franz to discard Cilly and take on his next unwanted ex-mistress, the words of this hymn occur for the first time (*BA* 163), clearly marking a turning point in relations between the two erstwhile friends, and alerting the reader to the danger latent in the man who is about to become Franz's antagonist. The words are repeated, infrequently at first, then with greater insistence, at key points when Franz faces (and ignores) opportunities to disown Reinhold: when recovering from his injuries in hospital (*BA* 201), deciding not to live off charity (*BA* 214), and later, when questioned about his employment (*BA* 241). Each time, the words provide reminders of Franz's vulnerability and his proximity to evil, which manifest themselves as a desire to cover up for Reinhold and to follow his example by living off dishonest earnings. Eventually, when the murder takes place in Book VII, the garbled words of this hymn accompany Reinhold's brutal actions and the last words of his victim: *Gewalt, Gewalt, ist ein Schnitter, vom höchsten Gott hat er die Gewalt. Laß mir los* (*BA* 317) ('Power, power, is a Reaper, from the Lord he receives his powers. Leggo of me').

In the ninth book, Reinhold reappears as the embodiment of the diabolical tempter, his death-like yellowish complexion having been an early pointer towards the function which he was later to assume. The symbol of the Reaper thus turns out to be related to a group of other motifs which suggest that, on one of its levels, *Berlin Alexanderplatz* has more in common with the morality play than with modern fiction.

8. THE BIBLE

On close examination, *Berlin Alexanderplatz* turns out to be shot through with quotations from the Bible as well as from other religious sources. Before Franz is arrested in Book VIII, two angels argue about his destiny, disagreeing with each other as to whether he should be abandoned or given further protection. It is as though Döblin wished to fly in the face of those who might choose to see him as a champion of the modern, secular, labyrinthine *roman trouvé*, and was determined to counterbalance the welter of fortuitous incidents with pointers towards a more elevated level of meaning.

The Bible was, without doubt, a major source-book for *Berlin Alexanderplatz*, and a curious one for Döblin to choose, given his intense interest in chronicling the lives of characters not noted for their interest in religious affairs. Its importance in the novel has encouraged those critics who see *Berlin Alexanderplatz* as a Christian work and give pride of place to the hero's belated conversion in their analysis of it (see p. 39, n. 26, below).

The quotations used by Döblin range from Genesis in the Old to Revelation in the New Testament. There are several points at which Döblin goes back to the very beginning of time, to the story of Adam and Eve, as he sets the scene for the 'new life' that Franz is about to embark upon following his resolution to become a decent citizen. The Garden of Eden is given pride of place in the opening section of Book II:

> *Es lebten einmal im Paradies zwei Menschen, Adam und Eva. Sie waren vom Herrn hergesetzt, der auch Tiere und Pflanzen und Himmel und Erde gemacht hat. Und das Paradies war der herrliche Garten Eden. Blumen und Bäume wuchsen hier, Tiere spielten rum, keiner quälte den andern.* (BA 37)

(Once upon a time there lived in Paradise two human beings, Adam and Eve. They had been put there by the Lord, who had also created beasts and plants, heaven and earth. And Paradise was the resplendent Garden of Eden. Flowers and trees grew there, beasts frolicked around, none tormented the others.)

The salient phrase is 'none tormented the others'. The idyll does not last, the world as we know it is flawed, and Franz must realise that the implementation of his resolutions is doomed to fail. By the time he is humiliated by his politically motivated provocateurs in Henschke's bar, the world has begun to look different:

> *In seiner Dämmerung graut er sich: es ist etwas nicht in Ordnung in der Welt, die stehen da drüben so schrecklich, er erlebt es hellseherisch.*
> *Es lebten aber einmal im Paradies zwei Menschen, Adam und Eva. Und das Paradies war der herrliche Garten Eden. Vögel und Tiere spielten herum.* (BA 81)

(In his twilight state he shudders: something is seriously wrong in the world, those people look so frightening, he senses with a flash of clairvoyance.
But once upon a time there lived in Paradise two human beings, Adam and Eve. And Paradise was the resplendent Garden of Eden. Birds and beasts frolicked there.)

The optimism of the opening paragraph is recalled, if only to be relativised; the reader now recognises that Franz lives in a 'fallen' world whose inhabitants appear to make a sport of 'tormenting the others'. The myth of Adam and Eve is used again in the context of Gerner's thefts (BA 131), in Eva's name, and in the casual reference to stolen goods as 'fruit'.

Franz Biberkopf is likened to various figures from the Old Testament at important points in the novel. The story of Abraham's attempt to sacrifice Isaac (Genesis XXII: 1–19) is interpolated into the narrative after Franz has revisited Tegel prison. On the way home, he falls asleep in the taxi and experiences a veridical dream; again this vision seems connected with Reinhold, as it precedes his decision to resume their relationship (255f.). The dream is a warning which 'tears open his eyes' (BA 255), but Franz fails to recognise himself in the guise of the victim, Isaac.

The figure whose misfortunes come closest to his own is the Old Testament sage Job, sorely tried and repeatedly shaken. Job is the character who is put to the test in the most powerful poetic theodicy in the Bible, where the Lord and Satan strike a deal which gives Satan the authority to attempt to lead him astray. Job's life, more than that of any other biblical figure, becomes a battleground for the clashing forces of good and evil. The battle is close, and there are periods when it looks as though evil will gain the upper hand. Although Job loses everything in the course of his trials, he ends up acknowledging God's greatness, having attained insight not through rational arguments but via a vision which transcends Reason, the so-called 'Voice in the Whirlwind'. But before he reaches this position, he goes through periods of despair, and it is in this respect that Franz is first compared to him (BA 124–7). Biberkopf and Job are strong men overcome by a succession of misfortunes which they cannot comprehend from the point of view of their terrestrial lives; their eventual triumph is due, in large measure, to a miraculous vision. The parallel becomes explicit in Book VIII: *Du hast nicht soviel verloren wie Hiob aus Uz, Franz Biberkopf, es fährt auch langsam auf dich herab* (BA 342) ('Franz Biberkopf, you have not lost as much as Job from Uz, but you, too, are soon to be struck down'.)

A more pessimistic note is struck by allusions to the Lamentations of Jeremiah. With Franz about to embark on his first night as a reluctant burglar, a warning is given against reliance on unsuitable companions:

> *Verflucht ist der Mann, spricht Jeremia, der sich auf Menschen verläßt, der das Fleisch zu seiner Stütze macht und dessen Herz von Gott abfällt. Er gleicht einem Verlassenen in der Steppe und gewahrt es nicht, wenn Gutes kommt.* (BA 175; cf. Jeremiah XVII: 5-9)

(Cursed be the man, saith Jeremiah, that trusteth in man and maketh flesh his support, and whose heart foresaketh the Lord. For he shall be like one abandoned in the steppes, and shall not see good when it cometh.)

Jeremiah is also relevant to *Berlin Alexanderplatz* in respect of his warnings about the wickedness of Babylon, first heard shortly before Franz is given the parable of Zannowich: *Sprach Jeremia, wir wollen Babylon heilen, aber es ließ sich nicht heilen* (BA 14; cf. Jeremiah LI: 9:9), ('Quoth Jeremiah, "We would fain heal Babylon, but she will not be healed"'). The wider implications of this apparent interpolation will not become obvious until much later on in the novel, when Berlin is identified as the Modern Babylon.

The association of Berlin with the biblical stronghold of sin, strife and oppression is part of the fundamental design of Döblin's novel – hence the concentration on low-life characters and the underworld. The moral anarchy of the city is epitomised by the biblical figure of the Whore of Babylon, who confronts the hero as he is beginning to recover from his accident: *Die große Hure, die Hure Babylon, die da am Wasser sitzt* (BA 211; cf. Revelation XVII: 1–9) ('The great Whore, the Whore of Babylon, that sitteth beside the waters'). She becomes a cipher for Berlin, laughing with glee as Franz turns to dishonest occupations (BA 226), and exhibiting delight as he sets off to resume his relationship with Reinhold: *'Jeder Schritt von dir freut sie. Trunken ist sie vom Blut der Heiligen, die sie zerfleischt ... Wie sie dich anlacht'* (BA 262) ('Each step you take delights her. She is drunken with the blood of saints whom she tears asunder ... And she laughs in your face'). Rearing her seven heads and ten horns, she gloats over the progress of her latest victim. It is only when Franz lays the spectre of death, curses Reinhold and weeps for the evil he has done, that the Whore is banished:

> *Das Weib mit den sieben Köpfen zerrt an dem Tier, das Tier kommt nicht hoch ... Die große Babylon kann endlich ihr Tier hochzerren, es kommt in Trapp, es rast über die Felder, es sinkt in den Schnee. Sie dreht sich um, heult gegen den strahlenden Tod. Unter dem Tosen bricht das Tier in die Knie, das Weib schwankt über dem Hals des Tiers.* (BA 401)

(The woman with seven heads tugs at the beast, but the beast cannot raise itself ... Now the great Babylon at last manages to force it to stand, its starts trotting, races across the fields, sinks into the snow. She turns round, rails at the shining figure of Death. Her furious screams cause the beast to stumble onto its knees and the woman tumbles over its neck.)

This is the point at which the lure of the darker side of city life is overcome; from now on, Franz Biberkopf is able to look on with detached equanimity as the citizens march past him towards their ominous rallies.

9. MAN AND BEAST

Our survey of the biblical elements used in *Berlin Alexanderplatz* has shown that the novel does not attempt to glorify city life; to preserve his integrity, man must withdraw and opt out of overt involvements in favour of a position of contemplative isolation. Franz discovers the truth about the world while confined to a mental hospital, echoing Nietzsche's prophesy that 'the last man' would seek voluntary admission to an asylum.[16] Only other social outcasts, such as the Jews in Book I, had tried to warn him against committing himself to the values of contemporary society. Withdrawal from the world is a significant theme in twentieth-century German fiction, and we shall observe that several later writers take the theme further and question whether the self-imposed isolation of the individual is a legitimate reaction to the ills present in society.

An image which is closely connected with the biblical reminiscences on the one hand, and with city life at its most basic level on the other, is that of the abattoir. It brings together the mythical and the realistic strands in a remarkably successful synthesis. Parallels between man and beast are drawn gradually and unobtrusively in the context of an almost pedantically detailed visit to the central abattoir of Berlin. The chapter is located prior to the conversation with Job, after Franz has been deceived by Lüders; its heading derives from Ecclesiastes III: 19.

Day-to-day activities are sketched in: a feeble horse, nibbling at a tree, is disposed of for fifty marks and a round of drinks, and dragged off in haste. Little details draw attention to the human parallel, hinted at in the chapter-heading: an obelisk in honour of the war dead is sighted near the slaughter rooms for animals. A pig's-eye view of the whole process is put before us, in which the unfortunate animals are seen entering a steam bath:

> *Da bist du im Dampf wie in einem Bad, da nehmen die Schweine vielleicht ein russisch-römisches Bad. Man geht irgendwo, du siehst nicht wo, die Brille ist einem beschlagen, man geht vielleicht nackt, schwitzt sich den Rheumatismus aus, mit Kognak allein geht's nicht ... Da sind ja schon Schweine, da hängen ja welche, die sind schon tot ...* (BA 119)

(You're surrounded by steam as in the baths, maybe the pigs are taking a Turkish bath. You wander along, you can't see where you're going, your glasses are steamed up, perhaps you're naked, sweating out your rheumatism, brandy on its own is ineffective ... Here are the pigs, some of them are hanging there, they're dead already ...)

At the end of their journey, the pigs lie there 'in their neat white shirts, relaxed as though they had just emerged from a tiring bath, a successful operation or a massage' (BA 120).

The anthropomorphisms abound: blood pouring out of a stunned bull is compared to some merry party of guests 'trickling' out of a house, dancing out into the open. The scene remains gruesome and realistic; the later references to a hammer crashing down on Franz Biberkopf make it clear that, without insight, he was indistinguishable from the beasts who are slaughtered each day in the city's abattoirs. Comparisons between Franz and beasts such as pigs (BA 265) no longer seem fortuitous. The section ends logically with a view of the animals' trotters laid out in orderly fashion in a butcher's shop, leaving the reader to reflect on the connection between what we eat and what we are.

The name of Döblin's hero contains further pointers in this direction. 'Franz' recalls St Francis, who treated man and beast alike, while the curious surname 'Biberkopf' is evidently composed of the two elements *Biber*, a beaver, and *Kopf*, a head. The resulting compound brings instinct and rational powers together, drawing attention to a fundamental polarity in the man's character, where a permanent conflict is being waged between natural impulse and cerebral reflection. Franz is repeatedly referred to by others as some kind of animal (an ox, a camel, a pig); the narrator describes him and a friend as *zwei große ausgewachsene Tiere in Tüchern* (BA 72) ('two fully-grown large animals in cloth'). And animal welfare is not the least of Franz's many concerns, as his sympathy for the caged goldfinch in Henschke's bar reveals – this creature provides another emblem of his own imprisonment in an unhealthy environment (BA 74f.).

Mieze's name is no less significant. Her real name was Emilie, but she styles herself Sonia, possibly as a tribute by Döblin to Dostoevski, who uses the name for the prostitute at the centre of *Crime and Punishment*. Eva addresses her as Sonia, but the name sounds too 'foreign' to Franz, who would like a girl called Marie, recalling both Mary the Virgin and Mary Magdalen. But even this name proves too much of a mouthful to him, and so he opts for the diminutive 'Mieze' or 'Miezeken' ('pussy-cat'):

Die heißt aber bei ihm bloß einen Tag Sonja, dann bettelt er, er kann so fremde Namen nicht leiden ... Er hätte ja schon viele Mädels gehabt ... aber noch keene, die Marie hieß. Sone möchte er gern haben. Da nennt er sie denn nun 'sein Miezeken'. (BA 229)

(But he can only bear to call her Sonia for one day, then he starts pleading – he can't stand these foreign names ... He's had loads of girls before, but not one was called Marie ... He'd love to have one all to himself. And so he ends up calling her 'his Miezeken'.)

And so the name chosen for Reinhold's principal victim is associated with three distinct spheres: the divine, the human and the bestial, and the language with which the murder is communicated conceals reminders of these levels of experience as they have already featured in the novel:

Seine Zeit! Seine Zeit! Jegliches seine Zeit ... ist ein Schnitter ... zusammen zieht sich ihr Körper ... Danach schlägt man mit der Holzkeule dem Tier in den Nacken ... Jegliches, jegliches. (BA 316f.)

(Its season! Its season! Unto everything its season ... there is a Reaper ... her body contracts ... Thereupon the animal receives a blow on the neck with a wooden club ... unto everything, everything.)

10. RECEPTION

Asked by a journalist for his opinion of Alfred Döblin, Thomas Mann is reported to have replied *Es gibt sehr wenige Leute, die Döblins Bücher bis zu Ende lesen können*[17] ('Very few people are able to read Döblin's books right through to the end'), a curiously dismissive comment from one whose novels are neither short nor easy to follow. The volume of mail received by the *Frankfurter Zeitung* which originally serialised *Berlin Alexanderplatz* suggests that many readers had in fact read all instalments. Some were far from edified. *Die Zeitung ist nicht das Forum zur Aufdeckung von Eiterbeulen, es genügen uns vollauf die Prozeßberichte* ('A newspaper is not the proper forum for the exposure of abscesses: law reports are quite adequate for that purpose'), writes one correspondent, tacitly confirming the verisimilitude of the underworld as it is portrayed in the novel. Some readers complained about what it might do to Germany's tarnished image abroad and implored the editor to hesitate before publishing such potentially damaging material, *doch auf das Ausland Rücksicht zu nehmen, dem man solche Einblicke in deutsches Leben nicht geben dürfe* ('to consider other countries who should not be provided with this kind of insight into life in Germany'). Again the implication is that such insights are not entirely fanciful.

There were many positive responses, ranging from *Bravo* and *Ja* to *ein Werk tiefster Reinheit* and *wir sehen unsere Verantwortung, unsere Machtlosigkeit, unser Verkettetsein* ('a work of great purity'; 'its shows us our responsibility, our helplessness, our dependence on circumstances'). An official of the judiciary was moved to comment *Erschütternd hat mir der Roman klar gemacht, wie fragwürdig selbst unsere modernsten Vorschläge über Strafvollzug sind* ('I was shocked to realise, on reading this novel, just how dubious even our most modern ideas about punitive methods are'). A theologian opined that 'the subject could not have been treated with greater integrity'.[18]

Yet there is a sense in which all these responses skirt round the questions which the novel raises in its final chapters, when Franz Biberkopf emerges from his ignorance to begin a new life. The causes and significance of this eleventh-hour conversion were of little interest to the early readers and remain controversial among today's critics. The sordid milieu and the literary devices have proved to hold greater interest than the conclusion of the novel, in which Franz is reduced to a representative of good sense; in this sense, Thomas Mann can be said to have identified the most controversial area of the novel: the fact that very few people read it 'right through to the end' and give serious consideration to the new Franz *Karl* Biberkopf who emerges on the final pages, preferring instead to view it as a vast showcase of twentieth-century *mores*.

That Döblin himself intended readers to think along different lines is evidenced by a passage from the retrospective *Epilog*, in which the idea of a 'sacrifice' is given prominence:

> *Das Opfer war das Thema des 'Alexanderplatz'. Die Bilder vom Schlachthof, von der Opferung Isaaks, das durchlaufende Zitat 'Es ist ein Schnitter, der heißt Tod' hätten aufmerksam machen sollen. Der gute Franz Biberkopf mit seinen Ansprüchen an das Leben läßt sich bis zu seinem Tod nicht brechen. Aber er sollte gebrochen werden, er mußte sich aufgeben, nicht bloß äußerlich.*[19]

(The theme of *Alexanderplatz* was that of the sacrifice. The images of the slaughterhouse, the sacrifice of Isaac, the recurring quotation 'There is a Reaper, Death, abhorred'

should have made people aware. The *good* Franz Biberkopf
with his lofty expectations of life cannot be broken except by
death. Yet he had to be broken, he had to surrender, in the
fullest sense of the word.)

These lines were written some twenty years after publication of
the novel; for better or worse, there are very few earlier comments
on it by its author. Scholarship seems divided on the fundamental
question of whether *Berlin Alexanderplatz* provides little more than
a sweeping panorama of urban life, or whether the seemingly
random succession of events adds up to a rational explanation of
the changes which its hero undergoes at the end. In other words,
is the title, *Berlin Alexanderplatz*, suggestive of a kaleidoscopic
survey of the city, more appropriate than the subtitle 'The Story of
Franz Biberkopf'?

We know that *Berlin Alexanderplatz* was Döblin's original title
for the book, and that the subtitle was added at the insistence of
his publisher, Samuel Fischer; it is therefore not surprising that
several authorities stress the importance of the city at the expense
of the novel's characters. It has become commonplace to speak of
this novel as *der erste deutsche Großstadtroman* ('the first urban
novel in the German language'), suggesting that the milieu is all-
important. Volker Klotz has provided a cogent reading of *Berlin
Alexanderplatz* from this point of view in his study of literary
townscapes *Die erzählte Stadt* (1969). Pride of place is given to the
metropolis, and Franz is seen as a specimen culled from the
collective life of Berlin. He is an Everyman, or a modern Faust
tempted by a Mephistophelian city. The battle between the individual and the collective results, according to Klotz, in victory for
the metropolis, and he appears to doubt whether much credence
need be given to the reborn hero:

> *Die gegenständliche Fülle der Stadt, ihre multiplen Bewegungen
> und Gegenbewegungen, das erzählerische Aufgebot ihres faßbaren
> Bestands, der weder tieferen Sinn noch höhere Botschaft kennt,
> siegt endlich über die lehrhafte Parabel … Die Dampframme am
> Alexanderplatz überhallt den mythischen Gang des Sturmwinds,
> die Straßenbahn Nr. 47 überfährt die Hure Babylon, die
> Litfaßsäulen überschatten den geschlagenen Hiob.*[20]

(The all-embracing city with its multitude of currents and
cross-currents, the narrative inventory of its tangible content, conveying no deeper significance nor lofty message,
triumphs in the end over the didactic parable … The steam
pile-driver working on Alexanderplatz drowns out the

mythical Voice in the Whirlwind, tram number 47 runs down the Whore of Babylon, and the columns covered in advertising slogans overshadow Job in his defeat.)

There is little room here for reflections on Franz Biberkopf as a character; whether he may or may not be in a better position to master the vicissitudes of his life is not discussed by Klotz in this study.

The label *der erste deutsche Großstadtroman* suggests that there is a tradition of novels chronicling urban life in other countries, and that *Berlin Alexanderplatz* is the earliest representative of the genre in German. In fact, only *Ulysses* and John Dos Passos's *Manhattan Transfer* are ever cited as precedents in this respect, both having appeared in German translation in 1927. It is not known whether Döblin had read *Manhattan Transfer* before 1929, but *Ulysses* is mentioned with enthusiasm during 1928, when most of *Berlin Alexanderplatz* was written: *Zunächst hat jeder ernste Schriftsteller sich mit diesem Buch zu befassen* ('The first duty of any serious writer is to come to terms with this book'). Breon Mitchell claims to have found evidence to the effect that many techniques which Joyce pioneered (use of advertising slogans, inner monologues and other devices) were inserted into the manuscript of *Berlin Alexanderplatz* after the first quarter had been written.[21] Klaus Müller-Salget does not see Joyce as a major influence, but admits that Döblin had originally used speech-marks, apostrophes and other typographical conventions until a late stage in the novel's composition, when they were suddenly excised. It is therefore not unlikely that Döblin did, in fact, make substantial changes to the book after reading Joyce, but these changes do not imply that the urban setting became more important than the character of Franz Biberkopf, whose fortunes are the subject of the recurring chapter-headings and summaries. It is reflected in the structure of the novel and accounts for ninety per cent of the text; in this sense, *Berlin Alexanderplatz* must be viewed as a novel of character development.

This is not to suggest that Franz is the only centre of interest in the book or that his psychology remains consistent or convincing throughout. The repeated ups and downs of his career come to appear contrived, and the ending stands out as an unexpectedly hopeful conclusion to an otherwise bleak fable. The all-too-brief glimpse of the new Franz may have encouraged readings which stress the role of the city; and readers who attempt to come to grips with Biberkopf's conversion face another controversy, which can be summed up in the following questions: is the world depicted by Döblin an unholy bedlam, where Franz belatedly discovers that he can only survive by isolating himself? Or does he learn to establish a better relationship with his fellow men? In short, does he withdraw from or accept integration into the human community? The commentators have been unable to agree on this question, and those who concur that Franz does find a useful niche for himself within the world are divided as to whether his development has taken place on a political, religious or moral level.

11. POLITICS

Socialist and Marxist critics were unwelcoming in their initial responses to *Berlin Alexanderplatz*. The main complaint was that Döblin had denigrated the working classes: *Döblin macht den bewußten Versuch, den Typus des Arbeiters unsrer Zeit ... mit einem Zynismus sondergleichen zu verhöhnen und lächerlich zu machen*[22] ('With unparalleled cynicism, Döblin makes a conscious attempt to mock and ridicule the figure of the working man of today'). The poet Johannes R. Becher saw it as 'a crazy, unviable construction', and the leading Marxist literary historian of his time, Georg Lukács, commented on what he took to be a clash between innovatory methodology and threadbare ideology: *Auch hier kommt er den brennenden Problemen des Tages und der Epoche nie wirklich nahe. Mit vollkommen neuen Mitteln des Surrealismus entsteht ein altes, ja fast banales Ergebnis*[23] ('Here, too, he never really gets to grips with the burning issues of his day and age. The completely new methods of Surrealism are used to produce a familiar, almost banal result').

These attacks from the left were short-lived. After the Second World War, socialist critics in the GDR could argue that *Berlin Alexanderplatz* was a prophetic document in which the perils of Fascism were sketched out in remarkable detail. Far from constituting a slur on the working man, the novel opens our eyes to the lives of displaced, classless members of the *Lumpenproletariat* in a pre-revolutionary city, and exposes the true face of capitalism, which drives ordinary people into crime. Reinhold is the representative of National Socialism, and the education which Franz receives is to learn to beware of Fascism.[24]

Writing in *German Life and Letters* in 1968, J. H. Reid put forward the view that Franz might be seen as an allegory of Germany as she was in the aftermath of the First World War, subject to repeated truncations and reversals, but still displaying great strength and vitality. The lost arm may well stand for the loss of territory sustained by Germany after the Treaty of Versailles. Undirected energy leads Franz astray: his reckless pursuit of false friends is seen as analogous to Germany's peremptory quest for recognition among the nations of Europe, which is doomed to fail unless undertaken with circumspection. Döblin pulls his hero back from the brink in order to show that the creation of a more natural social organisation is still possible.[25]

Reid's approach is useful in that it highlights several important connections between Franz's behaviour and conditions in Germany. As we have seen, Döblin deliberately refers to his hero's service in the war, to his political ambivalence and to contrasts between the German police state and conditions in other countries. As was suggested above (pp. 6–12), many of Franz's psychological qualities, like those of Adrian in Mann's *Doctor Faustus*, correspond to national stereotypes. The crass realism of the factual background compels the reader to look for statements about the direction in which the country itself is heading. Having observed so many aspects of a life in her capital city, it would not be unreasonable to search the text for evidence about the health of the nation as a whole.

12. RELIGION AND MORALITY

There are good grounds for suggesting that Christian ideas are important in this novel. The conclusion, in which Franz is reborn and renamed, seems to offer a solution in which grace has played its part and a kind of baptism is enacted. The designation of the book as a 'novel of conversion' is attractive in view of Döblin's own conversion from Judaism to Roman Catholicism in 1941. The good and evil angels, the biblical language and motifs, the author's condemnation of vain pursuits and worldly ideals, can be adduced in support of the claim that *Berlin Alexanderplatz* is a religious parable appropriate to the modern world, especially as Döblin later stressed his hero's 'sacrificial' role. However, it has to be acknowledged that this line of approach does benefit considerably from the level of hindsight which its advocates – who include the book's original editor Walter Muschg – enjoy. It should be noted that the overwhelming majority of the scriptural references are from the Old rather than from the New Testament; the theme of man's captivity in Babylon is likely to have greater significance for a Jewish than for a Christian writer. The ending seems to offer little support for the view that a specific religious doctrine is here being preached.[26]

Instead, Döblin repeatedly focuses on a 'learning process', *ein*

Enthüllungsprozeß besonderer Art (BA 409), suggesting that a more
general lesson about life is to be drawn from the story. Although
Franz Biberkopf is transformed, the direction in which the new
man develops at the end remains ill-defined and has perplexed
the critics. Albrecht Schöne believes that the principle of integration is at stake, *das Prinzip der Ergebung, der Einfügung in ein
umgebendes, kollektives Ganzes*[27] ('the principle of submission, of
integration into an all-embracing collective whole'). Hartmut
Becker and Leo Kreutzer disagree, since this would imply that
'the reality of city life is founded upon rationality and that
Biberkopf espouses this rationality in the end'.[28] Many recent
authorities view the open ending as constituting a direct appeal to
the reader to recognise what Erwin Kobel calls *die Uneigentlichkeit
seines Daseins*[29] ('the false qualities of his own existence').

By contrast, Klaus Müller-Salget has argued strongly in favour
of accepting the inner unity of the work. In his view, Franz over-
comes the sin of pride, but in doing so he neither plunges headlong into the community nor isolates himself from it, but simply
acknowledges his relative position in the world: *Erst der Mensch,
der seine Schwäche erkannt hat, weiß auch um seine Stärke*[30] ('Only
through recognising his weakness does a man become aware of
his strength'). There is some doubt as to whether Döblin himself
intended to conclude the novel with this degree of optimism; his
letter to Professor Julius Petersen of 18 September 1931 suggests
that the work should be seen as a fragment in which the dualism
of earthly life remains unresolved (see p. 42, n. 32, below).

13. EVALUATION

Sociopolitical, Christian and moral strands have been isolated and
emphasised by different readers, and it may seem convenient to
accept that each of these themes has played a part in shaping the
diverse facets of the novel. Individual episodes within the book
can, however, be subjected to mutually irreconcilable interpretations if one or another of these approaches is accepted unconditionally. Take the case of Otto Lüders, the man who intimidates
and robs the young widow whom Franz befriended when he was
hawking goods around the tenement blocks. At first sight, Lüders
seems to be an unprincipled scoundrel motivated by jealousy and
greed. But if we view *Berlin Alexanderplatz* as a social study, then
Lüders becomes an example of a victim of the Depression. We are
told that he has been unemployed for two years and that he has a
sick child, and may conclude that he was driven to act in the way
he did by unfavourable economic circumstances. In this sense, he

becomes a parallel to Franz Biberkopf, reflecting the brutalising forces which were at work during the latter years of the Weimar Republic. Seen from a Christian point of view, Lüders must assume a very different role. His treachery conveys a message for Franz; like a figure from a moral fable, he warns Franz to avoid ephemeral physical pleasures and vainglorious boasting. The Lüders episode would then be less closely related to the milieu sections of the *Großstadtroman* than to recurring reminders of the proximity of Death and the prophetic sections of the novel. The more general moral approach represented by Müller-Salget does not oblige us to make any such sweeping connections but merely sees in Lüders the uncle of Lina, Franz Biberkopf's current girl-friend. This 'uncle' is annoyed to hear Franz boasting about his conquest of another woman and resolves to teach him a lesson. Instead of paying more attention to the relationships which he has already forged, Franz obdurately ignores the warning and retreats into an attitude of self-pity.

The world of *Berlin Alexanderplatz* is too complex to permit it to be reduced to a simple formula. A parallel of sorts exists between the city and its inhabitants. Just as Berlin can only be represented by arrays of disjointed sensory impressions, Biberkopf's struggle for survival is conducted on many levels. The impersonal force of which the narrator speaks, *etwas, das von außen kommt, das unberechenbar ist und wie ein Schicksal aussieht* (*BA* 7) ('something coming towards him from outside, something incalculable that looks like a destiny'), demands decisions on many levels: political, spiritual and sexual. Franz is unable to win his battle against evil by acquiring an insight into any one of these spheres without paying due regard to the others. *Anständig sein* may be the right decision from a social and moral point of view; but, since it impels him towards the right wing of the political spectrum, it may be the wrong decision at this point in time, as events in Henschke's bar demonstrate.

The urban transport system which features prominently in the novel provides a vital analogy to Döblin's narrative method. Its criss-crossing routes reveal the 'runic' mysteries of modern life (*BA* 148). As Axel Eggebrecht remarked in an early review article: *Döblin benutzt jeglichen Stil wie eine Straßenbahn; er fährt nie zu weit; wenn er da ist, wo er hin will, springt er ab*[31] ('Döblin uses each literary style as one might use a tram-car – he never goes too far, and when he gets to his destination, he jumps off'). The tramline is, indeed, an important analogy to the journey undertaken in this novel. From its appearance at the start of the narrative to the final assurance that the trams are still running (*BA* 8, 405), the tramway symbolises a system that functions according to strict rules, and yet has no centre and no terminus. This principle must also apply to the novel *Berlin Alexanderplatz*, which by its author's own admission was destined to remain a fragment, demanding a conclusion which it was beyond his powers to supply: *Der Schluß müßte – eigentlich im Himmel spielen ... na, das war nicht möglich*[32] ('The ending ought really to take place in heaven ... well, that just wasn't possible').

14. THE NEW MAN

Literary historians may find it difficult to accept the lack of direction in the final pages of this novel because so many of the author's comments, in the chapter-headings and elsewhere, appear to indicate that a powerful force is driving Franz inexorably towards his ultimate confrontation with evil. There is an undeniable clash between the clearly defined structure of Franz Biberkopf's life with its ups and downs, and the open end of the novel. The inner logic of the narrative machinery seems at variance with the unresolved human problems that linger on, even after the 'new man' emerges from the mental hospital at Buch.

Franz Biberkopf's recovery is communicated through paradoxes. Twice we are told that he is dead, *Gestorben; bis zu seinem Ende in der Irrenanstalt* (*BA* 399) ('died'; 'up to his demise in the psychiatric clinic'). At this point, the 'other' character appears, equipped with the same documents: *Der andere hat dieselben Papiere wie Franz* (loc. cit) ('The other man has the same papers as Franz'). When referring to Reinhold, the author seems undecided whether the new life is or is not a continuation of the old: *der früher in seinem Leben, in seinem früheren Leben eine Rolle gespielt hat* (*BA* 402) ('who played a part earlier in his life, in his earlier life'). The reason for this hesitation appears to be that the new man is, as yet, dormant: *Der alte Biberkopf ist hin, der neue schläft und schläft noch,* (*BA* 402) ('The old Biberkopf is gone; the new one is in a deep sleep').

The new middle name 'Karl' (cf. Old Norse *karl*, a man) suggests a new beginning, but the new departure is denied by a note to the effect that Franz had been given this second name at baptism, in honour of his grandfather (*BA* 404). His old buoyancy is underscored by the phrase *Biberkopf ist wieder da* ('Biberkopf is back again'), which specifically recalls his reckless exploits of the past, cf. *Franz ist wieder da* (*BA* 404, 32): Döblin seems at pains to stress that the links with the past have not been broken.

A major factor in Franz Biberkopf's misfortunes had been provided by his sexual appetite and specifically by the naive pride
which he took in his sexual conquests. Although there are indications that his behaviour may have become more balanced in this
respect, the absence of a new female figure at the end of *Berlin
Alexanderplatz* suggests that he may still be vulnerable in this area.
The theme is disposed of with an innocuous image of Franz
consuming cream cakes with Eva in a coffee shop, after a visit to
Mieze's grave, and a reference to a child that was lost:

> *Gegenüber sitzt er mit ihr in der Konditorei, ißt Bienenstich,
> Mieze zu Ehren, weil die nicht genug davon haben konnte ... So
> redet Biberkopf mit der Eva und ißt Bienenstich.*
>
> *Seine Freundin wollte Eva früher werden, aber jetzt, jetzt will
> sie selbst nicht mehr. Die Sache mit Mieze und dann das
> Irrenhaus, das war ihr zu viel, so gut sie ihm ist. Und das Kleine,
> das sie von Ihm erwartet hatte, ist auch nicht gekommen, sie hat
> gekippt ... So sitzen sie ruhig nebeneinander und denken
> rückwärts und vorwärts, essen Bienenstich und einen Mohrenkopf
> mit Sahne.* (BA 407)

(He is sitting with her in the coffee-shop across the road,
eating a cream roll in honour of Mieze, who could never get
her fill of that sort of thing ... Biberkopf goes on chatting to
Eva while eating a cream roll.

Long ago, Eva had wanted to be his girlfriend, but now,
well now she has changed her mind. That business with
Mieze and then the madhouse, that was too much for her,
though she still likes him. And the little one she had been
expecting didn't come along either, she miscarried. ... So
they sit there next to one another quite calmly, thinking of
the past and the future, eating a cream roll and a chocolate
truffle cake with cream.)

Given the previous disasters in his life, this idyllic tableau has an
almost laughable quality. The ending is open, perhaps even
comic. In his explanatory letter to Professor Petersen, Döblin admits that he was unable to provide the second volume which he
had hoped to write: *der Schluß ist sozusagen eine Überbrückung, –
aber das andere Ufer fehlt* ('the end is, as it were, a bridge – but the
other side doesn't exist'). Here the author acknowledges that
'dualism', the tension between the spirit and man's inherent sensuality, is the main theme, but also that it is beyond his powers to
resolve the ensuing tension:

Gegen meinen Willen, einfach aus der Logik der Handlung und des Plans endete das Buch so; es war rettungslos, mir schwammen meine Felle davon. Der Schluß müßte – eigentlich im Himmel spielen ... , na, das war nicht möglich, aber ich ließ es mir nicht nehmen, zum Schluß Fanfaren zu blasen, es mochte psychologisch stimmen oder nicht. Bisher sehe ich: der Dualismus ist nicht aufzuheben.[33]

(Against my will, simply by the logic of the plan and the action, the book had to end as it does; there was nothing more I could do, my hopes were dashed. The conclusion needs to be set – in heaven ... , well, that couldn't be done, but there was nothing to stop me from sounding fanfares at the end, whether or not it made sense from a psychological point of view. So far I have realised one thing: dualism cannot be overcome.)

As a character study, then, the novel breaks off with Franz's discharge from hospital. This provides the book with a circular structure, since it mirrors the discharge from prison at the beginning (even tram 41 is mentioned again). But the last few paragraphs reveal that this novel is more than a collection of ephemera held together by a figure whose moral regeneration is, in the end, sketched out for us but never effectively demonstrated. It is the ending of *Berlin Alexanderplatz* that yields the most decisive evidence of the novel's status as a historical document which investigates the social and political climate of the years 1927–8, and eventually provides a very tentative glimpse of a troubled future. It is this aspect of Franz Biberkopf's career that demands consideration on the final pages.

Much emphasis is placed on the fact that our hero is no longer alone at the end of the novel, as he had been at the very beginning. *Er steht nicht mehr allein am Alexanderplatz ... Es sind welche rechts von ihm und links von ihm, und vor ihm gehen welche, und hinter ihm gehen welche* (BA 409) ('He no longer stands on his own in Alexanderplatz ... There are people on his right and people on his left, and people walk in front of him and people walk behind him').

The references to 'right' and 'left' have distinct political associations which are reinforced by their use in the martial language of the last chapter heading ('right and left and right and left'). It would be encouraging to think of Franz Biberkopf as occupying a middle position between the extremes of right and left. The columns of marching men who frequently pass his window 'with flags and music and singing' (BA 410) leave him unmoved. But his condition is still precarious: sooner or later he will be swept along with the tide. Many critics, including Eggebrecht and Keller, share the view that the new Franz is still at the mercy of those forces with which he has but recently engaged in battle.[34]

There are strong indications to the effect that Döblin was himself well aware of the unresolved tensions which remain at the end of *Berlin Alexanderplatz*. The 'right companion' mentioned on the cover of the first edition does not materialise; the dangers of isolation are spelled out within the text: *Viel Unglück kommt davon, wenn man allein geht ... es ist auch schöner und besser, mit andern zu sein* (BA 409) ('Great misfortune arises from going it alone ... it is also pleasanter and better to be with other people'). But who are these 'other people'? The only others envisaged in this chapter are the anonymous hordes of marching men, their very movements ('right and left and right and left') seeming to echo the political divisions by which the country was racked at the time. These are the divisions that will lead to further strife: *Wir ziehen in den Krieg* (BA 411) ('We are marching into war'); there is, here, a regretful acknowledgement that the other people by whom Franz Biberkopf finds himself surrounded at the end do not and cannot share his new-found pacifism.

Endings supply the grounds for endless controversy in all novels, be they 'open' as here in *Berlin Alexanderplatz* and in Grass's *The Flounder*, or marked by a decisive event such as the death of a principal character. Döblin's recognition that the dualism of life cannot be overcome obliges him to opt for an ending that is provisional rather than definitive. This need not be seen as a failing. It shows a respect for the complexity of life, that very complexity that gave the earlier parts of the novel their vibrancy and kaleidoscopic texture. Clashes between the *Biber* and the *Kopf* elements, between sensual and rational forces, are essential factors of every life. The marching columns whom Döblin places at the end of his book leave the reader with a telling image betokening both passion and discipline, chaos and order at the same time. In the final paragraph, the persistence of the battle between mind and instinct is put into words, before language itself disintegrates into mere sound: *widebumm, widebumm*. Whether these sounds evoke the beating of the human heart or the exploding of shells in an apocalyptic conflict remains unanswered and probably unanswerable.

NOTES

1. The 'epic' qualities of *Berlin Alexanderplatz* have often been discussed in the context of theories formulated by Döblin and Brecht; see Best, 1972; Keller, 1975, 1980; Durrani, 1981.
2. *AZL*, p. 21.
3. *AZL*, p. 390.
4. Prangel, 1975, p. 54.
5. Müller-Salget, 1987, pp. 310, 316f., 324.
6. *La chute*, 1956, p. 9.
7. Prangel, 1975, p. 111.
8. Schwimmer, 1975, pp. 130–42.
9. Stenzel, 1972, pp. 39–44.
10. Kracauer, 1947, pp. 182–8, 223f.; Prangel, 1975, pp. 237–44; Fassbinder, 1980.
11. *AZL*, p. 387.
12. *AZL*, p. 391. ⸺
13. Prangel, 1975, p. 44.
14. *AZL*, p. 15.
15. Arnim and Brentano, 1957, p. 37f.
16. Nietzsche, 1955, vol. 2, p. 284.
17. Prangel, 1975, p. 72.
18. Ibid., p. 60f.; see also Durrani, 1987.
19. See n. 12, above.
20. Klotz, 1969, pp. 409, 417.
21. Mitchell, 1976, pp. 131–50; Müller-Salget, 1987, pp. 286–92.
22. Prangel, 1975, p. 87f.
23. Ibid., p. 93; Lukács, 1947, p. 56.
24. Links, 1965, pp. 86, 93, 78; there is less emphasis on this aspect in Links, 1981.
25. Reid, 1967/8, pp. 214–223.
26. In his postscript, Muschg describes the novel as 'Döblin's first Christian work', *BA*, p. 423. See also Jennings, 1959, and Weymbergh-Boussart, 1970.
27. Schöne, 1963, p. 324.
28. Becker, 1962, pp. 76–9; Kreutzer, 1970, p. 123.
29. Kobel, 1985, p. 280.
30. Müller-Salget, 1987, p. 324.
31. Prangel, 1975, p. 65.
32. Ibid., p. 42.
32. Loc. cit.
34. Ibid., p. 64; Keller, 1980, p. 196.

CHAPTER TWO

Hermann Hesse: *The Glass Bead Game* (1943)

'Interessantere Lebenserscheinungen', erwiderte er, 'haben wohl immer dies Doppelgesicht von Vergangenheit und Zukunft, wohl immer sind sie progressiv und regressiv in einem. Sie zeigen die Zweideutigkeit des Lebens selbst.'

(Thomas Mann: *Doctor Faustus*, chapter 22)

('The more interesting of life's phenomena', he replied, 'will always tend to have this double perspective, facing the past as well as the future, and will always tend to be progressive and regressive at the same time. They display the ambiguity of life itself.')

1. CONTRASTS

A comparison of the novels *Berlin Alexanderplatz* and *The Glass Bead Game* does not, initially, indicate many points of contact between Alfred Döblin and Hermann Hesse. The earlier novel was set in a throbbing contemporary metropolis, while Hesse locates *The Glass Bead Game* in a quiet, quasi-monastic province at some point in the remote future. Franz Biberkopf was a sensual being with a zest for food, drink and women; Josef Knecht seems the very antithesis: an ethereal scholar with little time for mundane pursuits, no love life, no involvement in anything other than the austere world of learning, where he reaches the sublime pinnacle of success as a Grand Master of the Bead Game. His existence is that of a revered professional sage and aesthete, and it is lived out within an idealised utopian state in which the acquisition of knowledge is the highest goal and few other pursuits are tolerated. He is an exemplary, almost saintly figure, treated with the utmost respect by a grovelling and obsequious narrator – a far cry indeed from the restless Franz Biberkopf and the margins of the corrupt urban society which he inhabited. *Berlin Alexanderplatz* was narrated at breakneck speed, changing themes and switching perspectives in mid-sentence, while Hesse seems content to linger over every detail in Knecht's life, ponderously piecing it together and often repeating himself in the process. There is little in the way of linguistic innovation here, no shocks or surprises, no verbal firecrackers, but rather the opposite: strings of worn-out clichés and pretentious empty phrases which have the effect of bathing the narrative in an atmosphere which is as sanctimonious as it is sterile. The contemporary social plasma, so important in *Berlin Alexanderplatz*, seems hardly worthy of mention in this futuristic fantasy.

Yet Hesse is undoubtedly one of Germany's most important and best-known authors, enjoying a much wider readership than Döblin and probably more famous outside Germany than any of her other twentieth-century novelists.[1] He won the Nobel Prize for literature in 1946 and quickly became a 'cult figure' in the United States, Japan and elsewhere. It seems improbable that he would have received this level of acclaim had he turned his back on the problems of the modern age altogether. He was no recluse, but a public figure who was not afraid to voice his opinions on the affairs of the nation, as he repeatedly did during the First World War.[2] *The Glass Bead Game* was written over a period of eleven years between 1932 and 1943, and it is not improbable that he would have wished to register some response to the events of those tragic years in the novel which kept him occupied at this crucial time in the history of modern Germany. In effect, a probing reading of *The Glass Bead Game* will reveal that the social context is vitally important in this novel. Like *Berlin Alexanderplatz*, it communicates the story of one man's struggle for survival in a world in which the citizen counts for little and subordination to an imperfect hierarchy is more important than individual self-fulfilment.

Josef Knecht may be a wiser and more responsible member of the community than Franz Biberkopf, but his biography reveals that he is also a rebel, an outsider whose integration into the self-contained republic of scholars is never fully effected. The name which he bears, *Knecht*, 'a servant', is suggestive of loyalty and obedience, but also, in a more ominous sense, of serfdom and slavery. The *Knecht* is the lowest member of the social hierarchy, the disenfranchised worker who must carry out orders and serve his master unquestioningly or bear the consequences. In the end he, too, faces a crisis which puts him at odds with the world in which he has hitherto enjoyed a protected life. The talents he has acquired provide little help when he has to survive in a world outside the province of scholars. Like Franz Biberkopf, he must re-examine his values and make an active decision to change his life, a task made extremely difficult for him on account of the highly restrictive social organisation to which he has been confined throughout his life. His options, in the end, seem narrower than Biberkopf's; the world has moved on, and Hesse is more pessimistic about its prospects than Döblin had been fifteen years earlier, before the advent of Fascism as a social and political system. The style in which Knecht's *vita* is put before us is idiosyncratic and experimental, although in a different way and for different reasons from Döblin's. It is my contention that many of the features of Hesse's style reflect changes which had come about in the political arena during the dark years of the 1930s and 1940s, and that despite its very different setting, structure, and themes, *The Glass Bead Game* is no less important a document of its era than *Berlin Alexanderplatz* had been.

2. FORMAT

The Glass Bead Game is Hesse's longest and most ambitious creation. Its structure is complex and raises questions as to what its central themes are, in a manner that recalls the debates about *Berlin Alexanderplatz*. Again, it seems uncertain whether Hesse would wish his readers to pay more attention to the life of the 'hero' or to the social and intellectual framework in which this takes place. The monolithic main title is modified by a subtitle in which the central character is named: *Das Glasperlenspiel. Versuch einer Lebensbeschreibung des Magister Ludi Josef Knecht ...* ('A Tentative Sketch of the Life of Magister Ludi Josef Knecht'). The impersonal game is immediately placed into the context of a specific human life, allowing the human and the abstract spheres to come together and vie for attention in a composite title.

The novel itself is in five sections: a motto, followed by a pseudo-scholarly description of how the Glass Bead Game came to be played. Then comes what most readers would take to be the 'main' section, an account, in twelve chapters, of the principal stages in the life of Josef Knecht, the celebrated Master of the Game, or *Magister Ludi*, to give him the Latin designation current in the province. There follow two corpora of posthumous writings attributed to Knecht, comprising thirteen poems and three fictional biographies. Knecht's life is thus illuminated from three distinct angles: the motto, the biography and the documents which its subject is said to have composed in his youth.

The anonymous narrative takes a linear course and traces Knecht's intellectual and moral development from his earliest childhood to his death, a procedure which inevitably invites comparison with the German *Bildungsroman* of the past. *The Glass Bead Game* is in some respects an extreme example of this narrative form, focusing single-mindedly on its hero's spiritual development and eschewing any references to characters or events that do not have a direct bearing on the hero's education. This part of the novel examines the tensions which arise out of Knecht's position as a product and leading member of the 'pedagogic' province of *Kastalien* ('Castalia' in its anglicised form), a social and political organisation comparable to a strict monastic institution.

The opening pages of the novel reveal that Josef Knecht's life story is put before the reader in a partial and defective format. Many factors combine to lessen the narrator's credibility. He treats his subject with a sense of reverence which makes it unlikely that he would repeat anything that might reflect badly upon him. His manner is sententious, his approach pedantic and repetitive. Also, as many years have evidently elapsed since Knecht's death, the sources used in compiling the biography are far from impeccable. The account of Knecht's last days, for example, is introduced as a 'legend', in a manner suggestive both of hero-worship and of authorial uncertainty. And there is another significant factor which compounds the ambiguity of the narrative before it has properly begun: the elitist province of Castalia is hostile to the very notion of a biography, to such an extent that the narrator must begin by remembering that *das Auslöschen des Individuellen* (GB 8) ('the obliteration of the individual') is one of the ruling principles on which the new state is founded. These are just a few of the factors that do not augur well for the authenticity of Knecht's biography, and predispose the reader to be suspicious of the 'truth content' of the text.

3. CASTALIA

Although Castalia is not mentioned by name in the first chapter, this historical section (GB 8–44) explains what the republic stands for and how it came into being. By the time of Knecht's life, several hundred years in the future,[3] the unnamed central European nation in which the novel is set has divided into two provinces – a world of commerce and strife much like our own, and a separate province dedicated to meditation and study, an independent community endowed with its own set of laws and regulations. In this sheltered environment, beyond the reach of the political manoeuvrings of the secular authorities, tolerated if not exactly encouraged by them, fraternities of art-lovers and intellectuals live in peaceful isolation like the members of some curious but essentially harmless endangered species. Here, they are free to play antiquated musical instruments, meditate, conserve artifacts, and teach each other about the cultural achievements of bygone generations. The denizens of Castalia look upon themselves as the guardians of a treasure house in which the accumulated wisdom of the past is stored.

This is a world in which some of the prognostications that have been voiced in our own century concerning the inevitable trend towards 'two cultures', by C. P. Snow and others, have come true. A polarisation has set in; the world of art has become distinct from the world of science; Castalia may exist side by side with the secular state, but it is self-governing, and run by an elusive 'Board of Educators' along lines which are at times reminiscent of a medieval religious order, but at times closer to the practices current in an inferior boys' boarding school.

In some respects, Castalia may therefore sound like the realisation of an age-old ideal, involving the complete liberation of the arts from any dependence on the practical demands of the community as a whole. Within the confines of this 'republic of scholars', the members of the Order are free from pressure: they need not fear unemployment or ridicule, and are provided with the necessities of life in return for a commitment to abide by certain rules. Their actual duties are few. As students, they enjoy the freedom to study more or less as they please, writing occasional exercises in the manner of Knecht's fictional autobiographies.

The narrator's eulogies of the system cannot, however, disguise one important circumstance: that Castalia is profoundly, almost wilfully, unproductive. Overtly creative compositions, be they poetic or musical, are not merely frowned upon but proscribed. The paradox at the heart of the Castalian experiment is that despite the long years which its scholars devote to the assimilation of knowledge, to all manner of accomplished performances and recitals, to the dedicated pursuit of excellence and to the study of all art-forms known to humankind, her thinkers are incapable of generating new ideas, her musicians no longer compose, her art experts have abandoned any pretence to genuine creative endeavour. The spontaneity of the active artist has been driven out and replaced by a new pursuit: mastery of the Glass Bead Game.

In these discussions, I have had to follow the Anglo-Saxon convention of turning *Kastalien* into 'Castalia'. The result is more euphonic than the original and may have the effect of rendering the organisation which it designates more attractive to the reader;

the feminine ending seems curiously inappropriate.[4] Although derived from the 'Castalian spring' on Mount Parnassus, reputed to be the source of eloquence, *Kastalien* is acoustically reminiscent of *Kasten* ('a box') and *Kasteiung* ('chastening', 'punishment'), as well as of castration. It is also of interest to note that the spring bears the name of the nymph Castalia who met her death there while fleeing from Apollo in a predicament that is comparable to the death, by drowning, of the fugitive Josef Knecht.

4. THE NATURE OF THE GAME

The Game itself is the central image of the novel. It is revered as the supreme cultural achievement by the population of Castalia, but, despite Hesse's application of the term 'utopia' to the novel (a concept to be discussed more fully on pp. 65–7), it is not consistently idealised. Rather, it appears to serve as a means enabling Hesse to express concern about many features of modern intellectual life: monolithic institutions, excessive attention to academic proficiency, and a feeling of sterility common to many modern artists. There is even a sense in which the Game stands for the modern novel, a reading supported by the close resemblance between 'Master Thomas von der Trave' and Hesse's contemporary, Thomas Mann (a native of Lübeck on the River Trave).

Readers expecting precise instructions and rules will be disappointed. The Game owes much to the principles of mathematics and music, enabling players to express 'the content ... of nearly all scholarly disciplines' (*GB* 12), and the objective would appear to consist of placing these ideas into new relationships with each other, so that the following claim can be made: *Das Glasperlenspiel ist also ein Spiel mit sämtlichen Werten und Inhalten unserer Kultur* ('The Glass Bead Game is thus a game involving the entire content and all values of our culture'). The player resembles an organist in control of a vast instrument 'of almost unimaginable perfection'. In theory, the entire intellectual content of the world can be reproduced by this means (loc. cit.).

Although its forerunners included Pythagoras, Novalis, Leibniz and Hegel, the Glass Bead Game resulted from developments in more recent times. Hesse's chronicler now refers to a fictitious historian by the name of Plinius Ziegenhalss, who is credited with having coined an apt phrase for the modern era: *das feuilletonistische Zeitalter* ('the Age of the *Feuilleton*') ('Literary Review'), or, to use a more up-to-date though slightly inaccurate rendering: 'the Age of the Colour Supplement'. This is the heyday of the crossword puzzle and of intellectual parlour-games

(*Bildungsspiele*) which Ziegenhalss associates with intellectual and moral decadence, distinguished by a demand for dissertations on obscure subjects like 'Nietzsche and Women's Fashions in the 1870s', or 'The Role of the Lapdog in the Lives of Great Courtesans'. What such diversions betoken is a gradual loss of interest in the true essence of things. Presentation and packaging became all-important. People stopped attending concerts for the sake of the music; they just went along to see a particular conductor or to listen to an individual interpretation. The concern which Hesse felt at the dilution of the nation's cultural life is obvious at this point in the narrative. As a reaction against these pernicious trends, a small group of high-minded music-lovers began to reconstruct old instruments and play the works of past composers in the original style, not as the fashion of the day dictated. In this context, a new form of notation was invented, involving multicoloured glass beads suspended on wires. Over the years, this contraption was adapted by many arts and sciences, so that it could eventually be used to express ideas in many fields of inquiry, all of which experienced a kind of renaissance, until the Age of the *Feuilleton* was overcome: *An der völligen Überwindung des Feuilletons und an jener neu erwachten Freude an den exaktesten Übungen des Geistes, der wir die Entstehung einer neuen Geisteszucht von mönchischer Strenge verdanken, hatte das Glasperlenspiel großen Anteil* (GB 33) ('The Glass Bead Game played a major role in the utter defeat of Feuilletonism and kindled a new delight in strict mental exercises which have led to the birth of a new intellectual discipline comparable to monasticism in its rigorous austerity').

If this is, indeed, a utopian vision of the future, it is one that has distinct, and paradoxical, affinities with the Middle Ages. The clock has gone forwards and backwards simultaneously, reflecting a not uncommon experience that society is capable of progressing and regressing at the same time. Movements such as National Socialism were characteristically ambiguous in their orientation 'back' towards nationalism and 'forwards' to a climate of greater social concern. The students of the Bead Game no longer indulge themselves in *ein Herumnaschen an den Hochschulen* (loc. cit.) ('taking a bite of this and that from what is on offer at university'), but adopt *eine büßerisch-fanatische Hingabe an den Geist* (GB 34) ('a fanatical and penitential subordination to matters of the spirit'). They must learn to renounce worldly possessions, fame, acclaim by the press and comfortable marriages to the daughters of bank-managers and industrialists if the sloppiness and dilettantism of the past are to be overcome.

The Glass Bead Game evolves over time into a means of harmonising and synthesising many scholarly pursuits with the assistance of a common set of symbols. The beads are eventually abandoned, replaced by carefully vetted ciphers. What began as an *aide-mémoire* is gradually elevated to an exercise in virtuosity, and finally provides the basis of a public ceremony. It comes to be revered as an end in itself. It is played in regular ceremonial meetings, the culmination of which is the *ludus sollemnis* which lasts for several weeks and is accompanied by rigorous exercises in meditation. The rules are best envisaged as resembling an infinitely complex game of chess, in which each piece, move or grouping of figures has a specific meaning or set of references associated with it (*GB* 131).

If descriptions of the Game fall short of providing a viable set of instructions, this is partly because its correspondences with many different forms of intellectual activity are of importance to Hesse. One such relationship is the link with religion. Of this, the narrator remarks:

> *Es ist kaum übertrieben, wenn wir zu sagen wagen: für den engen Kreis der echten Glasperlenspieler war das Spiel nahezu gleichbedeutend mit Gottesdienst, während es sich jeder eigenen Theologie enthielt.* (*GB* 41)
>
> (It would scarcely be an exaggeration to venture to declare that the small circle of genuine Glass Bead Players viewed the Game as virtually equivalent to a religious service, although it lacked any specific theological content of its own.)

Here, as so often, the narrator mentions, and immediately plays down, one of the less wholesome developments associated with the rise of the Glass Bead Game (see pp. 78–84).

The Game also influences the educational system in that special 'elite' schools are set up to teach its thousands of symbols to especially talented students, for some of whom it may well become a lifelong preoccupation or obsession. Each graduate cherishes the ambition of becoming a Magister Ludi, the quasi-divine High Priest whom they revere 'almost as a deity' (*GB* 43).

Before the reader has delved very far into the novel, questions arise as to whether the new society is in fact an improvement on the old. Sample titles of the kind of research undertaken by Castalian scholars suggest that the work done here is far more futile and spurious than the *Feuilleton* articles which were denounced by Ziegenhalss as having trivialised scholarship in the twentieth century. It has also been claimed that here, more than elsewhere in his writings, Hesse has chosen to turn his back on the pressing problems of his age and to retreat into a world where he can remain contentedly oblivious to the moral issues facing his German contemporaries. Why debate the pros and cons of an imaginary republic of world-weary aesthetes at a time when Fascism, not Feuilletonism, was subverting the cultural evolution of Europe? Could Hesse maintain his credibility as a sage after publishing a book in which a nebulous 'bead game' is held up as an answer of sorts to the aberrations of modern man, and this while the continent of Europe was in the throes of a World War? To answer this question will require a short excursus involving a look at the genesis of Hesse's manuscript.

5. LANKHAAR, SCHWENTCHEN AND LITZKE

Although Hermann Hesse had retreated to the mountains of Montagnola in Switzerland long before the outbreak of the war, he was by no means blind to the political realities of life in the 1930s and 1940s. His novel *Der Steppenwolf* of 1927 shows his concern with issues such as pacifism, though in a somewhat ambiguous manner.[5] But the most striking evidence of Hesse's political concerns in *The Glass Bead Game* has so far gone almost unheeded by the critics, despite having been readily available for inspection for many years. This is to be found in an early version of the introductory chapter, written in draft form in June 1932, less than a year before Hitler seized power. It reveals a bitingly satirical streak in the novelist and leaves little room to doubt that *The Glass Bead Game* was originally intended as a counterblast to certain distinctly worrying tendencies that were affecting the cultural life of contemporary Germany.

The opening chapter of this draft bears the heading *Vom Wesen und Herkunft des Glasperlenspiels* ('On the Nature and Origins of the Glass Bead Game'). It contains a similar diatribe against the almighty *Feuilleton*, followed by some striking examples of the abuse of scholarship by two named academic charlatans whose work considerably surpasses in deviousness that of the pretentious journalists who are ridiculed in the final version. These would-be scholars are no idle time-wasters, but perverse and irresponsible ideologues whose theses play into the hands of radical politicians. The text of this preliminary draft merits careful consideration:

> *Als Beispiele für die rührend-lächerliche sowohl wie für die verderbte Seite dieser Zustände an den Hochschulen (deren Schüler übrigens nach Belieben streikten, demonstrierten, die*

*Lehrer am Leben bedrohten usw.) nennen wir zwei um 1950
erschienene umfangreiche Bücher deutscher Professoren, welche
beide als Kuriosa eine gewisse Berühmtheit behalten haben. Das
eine, rührende, ist Professor Lankhaars zweibändiges, über 1,500
Seiten Quart umfassendes Werk 'Die Kriegsschuldlüge'. In diesem
Werk widerlegt Lankhaar gewisse, schon damals von der ganzen
Welt vergessene oder belachte Vorwürfe, welche während des
Weltkrieges von 1914 gegen das deutsche Volk, seine Führer,
seinen Charakter usw. von den damaligen Feinden erhoben
worden waren ... Dieser Gelehrte beweist also ... die vollkommene
Unschuld des deutschen Volkes, des deutschen Kaisers, der
deutschen Generalität und Diplomatie, und wies aufs deutlichste
und mit vielen Belegen die beiden einzigen Schuldigen nach,
nämlich den vor manchen Jahrhunderten verstorbenen
französischen König Ludwig den Elften und einen inzwischen
völlig vergessenen französischen Beamten namens Théophile
Delcassé ...*

*Weit schlimmer steht es mit einem anderen Buch, das ein
Hochschulprofessor Schwentchen damals herausgab, mit dem
Titel 'Das grüne Blut'. Es lebte damals ein Jugendführer,
Verschwörer und Abenteurer namens Litzke, der mehr als zehn
Jahre lang als Deutschlands 'heimlicher Kaiser' galt und sich
selber gern so nennen hörte. Er war es, der die durch Rassen-
legenden alles Denkens entwöhnte Jugend durch die neue, von ihm
erfundene Legende vom 'grünen Blut' beschenkte. Dies grüne
Blut, so hieß es, sei die mystische, einem heiligen Stigma gleich-
zusetzende Auszeichnung weniger, nämlich der aus mindestens
dreißig Generationen reinen Germanenstammes entsprossenen
echten Führernaturen. Viele der alten deutschen Kaiser hätten es
gehabt ... und natürlich besaß es auch Litzke, der heimliche Kaiser
... Professor Schwentchen ... zitierte darin Zoroaster und Manu,
entlehnte Worte aus dem Sanskrit, dem Sumerischen, dem
Griechischen, Wörter, die er selber gar nicht lesen konnte, denn
sein Fach war nicht Philologie, sondern die Wissenschaft des
Tennisspiels, für welche es damals Professuren gab ...* [6]

(We shall cite two examples of the sentimentally pathetic
and degenerate conditions obtaining in the universities of
the time (whose pupils, incidentally, were given to striking,
demonstrating and threatening the lives of their teachers as
they saw fit). These voluminous compilations by German
professors appeared around 1950 and have attained a certain degree of celebrity as curiosities. The more sentimental
of these two publications is Professor Lankhaar's two-

volume study *The Myth of War Guilt*, rnning to more than 1,500 sides of quarto. Here Lankhaar refutes certain allegations made during the World War of 1914 by Germany's enemies against her people, her leaders, her national character etc., allegations which by then had been forgotten or ridiculed by all and sundry … This scholar, having demonstrated to the entire world … the complete and utter innocence of the German people, the German Emperor, the German generals and diplomats, then indicated vociferously and with reference to a multitude of sources who the guilty parties were. There were only two: the French King Louis the Eleventh, deceased several centuries earlier, and a French official by the name of Théophile Delcassé, who has since been completely forgotten …

Far worse is the case of a book entitled *Green Blood*, published in those days by Schwentchen, a university professor. There was a leader figure enjoying some popularity among the youth of his time, a conspirator-cum-adventurer called Litzke, who for more than ten years wished to be regarded – as he was by his followers – as Germany's 'secret Emperor'. It was this man who bequeathed a new myth to a generation of young people already reduced to mindless stupidity by bogus racist doctrines: the myth of 'green blood' which he had invented. This so-called green blood was supposed to be a distinction conveying mystic properties, comparable to a holy stigma, which only very few people possessed, namely those genuine leader figures who were descended from at least thirty generations of unadulterated Germanic ancestry. Many of the ancient German Emperors had it … and so, naturally enough, had Litzke, the secret Emperor … Here, Professor Schwentchen … quoted Zoroaster and Manu, borrowing words from Sanskrit, Sumerian and Greek, words which he himself could not read, for his discipline was not philology, but the scientific study of tennis, for which they had professors in those days …)

These two arrogant scholars and their populist publications sum up Hesse's opinions of the chauvinist tendencies that were in the air in the aftermath of the First World War, attitudes whose appeal to the disaffected youth of the time helps to explain the widespread popularity of radical policies in the 1930s. Lankhaar speaks for many when he tries to belittle the role of Germany in sparking off the First World War and blames everything on the French, thus fuelling the notion of a 'hereditary enmity' between

France and Germany, here illustrated by references to figures from the distant past.[7] His was not a lone voice; Hesse's satirical account of these tendentious writings clearly draws on the then prevalent *Dolchstoßlegende*, the feeling that the German army had not been defeated in fair combat so much as betrayed or 'stabbed in the back'.

The 'far worse' Professor Schwentchen represents a different set of opinions which Hesse identifies as part of the social and political malaise of the time: the racist mysticism spread by the likes of Alfred Rosenberg, whose notorious pseudo-scholarly treatise *Der Mythus des 20. Jahrhunderts* ('The Myth of the Twentieth Century') had recently appeared, in 1930. Its aim was to provide legitimate-sounding credentials for some aspects of the National Socialist ideology. The identity of the conspiratorial adventurer named in the passage should now be more than self-evident.

Two reasons will have persuaded Hesse to abandon this preamble during the later stages of his work on *The Glass Bead Game*. His clever satirical sketch had patently been overtaken by events long before it could be published, and it was fast becoming clear that by 1950, Europe would be in a very different predicament from that envisaged here. Second, Hesse was determined to attempt publication of the novel in Germany as soon as it was completed, i.e. during the Second World War. Overtly satirical comments of the type mentioned above had to be excised. Some authorities have expressed surprise that he attached much importance to seeing the book through the press in Nazi Germany, but his determination to do so provides a valuable key to his view of its direct relevance to his war-torn country. While making no public statements either for or against the German regime, Hesse earned himself a temporary immunity from censorship. He did not lose sight of the role which he had traditionally played there, as a defender of personal integrity and champion of greater self-awareness.

Seen in this context, *The Glass Bead Game* appears in a new light. What began as a recipe for salvation in a world dominated by ideologues and demagogues of the worst kind was examined more critically and found to be no better than the malaise it was intended to cure. There can be little doubt that the extremely authoritarian province of Castalia, with its emphasis on discipline, empty rituals and personal purity, its insistence on unconditional obedience, its ruthless destruction of its enemies, and its generally dictatorial atmosphere, is a cryptic replica of the Fascist state, however much this interpretation may run counter to the intentions of its author prior to 1933. Originally, Hesse had proposed to conclude the novel with a confrontation between Knecht and a dictator who insisted on banning the Game.[8] Despite the rewriting of this and other sections, it is hardly surprising that the Berlin censor withheld permission to publish the novel in 1942, and that a general ban on all of Hesse's books followed shortly thereafter; the portrayal of the republic of Castalia was too close for comfort. Here, Josef Knecht is placed under almost constant surveillance, his freedom to travel is restricted, independent decision-making is impossible, boards and authorities watch over his every move, and creative endeavours are jealously scrutinised for signs of deviation from the norm. Whether the Game itself is anything more than empty ritual, an aberration rather than a utopian ideal, must be considered in the light of the protagonist's career.

6. THE MAKING OF A MASTER

Little is known about Josef Knecht's background; he may have been an orphan, or he may have been discovered in unfavourable family circumstances by the powerful *Erziehungsbehörde* ('Board of Educators'), removed from home and sent to a succession of special 'elite' schools. There is more than a hint at the beginning of the narrative that family life is incompatible with scholarly achievement. Through the intervention of the benign *Magister Musicae*, he is selected for promotion to the nation's top establishments, which are under the control of an elusive 'Board' composed of the 'Elite'. These authorities, spoken of with cringing reverence by the narrator-cum-biographer, are soon recognised to be sinister, monolithic institutions with little concern for the well-being of their charges.

After four years at the preparatory school of Eschholz, Josef moves on to Waldzell, which specialises in producing players of the Glass Bead Game (Chapter 2). His interest in art and music is stimulated, but the negative side of this education is conveyed by the Head Teacher, Zbinden, his name suggestive of 'binding', who treats Josef with cold severity, perhaps because he recognises that the boy's independent outlook is at variance with the rigid doctrines of Castalia. The sharpest criticisms of the 'Order' come from Plinio Designori, a pupil who enjoys strong connections with the outside world. Plinio is scathing about the Game, which is revered within the province at the expense of the genuine creativity of the individual. Josef is manoeuvred into defending the system, but remains uncertain as to where his true loyalties lie. He turns to the Music Master for advice, but is merely instructed to persevere with his studies and to turn his debates with Plinio into exercises in rhetoric. Permission to visit Plinio at home, outside Castalia, is curtly refused by the authorities.

During his 'Years of Study' (Chapter 3), Josef travels from one archive to another, amassing knowledge. His only duty is to compile one fictional autobiography each year, in which he has to project himself into a past epoch. Three such exercises are appended to the novel, as are several more or less illicitly composed poems; Hesse is known to have spent time on a fourth life concerning an eighteenth-century theologian, but this has remained a fragment, perhaps because it was coming to resemble a key to the novel as a whole.[9] The young man's sexual experiences are glossed over: after a period when youthful diversions are tolerated, chastity, or at least celibacy, becomes the norm, and for the true Castalian, marriage is no more than a 'curiosity' (*GB* 116f.). Josef spends time acquainting himself with Far Eastern culture and meets an engaging crank known as the 'Elder Brother', a man who has forsaken Castalia and taken up his abode in a remote bamboo grove where he prefers to live according to ancient Chinese traditions rather than see them incorporated into an empty ritual.

When his years of wisdom-gathering are up, Josef Knecht is selected for a diplomatic mission to the monastery of Mariafels (Chapters 4–5). At the instigation of the current *Magister Ludi*, Thomas von der Trave, Josef is dispatched there, ostensibly to teach the monks to play the Bead Game. Complex political motives appear to underlie this mission: he is instructed by Dubois, Castalia's Police Chief, to report back on noteworthy goings-on and is congratulated on his efforts in this direction. But while on this expedition, he hears the view that the Game is little more than a belated, secular offshoot of the Christian culture of the West, an opinion which is expounded in some detail by Pater Jakobus, the monastery's resident historian (*GB* 186).

He returns to Castalia a front-runner for high office and is duly elected one of the twelve highest-ranking 'Masters'. The vacancy occurs when the incumbent *Magister Ludi* passes away, an event that affords a disturbing insight into the way in which the elite officials control the political life of the province. A vicious campaign is mounted against the dying man's deputy, Bertram, and, once he has been disposed of, Knecht must fight hard to gain the recognition of an apparently implacable hard core of *Repetenten*, or candidates for high office within the system. Knecht asserts himself and presides over his first public Bead Game, which is based on the design of the Chinese house (Chapter 7). This is the apex of his career.

7. DECLINE AND FALL

There is much to suggest that within the strict hierarchy of Castalia, Knecht's style of office is more flexible and dynamic than that of the other officials. Lacking their intellectual arrogance, he is not averse to devoting himself to the needs of novices and assuming personal responsibility for instructing the very young, something he particularly enjoys. But in the chapter *Die beiden Pole* ('The Two Poles'), Knecht must admit that he is torn between two extremes: the conflicting priorities of service to the Game (and ultimately to Castalia as a political entity) on the one hand, and his own personal development on the other. The problem is that of establishing the appropriate balance between these twin poles:

> *Die beiden Grundtendenzen oder Pole dieses Lebens, sein Yin und Yang, waren die Tendenz zum Bewahren, zur Treue, zum selbstlosen Dienst an der Hierarchie, und andrerseits die Tendenz zum 'Erwachen', zum Vordringen, zum Greifen und Begreifen der Wirklichkeit.* (GB 299)

> (The two basic tendencies or poles of his life, its yin and yang, were, on the one hand, a tendency to preserve, to remain loyal, to serve the hierarchy unconditionally, and, on the other, an inclination towards a 'new awakening', a desire to apprehend and comprehend the real world.)

A chance meeting with Plinio in Chapter 9 reveals that his erst-while schoolmate has been dogged by misfortune in the outside world, but at least he has seen both sides while Josef Knecht has remained a virtual prisoner within a narrowly circumscribed institutional existence. After eight years as *Magister Ludi*, he resolves to quit the province and attempt to start a new life outside it, initially as a tutor to Plinio's rather wayward son, Tito. That he should wish to resign is unheard of in Castalia, and its bureaucratic machinery is unable to respond to his request. Knecht issues an 'open letter' – written in part by a slightly neurotic friend, Tegularius – in which the Game is criticised on the grounds that it is an ephemeral cultural phenomenon, subject to the vicissitudes of time and to the goodwill or otherwise of the secular governments on whose financial support the republic of aesthetes is totally dependent.

By the time he reaches the twelfth chapter of his biography, the never very confident narrator has to admit that he is merely reproducing a 'legend' about his subject, warning his readers that what he is placing before them could well be the result of fanciful speculation. Knecht seeks a final interview with the over-all Head of the Order, Master Alexander, who refuses to grant him leave of absence. According to the 'legend' of the Master's last days, Knecht accompanies young Tito to Belpunt, the family's summer retreat in the mountains. The boy goes for a swim, challenging his tutor to emulate him. Not wishing to seem uncomradely, Knecht follows him, but is quickly overcome by the icy cold water of the mountain lake. Tito is left to contemplate, and learn from, the tragic scene for which he considers himself responsible:

> *O weh, dachte er entsetzt, nun bin ich an seinem Tode schuldig! Und erst jetzt, wo kein Stolz zu wahren und kein Widerstand mehr zu leisten war, spürte er im Weh seines erschrockenen Herzens, wie lieb er diesen Mann schon gehabt hatte. Und indem er sich, trotz allen Einwänden, an des Meisters Tode mitschuldig fühlte, überkam ihn mit heiligem Schauer die Ahnung, daß diese Schuld ihn selbst und sein Leben umgestalten und viel Größeres von ihm fordern würde, als er bisher je von sich verlangt hatte.* (GB 471)

(Alas, he thought in utter horror, now I am guilty of causing his death! And now that there was no pride to preserve, no resistance to offer, he began to feel, in the depths of his grieving heart, how fond he had grown of this man. Despite all arguments to the contrary, he knew that he was partly to blame for the Master's death, and a shudder of awe came over him, making him realise that this guilt would transform him and reshape his life, demanding far more of him than he had ever before demanded of himself.)

8. NARRATIVE STRATEGY

The introductory chapter outlining the evolution of the Game was, along with the Rainmaker's biography, the first part of the novel to be written. After several revisions, Hesse felt it could be published in Nazi Germany without attracting the disapproval of the authorities, and it duly appeared in *Die neue Rundschau* in December 1934 with a note indicating that it could have been written 'sometime around the year 2400'. In a letter to Gottfried Bermann Fischer, Hesse explained that he had no intention of escaping into the past or into the timeless world of the fairy-tale.

The opening chapter would compel his readers to decide whether to 'put the book away, or to accompany the author into the clean but rarefied atmosphere in which it is set'.[10] Progress on the remaining chapters was excruciatingly slow and was hampered by illness and by Hesse's endeavours on behalf of refugees from Germany. The last twenty pages of 'The Legend' took one year to write.[11] Hesse continued to place extracts with two literary periodicals, *Die neue Rundschau* and *Corona*, right up to 1942, which demonstrates how close he must have come to realising his ambition to see the work through the presses in wartime Germany.

This is no fast-moving narrative in the manner of *Berlin Alexanderplatz*. The characters come across as shadowy figures with whom identification is difficult, as they tend to be heavily idealised (Knecht, the *Magister Musicae*, Pater Jakobus, Ferromonte), whimsical loners with neurotic propensities (the 'Chinese' Elder Brother, Tegularius, Petrus, Anton, Bertram), or essentially 'faceless' representatives of an impenetrable bureaucracy (Zbinden, Thomas von der Trave, Dubois, Alexander). The narrative is marred by some digressions and repetitions, and the immediacy of its impact is clearly lessened by the idiosyncrasies of the narrator-cum-chronicler, whose ponderous moralising seems calculated to prevent the reader from reaching an independent conclusion concerning the merits of Castalia and the hero's progress within it. These charges will be examined in greater detail on pp. 78–84 below.

Hesse is not normally thought of as a satirist, although several of his semi-autobiographical novels, especially *Peter Camenzind* and his chilling portrait of a boys' boarding school, *Under the Wheel*, contain more than a few satirical vignettes. It was in *Peter Camenzind* that Hesse sketched out a programme for the budding novelist which seems appropriate to *The Glass Bead Game*:

> *Die Menschen überhaupt waren mir von Kind auf weder sonderlich lieb noch notwendig gewesen, nun begann ich sie kritisch und ironisch zu betrachten. Mit Vorliebe erfand und erzählte ich kleine Geschichten, in welchen die Verhältnisse der Menschen untereinander lieblos und mit scheinbarer Sachlichkeit satirisch dargestellt und bitter verhöhnt wurden. Woher dieser verächtliche Ton kam, wußte ich selber nicht ...*[12]

(From my childhood onwards I experienced no great feeling of love for or dependence upon my fellow human beings in general, and I therefore began to regard them critically and with irony. I especially enjoyed inventing and narrating little stories in which human relationships were depicted without love and described from a satirical, seemingly matter-of-fact point of view, and subjected to bitter mockery. I had no idea where I had acquired this disdainful tone ...)

These lines read like a succinct description of the author's method of narration in *The Glass Bead Game*. The account of Castalia unfolds in an ostensibly factual manner; the history of the Game in the first chapter is certainly related from a 'seemingly matter-of-fact point of view'. The society that is investigated in the subsequent chapters is not based on love; here one need only think of the representatives of the so-called 'elite' and of their jealous machinations concerning Thomas's deputy, Bertram. This goes some way towards explaining the lack of conventional character portrayal in the novel; Hesse is less concerned with the direct depiction of 'reality' than with exposing pernicious tendencies which he sees as becoming ever more pronounced in modern times. In doing so, he is clearly extrapolating from experience.

The most obvious victim of this strategy is the narrator. He has been criticised on the grounds of being excessively pedantic, and there is no denying his addiction to well-worn clichés that grate on the ear and inspire scant confidence in his critical faculties, least of all when he is lavishing praise on Castalia's supposed excellence. Each of Knecht's formative experiences is hailed as something special: *ein schönes und bedeutendes Ereignis* (GB 76)('a beautiful and meaningful event'), *eine große und seltene Ehre* (loc. cit.) ('a great and rare honour'). *Mächtig spürte er den Zauber dieser Atmosphäre* (GB 90) ('He became powerfully aware of this enchanted atmosphere'), *Nun gaben tiefe Schichten seiner Seele Antwort* (loc. cit.) ('The deep recesses of his soul now responded'), or *die Sternenwelt des Glasperlenspiels* (GB 110) ('the starry realms of the Glass Bead Game') – here, language is overloaded; the effect is cloying, the imagery repetitive, sometimes in a manner that recalls some crudely penned, kitschy romance; compare *innig und freundlich klang die reine, innig heitere Musik mit ihren süßen Dreiklängen* (GB 173) ('the pure, delicately serene music with its sweet triads sounded so delicate and appealing'). Romantic pathos is evoked at every opportunity: *einen zarten Schmerz im Innern* (GB 190) ('a tender ache within him'), *von jenem Hauch des Wunders gestreift* (GB 221) ('touched by that breath of the miraculous'), and archaic formulae like *je und je* (GB 184, 186, 310, etc.) ('ever and anon') are particular favourites.

All this may seem tedious and off-putting; only when it is realised that the narrator is an important figure within the novel does Hesse's purpose become clear. The slow-moving style, so irritating to many a modern reader, is explicable as a necessary product of Castalia's decadent intellectual climate, incapable of innovation, and a striking symptom of its decline. The narrator must appear tedious and sententious in order to demonstrate that the vital sap has drained away from the province which he represents. How could he be expected to write dynamically when he is the product of a system where rote-learning and high-handed indoctrination are the principal methods of instruction? But this dry cabinet style reveals only one side of our Castalian scholar; there is another, perhaps more important aspect which remains to be investigated (see pp. 78–84 below).

9. UTOPIA

There are two important considerations that appear to militate against the contention that Hesse is using the society depicted in the novel as a mechanism for deriding aspects of life in modern Germany. The first of these is the motto which he placed at the very beginning of the book and endorsed as fitting the book 'with absolute accuracy'; the second is the label 'utopia' which is applied to it in several letters to friends. The motto was composed many years before the final version of the novel was committed to paper; by 1932, Hesse had arranged for it to be translated into Latin, and there are strong indications that at this point in time he still intended to let Castalia figure as a positive contrast to the realities of life in modern Europe, as *eine geistige Kultur ... , in der zu leben und deren Diener zu sein sich lohnt – dies ist das Wunschbild, das ich mir da malen möchte*[13] ('a culture of the spirit ... which is worth living in and serving – that is the ideal which I should like to depict'). The motto was not modified when the book was completed; in fact, Hesse went so far as to stress its singular relevance to the novel in its final form: *Sein Motto hat den Vorzug vor vielen andern, daß es haargenau paßt*[14] ('Its motto has one advantage compared to many others: it fits the book with absolute accuracy').

This short statement with which the book opens seems to suggest that Castalia is worth bringing 'one step' closer to fruition:

> *nichts ist doch notwendiger, den Menschen vor Augen zu stellen, als gewisse Dinge, deren Existenz weder beweisbar noch wahrscheinlich ist, welche aber eben dadurch, daß fromme und gewissenhafte Menschen sie gewissermaßen als seiende Dinge behandeln, dem Sein und der Möglichkeit des Geborenwerdens um einen Schritt näher geführt werden.* (GB 7)

(nothing is more essential than to confront mankind with a visual portrait of certain phenomena whose existence is neither demonstrable nor probable, but which, when treated as though they were real by dedicated and conscientious persons, are brought one step closer to reality and to the possibility of being born.)

The wording of this preamble helps to explain why literary criticism has been slow to acknowledge the manifest shortcomings of Castalia as a social and cultural entity. Undoubtedly, Hesse did much to deter the investigation of this aspect of the novel by supplying his readers with apparently favourable assessments of the province he had depicted, and notably by attaching the term 'utopia' to Castalia. The importance of her role as a custodian of spiritual values and an antithesis to the evils of the present is underlined in a letter from 1955:

> *Ich mußte, der grinsenden Gegenwart zum Trotz, das Reich des Geistes und der Seele als existent und unüberwindlich sichtbar machen. So wurde meine Dichtung zur Utopie, das Bild wurde in die Zukunft projiziert, die üble Gegenwart in eine überstandene Vergangenheit gebannt.*[15]

> (In defiance of the wicked sneer of the contemporary world, I felt obliged to show that the realm of the spirit and the soul was both real and invincible. Thus I created a utopia, projecting an image into the future and banishing the evil present by transposing it into a past which people had managed to survive.)

The term 'utopia' has given rise to the understandable expectation that the book conveys a positive alternative to the present and that Castalia must be inherently admirable. Most critics are reluctant to depart from this view. Joseph Mileck hails Castalia as 'a splendid possibility' threatened only by 'the fallibility of man and the atrophy of time', maintaining that Hesse believed in a kind of lay monasticism as depicted here. Mileck and Ziolkowski agree that a 'better tomorrow of 2400' is brought about after Knecht's untimely death.[16] Others speak of 'futuristic idealism' or see Castalia as an antithesis to National Socialist Germany.[17] A more circumspect view is advanced by Martin Swales, who views it as an embodiment of both positive and destructive aspects of the German mentality:

> [Castalia is] a world dangerously determined to insulate itself from actualities; it is an ivory tower, an elite province

which will not acknowledge its own embeddedness in history as the given dimension of human being and activity. In this novel Hesse offers an affectionate, yet deeply critical, examination of a familiar pattern in German thinking.)[18]

Few readers are prepared to go further than this in their condemnation of Castalia;[19] we are, it would seem, debarred from condemning the system outright by the seal of approval enshrined in the motto and by Hesse's application of the term 'utopia' to the finished work. What may have eluded attention so far is that the motto must apply to the book as a whole, not merely to one aspect of it, such as the Bead Game or the social and intellectual climate of Castalia. If it is to fit the book 'with absolute accuracy' (*haargenau*), then it must relate to Knecht's defiant departure, to his self-liberation, rather than to the monolithic institutions of the republic which he himself sought to abandon. It would therefore be appropriate to see the hero's attempts to challenge an inflexible system as something that is indeed worth bringing 'one step closer to reality and to the possibility of being born', in the words of the motto. This seems more likely, given Hesse's lifelong struggle in defence of individualism, to be the 'utopian' message of the book, which it is difficult to see as an endorsement of the Castalian constitution. The notion of a 'utopia' in any case implies a rejection of the present, and it is interesting to compare the way in which Hesse himself defined the term in 1944:

> *Das mit der 'Utopie', das heißt mit dem Verlegen in die Zukunft, ist natürlich nur ein Behelf. In Wirklichkeit ist Kastalien, Orden, meditative Gelehrsamkeit etc. weder ein Zukunftstraum noch ein Postulat, sondern eine ewige, platonische, in diversen Graden der Verwirklichung schon oft auf Erden sichtbar gewordene Idee.*[20]

> (In regard to the 'utopia', i.e. the transfer of the action into the future, that is obviously just a convenient device. In reality, Castalia, the Order, contemplative erudition, etc. are neither futuristic fantasies nor postulates, but the workings-out of an ever-present platonic idea that has often been experienced on earth in various stages of its evolution.)

Precisely when and where the social paradigms represented by Castalia have been 'experienced on earth' will become clearer in the light of a more detailed inspection of her cultural achievements.

10. THE REPUBLIC OF SCHOLARS

No interpretation of *The Glass Bead Game* would be complete without an analysis of the social framework within which the Game is played and its Master employed, yet the narrator is coy about many aspects of life in Castalia and leaves many matters of detail to be inferred. In view of the oblique manner in which the republic is portrayed, it is hardly surprising that, as soon as the novel appeared in Switzerland in 1943, two contrasting interpretations were put forward. According to Professor Faesi, writing in *Neue Schweizer Rundschau*, Castalia is a utopian state in a positive sense, while the other opinion, expressed by R. J. Humm in *Die Weltwoche*, sees the province as pervaded by symptoms of decline and decadence.[21]

Both points of view receive support from the text, where the optimism regularly voiced by the narrator contrasts sharply with Knecht's personal decision to withdraw prematurely from an oppressive, inward-looking professional hierarchy. Theodore Ziolkowski proposes an answer to the dilemma which involves distinguishing between three separate manifestations of Castalia: the fruitful community of intellectuals originally established as a bulwark against mediocrity, the restrictive bureaucracy into which this originally noble experiment degenerates, and a third Castalia, which Ziolkowski believes will have benefited from Knecht's example:

> The novel actually depicts, implicitly or explicitly, *three* visions of Castalia: the utopian spiritual realm portrayed in the introduction and *only* there; the Alexandrine republic of aestheticism, sharply attacked by Knecht and the narrator alike in the text of the novel; and finally a more balanced synthesis of life and the spirit represented by the narrator himself. It is necessary to distinguish sharply between these stages.[22]

The neat distinction proposed above is not borne out by the novel itself. The introduction is not concerned with the state of Castalia, which it does not mention, but only with the evolution of the Game. There is no direct evidence that the province has benefited from the Master's resignation and demise; the fact that those very institutions which cramped Knecht's freedom are still in existence shows that little has changed since his time. Castalia has not become an 'open' society; she still maintains 'secret archives' to which Knecht's latter-day biographer is denied access (GB 311), and he has to admit that his attempts to probe into the details of

Knecht's life are repeatedly frustrated, not least because his work as a biographer remains *einigermaßen im Widerspruch zu den herrschenden Gesetzen und Bräuchen* (GB 8) ('to some extent at variance with the prevailing laws and practices') of the province.

It is difficult to concur with the view that the new Castalia of the narrator is better than the old Castalia in which Knecht lived. The Game is in a state of decline during Knecht's life, the annual festivals get shorter (GB 220) and are regarded *als unlebendig, als altmodisch, als zopfisches Relikt der Vergangenheit* (GB 253) ('as lifeless and unfashionable, as a fossilised left-over from the past'). Many of Knecht's posthumous poems, by contrast, celebrate the inevitability of change; in them, life is envisaged as a constant flux, man as clay, kneaded into different shapes but never struck into a permanent form (*Klage*, 'Lament', GB 472). In *Stufen* ('Steps'), the poem which Knecht recalls on the eve of his final departure, we find a sustained outcry against the very notion of stability in life:

> *Der Weltgeist will nicht fesseln uns und engen,*
> *Er will uns Stuf' um Stufe heben, weiten.*
> *Kaum sind wir heimisch einem Lebenskreise*
> *Und traulich eingewohnt, so droht Erschlaffen.*
> *Nur wer bereit zu Aufbruch ist und Reise,*
> *Mag lähmender Gewöhnung sich entraffen.* (GB 484)

> (The Cosmic Spirit strives not to restrain us,
> But raises us by steps and stages.
> We scarce have time to call a home our own,
> A cosy place where we grow old and dreary –
> We must depart and journey on alone
> To shun routines that paralyse and make us weary.)

In the most pessimistic of these poems, *Der letzte Glasperlenspieler* (GB 476) ('The Last Glass Bead Player'), Knecht foresees the eventual destruction of Castalia, its culture superseded by wars and plagues, as the now redundant beads roll off into the sands, and the bees and ivy move in to claim the ruins among which the last Master Gamesman awaits the inevitable. Given the cyclic view of history which Hesse shares with many twentieth-century German novelists, the strengthening of Castalia after Knecht's defection does not seem a high priority. A far more interesting and subtle theme of the novel is to be found in Castalia's defence mechanism against Knecht's criticism. His defiant, rebellious gesture is simply amalgamated into the history of the province with no concern for the personal liberation he was trying to achieve; in the final analysis, the novel demonstrates the buoyancy of an authoritarian system by showing its ability to transmute the 'rebel' Josef Knecht into a 'legendary' figure, and to use this figure to foster the status quo.

The putative virtues of the republic of scholars need to be investigated further if we are to arrive at an opinion as to which of its features are worth preserving and refining. Castalia would appear to offer five major advantages over previous political and educational systems: (i) it can claim to have suppressed the Age of the *Feuilleton*; (ii) its members are dedicated to the study and the loving preservation of the world's greatest cultural products; (iii) within Castalia, worldly ambitions, the pursuit of wealth, fame and power are discouraged; (iv) education is the highest (and only) goal of the state; (v) the province fosters a sober and meditative lifestyle among its members.

It will be observed that in each of these areas, Castalia as portrayed in the novel has failed to put its ideals into practice; in some cases, the medicine seems worse than the disease. The Age of the *Feuilleton* may have been a time of benighted dilettantism in which we can all too easily discern the imprint of present-day sensationalism and pseudo-scholarship, but research as it is understood in Castalia is so idiosyncratic as to compare negatively with all that went before. The new learning encompasses, for example, the following fields of inquiry: the pronunciation of Latin at southern Italian universities at the end of the twelfth century, a translation of ancient Egyptian texts into ancient Greek and Sanskrit, and a comparison of the horoscopes of Goethe and Spinoza, accompanied by multi-coloured sketches (GB 65, 148). When the sage Chattus Calvensis II, described as *etwas wunderlich*, (GB 65) ('somewhat peculiar'), dies during his work on one such project, no-one can be found to complete it. The narrator himself applies the word *vergeuden*, (GB 66) ('to waste'), to the work of a Castalian scholar who has dedicated his life to the futile task of deciphering a single inscription. Everything goes, as long as the scholar does not offend against propriety: *[es gibt viele], welche ihr Leben lang die entlegensten und oft fast närrischen Studien betreiben, und niemand stört sie darin, solange nur nicht ihre Sitten entarten* (GB 75f.) ('[there are many] who devote their entire lives to the most abstruse and frequently almost crazy topics, and no-one will hinder them in their labours, just as long as their morals do not degenerate'). The expression 'frequently almost crazy' does little to inspire confidence in the work which the majority of these scholars undertake; barring moral lapses, Castalia offers its inmates an unlimited sinecure.

The care with which the creative work of the past is collected and stored in Castalia's archives has its darker side, too. Castalia has evidently become, by Knecht's time, little more than a vast and unwieldy repository of learning whose inmates are incapable of – or must be restrained from – undertaking creative work of their own. Those whose powers have not atrophied are subjected to ridicule and prohibition:

> *Denn wenn schon im allgemeinen Kastalien auf das Hervorbringen von Kunstwerken Verzicht geleistet hat (auch musikalisches Produzieren kennt und duldet man dort nur in der Form von stilistisch streng gebundenen Kompositionsübungen), so galt Gedichtemachen gar für das denkbar Unmöglichste, Lächerlichste, Verpönteste.* (GB 110f.)
>
> (For while Castalia has, in general, renounced the origination of works of art (even in music, composition is only known and tolerated there if it takes the form of strictly controlled exercises), the writing of poetry was viewed as the most unacceptable, ridiculous and punishable of activities.)

The benign *Magister Musicae* is naively optimistic about the manner in which the province is run, and apparently blind to many of its failings. Before Josef Knecht is old enough to form opinions on this question, the Master tries his best to make the boy reject the outside world altogether. With an 'almost sly smile' (GB 74) hovering around his lips, he instructs his protégé in the wicked ways of the non-Castalians, where he would quickly become *ein Sklave niedriger Mächte, er hängt vom Erfolg, vom Geld, von seinem Ehrgeiz, seiner Ruhmsucht, vom Gefallen ab, das die Menschen an ihm finden oder nicht finden* (GB 75) ('a slave of base powers, dependent on success, on money, ambition and on his own drive for fame, as well as on the extent to which he pleases or displeases other people'). What astonishes us about this contention is its utter naivety. The story of Knecht's life makes it abundantly clear that ambition, the pursuit of fame and recognition, and personal contacts count for more than scholarship in the distribution of high offices. Why else would Bertram be hounded out of Waldzell by a Machiavellian clique of players? As for the supposed absence of personal likes and dislikes, *Gefallen*, in the province, the Music Master need look no further than his own relationship with Knecht to discover just how much favouritism can achieve here. Words like *Schützling, Vorzugsschüler, Lieblingsschüler* (GB 241, 206, 56) ('protégé', 'favoured pupil', 'teacher's pet') abound in the book and endow the entire Castalian system with the unsavoury aura of nepotism.

When examined in practice, the educational system which the narrator is given to praise in the abstract turns out to be severely flawed in its operation. The overriding impression is of austere schools in which sinister men like Headmaster Zbinden hold sway, producing clashes between the pupils and their parents (GB 45, 61), and where seasoned pedagogues delight in exposing their young pupils' ignorance. A telling indictment occurs when the narrator registers his surprise that Knecht survived his secondary eduction without 'visible signs of damage' (*erstaunlicherweise aber nicht erkennbar geschädigt*, GB 122).

Signs of potential and real traumas are sprinkled throughout the text. The graduates of Castalia's famous schools tend to be shy and sexually retarded (GB 93), and the circumstances in which contact is made with the opposite sex are bizarre and improbable; few societies would regard marriage as 'little more than a curiosity' (GB 117) without the severest of doctrinal pressures being brought to bear upon them. Castalia is dominated by males; no female characters play any part in her affairs, and an anti-feminist attitude can be deduced from the third of Knecht's biographies, in which Pravati is blamed for Dasa's misfortunes: *Verführt von Pravatis Schönheit, bestrickt vom Weib und angesteckt von ihrem Ehrgeiz, hatte er den Weg verlassen, auf welchem allein die Freiheit und der Friede gewonnen wird* (GB 605) ('Seduced by Pravati's beauty, captivated by a woman and infected by her ambition, he had strayed from the only path that leads to the acquisition of freedom and peace').

The place of women is taken up by involvements with boys and other men: Petrus worships the Music Master, Anton is attracted to Knecht, who responds warmly to the Music Master and Tito. At Mariafels, Knecht becomes aware of strong feelings emanating in his direction from the novice Anton, and resolves to be more restrained than he would have had to be in Castalia (GB 170). The darker side of such attachments is seen when Petrus goes to pieces after the death of his idol: he is threatened with hospitalisation, possibly as a prelude to some severe punishment; there seems to be no mechanism for dealing with emotional crises in the province (GB 308).

It is interesting to observe the uses to which meditation is put in the province. Here, a process which should help an individual to achieve greater self-awareness is often abused as a means of disposing of unwanted emotions, as Plinio repeatedly maintains, likening the Castalians' love of meditation to a form of self-castration (*GB* 99, 341). The Order maintains a tight control over its subjects by recommending that material for meditation be taken from its own rule-book (*GB* 151). When Master Alexander is confronted by the prospect of Knecht's imminent resignation, he quickly performs a familiar 'emergency exercise':

> *Der Ordensleiter schloß die Augen und schien nicht mehr zuzuhören. Knecht erkannte, daß er jene Notübung vollziehe, mit deren Hilfe die Ordensleute in Fällen von plötzlicher Gefahr und Bedrohung sich der Selbstbeherrschung und inneren Ruhe zu versichern suchen ...* (*GB* 424).

(The Head of the Order closed his eyes and seemed to have stopped listening. Knecht realised that he was carrying out an emergency exercise with whose assistance members of the Order attempt to regain their self-control and composure when confronted by unexpected dangers or threats ...)

Here, meditation is not a means of attaining inner harmony, but a cheap cure-all, a last-ditch method of suppressing emotion. Alexander performs his exercise as one might light a cigarette or pour a drink.

Finally, the Game itself, which is at the very hub of the intellectual life of the province, partakes of a similar ambiguity. Although regularly spoken of as a great marvel, the reader must wonder where the fascination lies. When it comes to describing the social context in which it is performed, the narrator's eulogies sound most dubious. The first official ceremony over which Knecht presides is an example of the hypocrisy surrounding the entire institution. This Game concerns itself with the symbolism of the Chinese house, which is determined by factors such as the points of the compass, the calendar and other data which Knecht deduced from the *Book of Changes* (*GB* 265). Previously, it had been carefully noted that there was widespread ignorance about or, indeed, antipathy towards this very book among the teachers of the Game in Waldzell: *ein Gebiet ... von dem man im Lehrhaus wenig wissen wollte* (*GB* 133) ('an area ... about which the institute had no great desire to inform itself'). The only person in Castalia to know something about the subject is the Elder Brother, who refuses to attend the *ludus sollemnis*, not wishing to see it travestied in a public performance. When Knecht finally plays the first 'solemn' Game of his career, and the majestic ciphers are broadcast throughout the land (*GB* 285), it is highly doubtful whether anyone can make sense of them.

11. THE POLICE STATE

Obscurantism is just one of several grounds on which the Game as an institution is open to criticism. The atmosphere of intrigue surrounding the previous year's solemn rites, during which and because of which the incumbent *Magister Ludi* breathes his last, provides a chilling demonstration of Castalia's inability to harness the dark forces of rancour and envy. The circumstances in which Bertram, Thomas von der Trave's deputy, an innocent but no longer popular man (*GB* 226), is hounded out of Waldzell remind us of the political putsch rather than of the academic paradise of the preface.[23] That Knecht should feel no more than a slight sense of frustration (*GB* 222) in view of these clandestine intrigues is indicative of his naivety: he fails to realise that he is being used as a political tool, not only when in Mariafels but also when nominated Master of the Game, an event in which the Chief of Police plays a major part (*GB* 233, 235).

We must now consider the possibility that Castalia as a social and political entity is in no sense a utopia and that the novel contains material exposing some of the traits characteristic of the modern police state, a possibility rendered more convincing by the fact that early versions of Hesse's manuscript were directed specifically at the manifestations and ideology of German Fascism (see pp. 55–9, above). It will be necessary to look more closely at those features of life in Castalia which are most reminiscent of totalitarianism.

It is evident that life within the community is subject to many rules and that, in particular, personal relationships are governed by stringently enforced conventions. A well-defined hierarchy exists, with a pecking order determining who may associate with whom and on what terms. Certain forms of address are prescribed for certain relationships; the familiar pronoun *du* may not be used with someone of higher rank, no matter how close the ties of friendship. Thus the Music Master is only allowed to converse with Knecht on familiar terms after his retirement: *Ich konnte dir das nicht anbieten, solange ich im Amt war* (*GB* 156) ('I was unable to offer you the privilege as long as I held office'). Conversely, Tegularius must drop the familiar form when Knecht is promoted; protocol demands that the Master be addressed as *Ehrwürdiger* (*GB* 261) ('Your Reverence'), in private as well as in public. The falseness of such formalities is illustrated by an unintentional lapse on Ferromonte's part: *einem andern als dir – verzeiht, als Euch, Domine* (*GB* 280) ('to someone other than you – excuse me, to someone other than your illustrious self, *Domine*'). Once out of

Castalia, Knecht has to be reminded not to address everyone as *du* indiscriminately (*GB* 371). The individual is manipulated by the state to a very considerable extent. Knecht is dispatched to Mariafels for two years with no option of refusing. He returns with a foreboding that he will be forced into the diplomatic service, a fate he would bitterly resent (*GB* 199). Here, Hesse makes use of terms which possess distinctly unpleasant political overtones: *abgeschoben werden, Kaltstellung, Bonzen* (*GB* 199, 225, 234) ('axing', 'liquidation', 'top brass'). Such words help to build up the impression of a ruthless, dictatorial machinery as the driving force behind the republic. A similar effect is produced by the many references to the 'Order' and the 'Board of Educators' with its numerous *Kanzleien*, (*GB* 226, 419)[24] ('offices'). It is here, one senses, that the real power resides. The Board of Educators recruits the best brains for service within its ranks (*GB* 55) and supervises important rituals like meditation (*GB* 115). It is this office, the *Kanzlei der Erziehungsbehörde*, that rebukes Knecht for his supposedly over-imaginative third biography (*GB* 120) and demands above all else a binding sense of commitment (*GB* 151).

Doctrinaire rigidity, a familiar feature of many large organisations, is by no means the most disturbing aspect of life in the province. Specifically political malpractices can be discerned in many references to the way in which Castalia's citizens are being watched and monitored by her authorities. Constant surveillance and frequent recourse to various forms of espionage appear to be well-established traditions of the republic. Cultural missions turn out to be little more than pretexts for dubious forms of information-gathering. It gradually transpires that Knecht's first visit to Mariafels is nothing other than a carefully orchestrated attempt to infiltrate the Church, as all parties appear to recognise. The mission necessitates a lengthy period of vetting and briefing, most of which is carried out by the unsympathetic Monsieur Dubois, Castalia's Chief of Police, whose first impressions of Knecht are unfavourable (*GB* 193). His instructions to his envoy are transparent enough:

> *[du wirst] vermutlich im Kreis dieser ehrwürdigen Herren und ihrer Gäste auch politische Gespräche hören und politische Stimmungen verspüren. Wenn du mich davon gelegentlich benachrichtigen wolltest, wäre ich dankbar dafür.* (*GB* 159)

> ([you will] presumably hear some discussions on political topics and become aware of the general political mood while

you are in the company of these venerable gentlemen. If you
would from time to time relay their opinions to me, I should
be grateful.)

This discreet remark is followed by a heavy-handed instruction
not to consider himself a spy and by references to other 'sources'
which Castalia possesses, all of which merely alerts the reader to
this aspect of Knecht's work in the monastery. As things turn out,
he is commended on his return for the reports he has sent back
rather than for his teaching (GB 183, 187), and it is eventually
acknowledged that his pedagogic role was merely a cover for a
more vital diplomatic task (GB 197). The monastic institution of
Mariafels was not chosen arbitrarily to illustrate the republic's
crude diplomatic manoeuvrings. The manner in which Castalia
here seeks to win the recognition of the Vatican is, without any
doubt, a reminder of the way in which the National Socialists
attempted to win over the Catholic Church and eventually succeeded in obtaining diplomatic representation at the Vatican before Hitler's Germany was recognised by any other sovereign
state in the world.

While such diplomatic ventures may not seem incompatible
with the legitimate interests of the state, a more sinister note is
struck when it becomes apparent that Castalia routinely subjects
its own agents to surveillance. On returning from his mission to
Mariafels, Knecht becomes aware that he himself is now being
observed (GB 194). After his promotion, he is allocated an official
Einpeitscher und Kontrolleur (GB 246) ('coach and controller') who
watches over him hour by hour. Much later, when his professional doubts have become known, an elderly man, described as a
Beobachter and *Späher* ('observer', 'spy') appears in Waldzell with
the express function of reporting on Josef Knecht to the President
of the Order (GB 406).

This is the last we hear of Knecht before the start of the avow-
edly fictitious 'Legend' – an ominous conclusion to that part of his
research which Knecht's biographer claims he can verify. The
reader is obliged to speculate whether, given the acute political
sensitivity of the Order and the renowned vindictiveness of its
elite, Knecht will have met his end in some remote mountain spot
– as the unfortunate Bertram had, eight years previously – while a
fanciful legend was put about for public consumption. After all,
the narrator admits that he lacks access to the secret archives of the
Board (GB 311) and that he 'knows nothing about Knecht's death',
certain only that it will not have been determined by chance
(GB 47).

These events encourage us to concur with the narrator's admission that active democratic rights and duties are non-existent in the province: *aktive politische Rechte und Pflichten besaß man nicht* (*GB* 208). The affairs of the republic's citizens are hedged in by rules and conventions of the most cramping kind. One may sympathise with the embargo that is imposed on private travel by junior pupils at Eschholz (*GB* 76f.), but when the twenty-four-year-old graduate is 'laconically' forbidden to visit Plinio at his home (by a special committee set up to deal with such evidently unusual requests), we are made to feel that an injustice has been done, the more so as no explanation is forthcoming (*GB* 113). Police registration, *Meldepflicht*, is the rule, although occasionally waived on a discretionary basis (*GB* 194). Alcoholic beverages are forbidden (*GB* 183), and a bed-time hour is prescribed for all, even for the high and mighty (*GB* 210, 413). Such rules cannot be ignored with impunity; they are followed blindly, although many have not been revised or scrutinised for decades (*GB* 429).

An inevitable consequence of this strict regimentation will be perceived in the general lack of sincerity that characterises human relationships in the province. Teachers of the Game are fond of teasing their pupils and rejoice when they have tricked them into making mistakes (*GB* 123f.). When senior members communicate with one another, they have recourse to blatant irony: it seems that, wherever possible, they hide their true feelings behind a façade of lavish flattery or studied sarcasm (*GB* 173). Even during the final desperate altercation between Knecht and Alexander, euphemistic formulas like *die verehrte Behörde* and *Eure goldenen Worte* (*GB* 420–3) ('the revered Board', 'your golden words'), are traded between the two antagonists. Castalia's smiling mask conceals her true face. It may well be that this excessive irony results not so much from the aesthetic disposition of her scholars as from the ever-present threat of surveillance and intrigue. Hesse has here succeeded in recreating the atmosphere of universal suspicion which distinguishes undemocratic, absolutist regimes; he also shows us the natural response to such pressures when the inhabitants of this society defend themselves by expressing themselves cautiously and with many misleading rhetorical devices calculated to screen their intentions.

Irony is not the only such reaction present behind the pleasing exterior of the organisation. Knecht's friend Fritz Tegularius is presented as the most typical product of the system; indeed, he is referred to as the *Erzkastalier* (*GB* 294) ('arch-Castalian'). He is a highly problematic figure, demonstrating those inevitable

tensions that arise from his enslavement to an institution which
views his individualism as a character defect:

> *Was man seine Krankheit nannte, war schließlich vorwiegend ein
> Laster, eine Unbotmäßigkeit, ein Charakterfehler, nämlich eine im
> tiefsten unhierarchische, völlig individualistische Gesinnung und
> Lebensführung* ... (GB 294)

> (What was spoken of as an illness on his part, was in the end
> no more than a bad habit, a resistance to pressure, a flaw in
> his character, attributable to a profoundly anti-hierarchical,
> totally individualistic attitude and way of life ...)

Thus it becomes clear that most of his 'problems', his excessive
fervour for the Game, his passionate attachment to Knecht, his
incipient neurosis, follow on from a single root cause: the hostility
towards the individual that is rife in the province. The words with
which the narrator analyses his case could have come out of the
records of a psychiatric unit in a totalitarian state:

> *er war im Grunde unheilbar, denn er wollte gar nicht geheilt sein,
> er gab nichts auf Harmonie und Einordnung, er liebte nichts als
> seine Freiheit* ... (GB 295)

> (he was fundamentally incurable, because he had no desire
> to be cured; he placed no value on harmony and integration,
> he loved nothing other than his freedom ...)

There could be no more telling indictment of the state that abuses
its powers and arbitrarily limits the rights of its citizens than this
harsh denigration of the pursuit of personal liberty. Whether, in
fact, the narrator shares or derides the official attitude which he
communicates in his text is a matter which must now be considered.

12. THE WRITER AND THE CENSOR

Several narrative voices come together to make up a polyphonic
rendering of Knecht's life and development. The introductory
chapter incorporates details derived from many fictitious sources
including the historian Plinius Ziegenhalss and one of Knecht's
pupils. Elsewhere, the narrator quotes and borrows from different
authorities, some of which he himself views as untrustworthy.
Only in the poems and the fictions at the end is Knecht's voice
heard directly.

We know very little about the narrator, Knecht's anonymous
latter-day biographer. There is little indication of his position

within the hierarchy, and no reliable information that would help us to establish the time-lag between the Master's demise and the compilation of the present tribute to him. His motives are equally obscure: the book may be read as an attempt at a factual biography, an act of homage to Castalia, a study of a radical dissident, or as an exposure of the Order's latent shortcomings. The narrator effectively hides his identity behind a smokescreen of empty verbosity, and in view of his uncertain motivation many readers find him irritating. In the words of a recent critic, 'reverentially stiff ... longwinded, repetitious, humorless, preachy while struggling to be objective and modest, he is a pedant'.[25]

There have been attempts to explain why Hesse chose to make him so. Theodore Ziolkowski believes that irony is at the heart of that peculiar tension that exists between the narrator's ignorance of his subject and the deductions which the reader is obliged to make from the story:

> Since ... the narrator is incapable of fully comprehending the problematic genius of his biographical subject, an ironic tension is produced between the limited perspective of the narrator and the fuller vision that he unwittingly conveys to the reader.[26]

The discrepancy between the story as told and the story as read should have the effect of manoeuvring the reader into a clearer appraisal of Hesse's intentions. This suggestion is an attractive one, alerting us as it does to the tension that often exists between the surface meaning of a text and its underlying significance. However, it is at odds with Ziolkowski's own interpretation of the novel, shared by other critics, which is that Castalia has been reformed and revitalised since the Master's early death. In their view, Knecht had to sacrifice himself in order to bring about a much-needed reform within the province; the narrator represents a 'more balanced synthesis of life and the spirit' as if to demonstrate the improvement that has come about as a result of Knecht's death. Josef Mileck argues that 'the chronicler's better world of 2400' proves that Knecht's example was not in vain.[27] These explanations are incompatible with comments on the narrator's 'limited perspective' and incompetence; if Castalia has indeed improved since Knecht's time, then something of this improvement ought to have rubbed off on the only man representing the new face of the republic. Yet this is patently not the case.

The narrator's deficiencies are worth examining in detail. Unlike Serenus Zeitblom, the fictional author of Thomas Mann's

Doctor Faustus, the Castalian chronicler reveals little about himself, and, although also given to long-winded formulations, is at
more of a disadvantage since his sources of information are
unreliable: unlike Zeitblom, he cannot claim to have first-hand
knowledge of his subject. His greatest failing as a narrator appears
to lie not in his turgid style but in his sheer ignorance concerning
the details of Josef Knecht's life. Not only that: he does not
enjoy free access to the state archives containing documents vital
to his research, he seems to share in the general scepticism
towards facts which prevails in Castalia, and he is fond of
making exaggerated claims on behalf of the province and its
institutions. It would be difficult to conceive of a person less
suited to the task of researching and compiling a reliable and
impartial biography.

His underlying attitude to the factual accuracy of his account
comes close to indifference at times. By dropping hints about the
existence of a 'secret archive' from which he himself has been
debarred, he steers attention towards the uncomfortable suspicion that some vital piece of information is lacking; it is as though
he wants his readers to distrust him. The same happens when he
speaks of the 'Legend' as no more than a fantasy. Breaking off
with the disturbing picture of Knecht being pursued by a spy from
the Order's headquarters at Hirsland, he concludes *Über das Ende
dieses Lebenslaufes wird ein späterer Biograph ohne Zweifel noch
manche Einzelheit feststellen und mitteilen können* (GB 407) ('A later
biographer will undoubtedly be able to discover and communicate various further details concerning the end of this person's
life'), thereby strongly hinting that there is more to his story than
present circumstances will permit him to disclose. The same is
true of the apparent nonchalance with which he refuses to give his
own version, whatever that may be, of Knecht's end: *Wir
verzichten darauf, eine eigene Darstellung von des Meisters letzten
Tagen zu geben* (loc. cit.) ('We shall resist the temptation to provide
an original account of the Master's last days') and declares that he
is prepared to accept the legend, 'regardless of whether or not it is
no more than a pious fable' (GB 47). This smacks of more than
ignorance or wilful obscurantism: the narrator seems intent on
drawing the reader's attention to the cover-up in which he is
obliged to collude.

While Döblin pried into every aspect of his characters' lives, the
Castalian narrator mentions the prevailing 'ideal of anonymity'
with apparent approval (GB 8f.) and lists many areas of Knecht's
life which men of his age would prefer to ignore:

Uns Heutige interessiert nicht die Pathologie noch die
Familiengeschichte, nicht das Triebleben, die Verdauung und der
Schlaf eines Helden; nicht einmal seine geistige Vorgeschichte,
seine Erziehung durch Lieblingsstudien, Lieblingslektüre und so
weiter ist uns sonderlich wichtig. (GB 10)

(We people of today are not interested in our hero's pathology or family history, nor in his sensual life, his diet or
his sleeping patterns; not even his intellectual background
or the formative influence of his favourite studies, reading
material and so forth strike us as significant.)

And yet there is a declared commitment to 'truthfulness' and
'scientific methods' (*Wahrheit, Wissenschaft*, GB 8), and there are
times when the biographer pays attention to those precise matters
which, he claimed, strike his own generation as insignificant. An
interest in 'pathology' surfaces in the detailed accounts of the
nervous disorders from which Tegularius and Petrus are suffering
(GB 154–6, 293–9, 305–10). Although 'we know nothing about
Knecht's origins' (GB 45), the narrator will eventually speculate that
Knecht's father may have been a cobbler (GB 463). An interest in
family affairs is evinced when the narrator reflects on Plinio's
marriage and its deleterious consequences for young Tito (GB 354,
359). The effects of Castalia on the sensual development of its
residents give rise to various comments (GB 93, 341); Knecht's frugal
diet of bread, fruit and milk is often stressed, as is the ban on alcohol
(GB 79, 81, 183). The young man's reading matter also gets an
occasional mention: it includes Leibniz, Kant, the Romantics and
Hegel (GB 93). In all these descriptions, there is a tension between
the biographer's declared methodology and the resulting work.

He is at his most inadequate in his evaluations of the events
which he records. This is most obvious in the cheerful optimism
with which he presents many of the more dubious institutions in
the province. While prepared to concede that no more than 'a
minute proportion' of all Castalia's graduates show any serious
interest in the Game, he serenades it as the greatest cultural
achievement of all time (GB 43). Remarkable examples of rhetorical
understatement occur in this context: thus Chattus Calvensis II,
author of a monumentally futile four-volume study of the pronunciation of Latin in southern Italian universities during the
latter half of the twelfth century, is coyly characterised as *etwas*
wunderlich (GB 65) ('somewhat peculiar'), while the man who
found an occult meaning in the musical notation of the fifteenth
century is merely labelled a *Schwärmer* (GB 148) ('hot-head',

'enthusiast'). The unproductive extravagance of their labours is regularly played down; the narrator is not so much ill-informed or pedantic as excessively euphemistic. It is as though he does not wish to give offence by condemning these scholars outright.

In the end, it may be possible to take a more constructive view of the narrator's faults by regarding these descriptions as calculated attempts to further rather than to frustrate efforts to arrive at the truth about Castalia. We may assume that he does not wish to fall foul of the authorities and must choose his words carefully. When he speaks respectfully of *die mild geübte Kontrolle der Erziehungsbehörde* (GB 215) ('the benign exercise of restraint on the part of the Board of Educators'), in the context of their refusal to allow the twenty-four-year-old graduate to visit Plinio in his home outside Castalia, the reader will recognise how false these innocent-sounding words are. Again and again, our narrator lavishes praise on the elite and speaks uncritically of their most dubious practices. The Police Chief is referred to as *der freundliche Herr Dubois* (GB 187) ('kindly Mr Dubois'), despite his prejudices against Knecht and the intensive three-week vetting procedure to which he subjected him.

Another method favoured by the narrator is to reproduce fierce criticism of Castalia by citing other authorities and listing their complaints. Occasionally, one comes across a torrent of abuse directed at the clique of aspirants to high office within the ruling elite:

> *Für andere wieder war dieser erlesene Kreis von Prätendenten auf die höheren Würden in der Hierarchie des Glasperlenspiels etwas Verhaßtes und Verkommenes, eine Clique von hochnäsigen Nichtstuern, geistreich verspielten Genies ohne Sinn für Leben und Wirklichkeit, eine anmaßende und im Grunde schmarotzerische Gesellschaft von Elegants und Strebern, deren Beruf und Lebensinhalt eine Spielerei, ein unfruchtbarer Selbstgenuß des Geistes sei.* (GB 141)

(There were others who regarded the select inner circle of candidates for high office within the hierarchy of the Glass Bead Game as odious and degenerate, as a clique of supercilious idlers and brilliantly self-indulgent know-alls who lacked all feeling for the real world, an arrogant and fundamentally parasitic set of dandies and social climbers whose professional and personal ambitions revolved around a mere game and the sterile self-satisfaction of their intellectual faculties.)

Nowhere does the narrator personally associate himself with such trenchant attacks on the foremost citizens of the province; he is quite content to refer, vaguely, to other people who have expressed such opinions. Yet the mere mention of these heretical ideas must implant doubts in the reader's mind as to whether there might not be some justification for this tirade. Elsewhere, Castalia is said to provide a haven for people unsuited to life in the raw *wegen Charakterungleichheiten oder aus anderen Gründen, etwa wegen körperlicher Mängel* (GB 64) ('on account of an unevenness of character or for some other reason, such as physical disabilities'). This adds another unsavoury dimension to the organisation, and it should perhaps be recalled that many of the top National Socialists were men of uneven or unstable character, and several, such as Goebbels, had physical disabilities as well. On the question of ambition, contradictory information is supplied at different points in the book. The Music Master dismisses the idea that ambition is to be found in Castalia (GB 176), but by and by it transpires that fierce competition for high offices is a regular feature of life in the province and that favouritism is a major factor in the decision-making process:

> *Ein Plus oder Minus an Ehrgeiz, an gutem Auftreten, an Körpergröße oder hübscher Erscheinung, ein kleines Plus oder Minus an Charme, an Wirkung auf Jüngere oder Behörden, an Liebenswürdigkeit war hier von großem Gewicht und konnte im Wettbewerb entscheiden.* (GB 162)

> (A modicum too much or too little in terms of ambition, demeanour, physical size or good looks, the tiniest surplus or shortfall in matters of personal charm, influence over young people or officials, general affability – were factors of great weight and could determine who was selected.)

Enough has now been said about the narrator's tendency to disseminate scepticism about the value of Castalia's most prized institutions and about the manner in which the affairs of the little republic are run. Cautiously and guardedly, he manages to expose a picture of a hypocritical and ruthless hierarchy intent on defending its power-base. Its social and political organisation reproduces many aspects of the realities of life in the totalitarian states of the 1930s and 1940s, whose readers, especially within Germany, Hesse sought to address. He is known to have had reservations as to whether readers outside Germany would be able to make much sense of his work.[28] Döblin surveyed the hustle and bustle of life in the streets of Berlin, while Hesse projects many of her intellectual pretensions and political deficiencies into a future in which the familiar patterns of the present are clearly discernible. The outlook for the individual is much bleaker here than it was at the end of Berlin Alexanderplatz; time has moved on and an optimistic or an open ending is no longer acceptable. Knecht's quest for self-fulfilment is thwarted, and he dies prematurely in tragic circumstances which the ironic text can only hint at. The narrator abdicates before a fanciful legend, reminding us again of his status as a victim of an organisation given to crushing the aspirations of the individual.

13. EVALUATION

If Castalia's function were to confront the modern reader with a haven of security in a positively utopian state, free from the stresses of modern life, the dilettantism of sensation-seeking media and the failings of our educational system, the true heroes of the novel would have to be its most loyal servants, teachers like Zbinden and important officials such as Thomas, Alexander and Dubois. In the final form taken by the novel, there is little to instil confidence in these somewhat frosty representatives of officialdom. Only the Music Master is endowed with likeable traits, yet he, too, does Knecht a disservice by claiming that Castalia is governed by more noble principles than will prove to be the case.

There is, on the other hand, an attitude of sympathy towards Castalia's many victims, which arises from the curiously offhand statements with which the narrator judges them. Comments on Tegularius, who suffers from an 'incurable' love of freedom, or Petrus, who needs hospitalisation and punishment for grieving at the Music Master's death, bring home the ruthlessness of the all-powerful authority that holds the province in its grip. Only a few are lucky enough to escape: Plinio, by being an outsider and a benefactor, and the dissenting 'Elder Brother', who lives by the *I Ching*, and will not travesty it in empty rituals which the public will not be able to understand. Bertram is a less fortunate type of victim: a man who once enjoyed the patronage of a great public figure, and is disposed of in highly dubious circumstances. His is the fate of a player on the political stage who lacks the support of the up-and-coming generation.

Knecht is himself associated with the regime and attuned to its ways. There is a sense in which he, too, is tainted by corruption. His talent for flattery and self-ingratiation played a major part in his climb to fame; as Thomas puts it to him: *du hast eine gewisse Gabe, dich angenehm und beliebt zu machen, ein Übelwollender könnte dich beinahe einen Charmeur nennen* (GB 199) ('You possess a certain talent for making yourself pleasant and popular; an ill-wisher might almost go so far as to describe you as a sycophant'). The system may have moulded him in this respect. It is also worth noting that once he has come into real power, Knecht is not beyond displaying his strength to those weaker than himself; the narrator speaks of this as *die Versuchung, den an Kraft, aber nicht an Liebe Schwächeren gelegentlich seine Macht fühlen zu lassen* (GB 161) ('the occasional temptation to make a man [Tegularius] weaker than himself in terms of strength, though not of love, conscious of his powers'). Observations of this type convey the impression that Knecht is inclined to reject friends such as Tegularius after his own promotion. Here again, the corrupting influence of power is manifest, with the implication that the illiberal, inward-looking regime has conditioned these responses in its subjects.

It is difficult to isolate individual character traits in Knecht, as was attempted apropos of Franz Biberkopf (see pp. 6–12, above). Aspects of his behaviour may well have been derived from those who influenced him – the quiet serenity of the Music Master, the cool rationality of Thomas von der Trave, the emotionalism of Tegularius, as well as Plinio's critical detachment. He is not the uncomplaining servant that his name suggests, in antithesis to the *Meister* ('Master') of Goethe's *Bildungsroman* (*Wilhelm Meister*), nor a leader figure given to command in the manner of Alexander or Dubois. His tragedy is to be caught up in a system which is governed by hierarchies, and where an unconditional commitment to one side or the other is required to ensure his survival. Here, in his unwillingness to give this commitment, he comes close to the position of watchful isolation which Biberkopf eventually attains.

At his school, Knecht had tried to be both a conscientious pupil and a champion of his classmates against their authoritarian masters. From the time of his youth, he is disposed to identify with the 'rejects', with those who forsake the lofty ideals of the province, comparing them, in a strangely positive way, with the 'fallen angel' Lucifer (GB 77). Later, when he is about to resign, Alexander speaks of his departure in similar terms, as a betrayal or an act of apostasy: *'erzählt mir die Geschichte Eures Abfalls ... Sei es als Beichte, sei es als Rechtfertigung, sei es als Anklage, ich will es anhören'* (GB 432) ('"tell me the story of your apostasy ... Be it a confession, a justification or an indictment – I wish to hear it"').

Only once is a description of Knecht's exterior attempted. It is worth considering in detail:

unter manchen andern Eigenschaften war es gerade Knechts Gang gewesen, den er gerngehabt hatte, ein bestimmter und taktfester, aber leichter, ja beinahe schwebender Schritt, zwischen würdig und kindisch, zwischen priesterlich und tänzerisch, ein eigenartiger liebenswürdiger und vornehmer Schritt, der ausgezeichnet zu Knechts Gesicht und Stimme paßte. Er paßte nicht minder zu seiner so besonderen Art von Kastalier- und Magistertum, seiner Art von Herrentum und von Heiterkeit, welche manchmal ein wenig an die aristokratisch gemessene seines Vorgängers, des Meisters Thomas, manchmal auch an die einfache und herzgewinnende des Alt-Musikmeisters erinnerte. (GB 448)

(among other qualities which appealed to him, he [Alexander] had always liked Knecht's way of walking: a firm, rhythmic step so delicate that there were times when he almost seemed to be floating. It could be both dignified and like that of a child, reminding one of a priest, and also of a dancer: a strangely likeable and noble way of walking, which was well attuned to Knecht's looks and voice. It was no less suited to his very distinctive qualities as a Castalian and a Magister, his style of leadership and his serenity, which sometimes recalled the aristocratic self-discipline of his predecessor, Master Thomas, and sometimes the simple, heartwarming manner of the retired Music Master.)

Here, he is placed halfway between extremes. He is portrayed as being both serious and serene; he resembles a priest and, at the same time, a dancer, a leader of men and yet also a child. The effect is to create the impression that Knecht bridges the divide between the world of reason and the realm of the imagination, the distinct poles which had been symbolised by the *Biber* and the *Kopf* elements in *Berlin Alexanderplatz*. It is a synthesis too perfect to be compatible with reality. A world as rigid as Castalia, the police state masquerading as a liberal republic, demands loyalty and unquestioning commitment, and will not tolerate a man who is not inclined to submit to its authority. Knecht comes to grief in Belpunt ('the place of the beautiful bridge'), and his death is, as Hesse always maintained, a sacrifice,[29] but, like that of the Rainmaker, one extracted from him by an uncompromising society.

Hesse never wrote the continuation which some readers believed would concentrate on young Tito and his attempts to revitalise the province. Only a complete reorganisation of its affairs would satisfy the demands that are implicit in the tale of Knecht's ousting and in the legend of his death. This has patently not occurred by the narrator's time. To have suggested that one temperamental adolescent might somehow challenge the entrenched bureaucracy of the nation is perhaps the culminating irony of the book. Yet Hesse was undoubtedly addressing himself to the youth of his time and indicating to them that the private wisdom gained by this young man is more important than the accumulated knowledge of a power-hungry elite. To ignore this dimension and to read the book solely in the light of the 'surface' meaning of its teasing Latin motto is to align oneself with the materialistic Castalians, who figure in the novel as the enemies of those values which Hesse championed throughout his career: poetry, the imagination, integrity and true emotion.

Many critics view the novel as flawed on account of its long gestation, during which Hesse's attempts to conclude it were subject to continuous interruptions.[30] These had the effect of diminishing his enthusiasm for Castalia and causing him to dwell on what he later called 'the relativity and transitoriness of even the most ideal of worlds'.[31] As we have seen, the original foreword and conclusion had to be rewritten; the general opinion is still that the novel suffered as a result of these revisions. My contention is that it has gained considerably by virtue of the changes that Hesse was obliged to make in response to the events that dominated the political arena of his time. By showing us an ideal that is not merely tinged with the traces of human frailty, but abused until it becomes more pernicious than the evil it had sought to combat, Hesse has succeeded in creating a world of Shakespearian ambivalence in which the sublime and the heinous become inseparable. Knecht cannot, as he naively hopes, separate the positive intellectual legacy of Castalia from the oppressive social framework upon which it depends for survival. The creative faculty is shown to be vulnerable to the darker forces which have a controlling effect on society: ambition and the thirst for power. In his maturest work, Hesse portrays man's spiritual potential against a distressingly real background of authoritarianism and political intrigue. Castalia needs the Game in order to give itself credibility, and, since all culture presupposes social organisation, the Game depends on Castalia.

The Glass Bead Game is 'utopian' only in its grasp of this paradox. It records a yawning discrepancy between the intellectual and the social sphere which people of the twentieth century have experienced in states which treat them as subjects, not as citizens. It does not portray the future, but replicates a social matrix all too familiar from its author's own time. In this respect, it has affinities with some of the 'negative' utopias, sometimes referred to as 'dystopias' or 'cacotopias', of which *Brave New World* and *Nineteen Eighty-four* are the best-known examples. Essentially a product of the prewar tensions, enriched by Hesse's observation of developments in Fascist Germany, the book warns against entrenchment, extremism and subservience to such superficially lofty, collectivist ideals which serve as convenient power-bases for unscrupulous tyrants. Hesse's personal antagonism towards the collective principle, be it of left- or right-wing inspiration, is well attested in outspoken personal letters.[32]

Knecht embodies ideas which have found their way into many other German novels of the twentieth century: like Franz Biberkopf, he believes that a simple formula of personal integrity will protect him among people dominated by ambition and greed. Like Josef K. in Kafka's *The Trial*, he delays too long in resisting his self-imposed jailers. He attaches so much importance to his cultural, intellectual interests that he becomes unable to survive outside the hot-house of Castalia, inviting comparison with Adrian Leverkühn's isolationism in *Doctor Faustus*. His own naivety, like that of Oskar Matzerath in Grass's *The Tin Drum*, reflects the crushing immaturity of the world into which he is placed. I hope to have demonstrated that Hesse has successfully combined many of the themes most characteristic of the fiction of his age and of his nation in this, his last and maturest novel, which puts forward a sober, cautionary image of the present rather than a naively optimistic speculation about what the distant future might hold.

NOTES

1. See Mileck, 1978, and Pfeifer, 1977, for information about Hesse's image and sales figures in the non-German-speaking world.
2. See the article 'O Freunde, nicht diese Töne', September 1914, GS vol. 7, p. 47.
3. Stern, 1980/1, p. 100, assumes that Knecht lived 'in the year 2200'; other critics place him somewhere in the twenty-third century or 'around 2300' (Michels, 1974, vol. 2, pp. 125, 115).
4. Tusken, 1992, p. 632f.
5. See Hollis, 1978.
6. Michels, 1973, vol. 1, pp. 18–20.
7. Louis XI reigned 1461–83; Delcassé was Foreign Minister of France in 1898–1905 and 1914–15.
8. Michels, 1973, vol. 1, p. 326.
9. Boulby, 1966; White and White, 1987.
10. Michels, 1973, vol. 1, p. 61.
11. Ibid., p. 223.
12. GS, vol. 1, p. 280.

13. See n. 10, above.
14. Michels, 1973, vol. 1, p. 240.
15. Ibid., p. 296.
16. Mileck, 1978, pp. 285, 268, 307; Ziolkowski, 1965, p. 302.
17. Norton, 1973; Koester, 1975, p. 61.
18. Swales, 1978, p. 141.
19. See Negus, 1961.
20. Michels, 1973, vol. 1, p. 241.
21. Michels, 1974, vol. 2, pp. 7–27.
22. Ziolkowski, 1965, p. 302f.
23. 'Though these men are the hierarchy's finest members ... they nevertheless do not shy away from what amounts to an act of collective murder', Friedrichsmeyer, 1974, p. 284.
24. The word *Kanzlei* recalls Kafka, whom Hesse was reading 'with enjoyment' at the time (Michels, 1973, vol. 1, p. 109); the term *Behörde* is used negatively in Hesse's private correspondence (ibid., pp. 188, 191).
25. Friedrichsmeyer, 1980, p. 261.
26. Ziolkowski, 1969, p. viii.
27. See n. 16, above.
28. Letter to Morgenthaler, *GS*, vol. 7, p. 731.
29. Michels, 1973, pp. 241, 279, 291.
30. Ziolkowski, 1965, p. 294; Boulby, 1967, p. 262.
31. Letter to Professor Faesi, in Michels, 1973, vol. 1, p. 232.
32. Letter to Rutishauser of December 1935, in ibid, p. 135.

CHAPTER THREE

Thomas Mann: *Doctor Faustus* (1947)

Und als bös und teuflisch erscheint mir, der ich gar kein Politiker bin, diese ganze Gesinnung des Dritten Reichs, wobei ich jedem Einzelnen das Recht der bona fides und des Verblendetseins zugestehe, auch den Führern. Es scheint mir sehr wichtig und kennzeichnend, daß die protestantische Kirche diese Bewegung sich sofort zu eigen gemacht hat und im Begriff zu sein scheint, sich als eine deutsche, germanische, nicht mehr römische, auch nicht mehr christliche Organisation bedingungslos den Männern mit hohen Titeln und schönen Uniformen zur Verfügung zu stellen. Alles Anrüchige des Protestantismus, vom Fürstendienertum Luthers bis zur Vergötterung des rein Dynamischen in der jüngeren Theologie, vereinigt sich hier und wird Ausdruck für eine bestimmte, eben für die deutsche und protestantische Form des blinden Nationalismus. Dazu paßt die Selbstanbetung des heutigen Deutschen, der tiefe Ehrfurcht vor seiner 'tragischen' und 'faustischen' Natur hat und darunter versteht, daß er, Auserwählter und zugleich Gezeichneter unter den Völkern, nun einmal dazu bestimmt sei, über die kleinlichen Schranken der bloßen Vernunft und bloßen Moral hinweg das Große und Ungeheure zu tun, nämlich seine Triebe auszuleben und seine Gelüste zu befriedigen.

(Hermann Hesse: diary entry for July 1933)

(And I, who am no politician, view the whole attitude of this Third Reich as evil and diabolical, although I concede that every individual, leading personalities included, has the right to act in good faith, even when under a delusion. It strikes me as highly significant and characteristic that the Protestant Church has espoused this movement from the outset and now appears to be on the point of placing itself unconditionally at the disposal of those men with their exalted titles and pretty uniforms, presenting itself as a German, Teutonic, no longer Roman and no longer Christian organisation. All the dubious aspects of Protestantism, from Luther's servility towards the princes right down to the apotheosis of unconstrained dynamism in its recent theology, come together here and serve to express a specifically German manifestation of blinkered nationalism. This goes hand in hand with the self-adulation prevalent among today's Germans, who are deeply in awe of their supposedly tragic and Faustian destiny and see themselves as chosen and marked out among the peoples of the world, and as predestined to rise above the trivial confines of mere reason and conventional morality so that they may achieve something great and unheard of: to live in accordance with their instincts and to satisfy their innermost desires.)

1. THE NOVEL AND ITS TITLE

The title of this novel yields the first indication of its purpose: it alludes to a semi-fictitious scholar and master of the black arts who is said to have lived in the first half of the sixteenth century. The monolithic formulation *Doctor Faustus* is, however, modified by a few explanatory words not dissimilar to those used by Döblin and Hesse, which focus on an individual and help to deprive the initial title of some of its more ominous reverberations. Like the impersonal formulae *Berlin Alexanderplatz* and *The Glass Bead Game*, the name of Doctor Faustus is quickly thrown into relief by the mention of another, more modern character in the following phrase: *Das Leben des deutschen Tonsetzers Adrian Leverkühn, erzählt von einem Freunde* ('The Life of the German Master-Composer Adrian Leverkühn, Recounted by a Friend').

The name of Faustus takes us back to the turbulent days of the Reformation in Germany when a sorcerer by that name is said to have entered into an alliance with the devil after abandoning the study of theology.[1] Some would see him as a charlatan, others as a sincere seeker after knowledge. His unequal partnership with Mephostophilis, the Mephistopheles of later traditions, is said to have lasted for a period of twenty-four years, after which the reckless magus was damned to the fires of hell, but not before finding time to warn his friends against following his example. This story found its way into a *Volksbuch* ('chapbook') that was first published in 1587. It was a propagandist work written in support of certain Lutheran doctrines such as justification through faith, but perhaps because it told of a desperate relationship between a man and an immortal spirit, it fired people's imagination more than other tracts of this type and was widely read, imitated and translated. By the more rational eighteenth century, interest in it had begun to wane, and it might well have been consigned to oblivion long ago had not a later generation of writers taken an interest in it for reasons very different from those which led to its original publication. At a time when large sections of the German public were beginning to tire of the predomination of French influence on the arts, it was suggested, initially by the critic and playwright G. E. Lessing, that this story would provide a valuable subject for a German national drama. The impact of this recommendation, first made in Lessing's seventeenth 'literary epistle' of 1759, was tremendous, and within a few years many of Germany's leading writers, including Goethe and Lessing himself, had produced scenes for dramatic works about Faust or even completed tragedies on this theme. Eventually the cautionary tale of the unbridled magician was elevated into something resembling an emblem of the German national character.

For this reason alone, *Doctor Faustus* by Thomas Mann is more obviously and more relentlessly an investigation of the German mind than any of the other novels considered in this study. By choosing to refer back to the Faust tradition at many points in the novel, and by allowing the life story of the fictitious modern composer Leverkühn to intertwine with that of the sorcerer, Mann obliges his readers to consider his protagonist as a modern Faust and thus as a representative of the salient qualities of the German nation.

The subtitle would initially seem to direct the reader away from the world of superstition and magic in which the Faust myth is rooted. The words appended to the main title indicate that the book will not, in fact, deal with the hero of the sixteenth-century chapbook, but merely with one Adrian Leverkühn, a German composer whose life has been chronicled by a close acquaintance. This formulation has the effect of rendering the name of the book less forbidding; that its hero should possess what looks like an ordinary German surname, a respectable vocation and a friend disposed to commit his life story to paper would seem to reduce the ominous overtones and cut the plot down to size.

But there are also some indications to the contrary: the subtitle is not as innocent as its sounds. Why would Mann emphasise his hero's German nationality – an apparently superfluous detail – were this not one of the focal points of the novel? The word *Tonsetzer*, 'he who sets down the tones', is a curiously archaic designation for a composer, a term that sounds both pedantic and cryptically meaningful: it conveys the idea of a 'trend-setter' or a 'pace-maker'. The composer's surname is another unusual compound which, like 'Biberkopf', triggers off specific associations. 'Leverkühn' would appear to be derived from two elements, *leben* ('to live') and *kühn* ('bold', 'daring'), and therefore to suggest someone who lives a bold or reckless life, someone who 'lives dangerously'. This catchphrase, *gefährlich leben*, points to another important constituent of the novel, the late nineteenth-century philosopher who was responsible for coining it, Friedrich Nietzsche.[2]

Five distinct strands vie for attention in the novel's composite title. *Doctor Faustus* supplies the mythical background: the twenty-four-year pact between the half-titanic, half-pathetic sorcerer and his evil genius, which provides a much-revised story held to contain certain penetrating insights into the German national character. Quite what these characteristic qualities amount to is a matter for debate. The term 'Faustian' has been applied loosely to convey the idea of a nation destined for great things, spurred on by a combination of restless, single-minded endeavour and a thirst for knowledge, but also characterised by a tendency to ride roughshod over the principles of morality as well as by a ready response to erotic stimuli. Viewed objectively, these are for the most part dubious qualities, but that did not deter the National Socialist propaganda machinery from making reference to Germany's 'Faustian' mission and destiny (see pp. 98–112, below).

The term *deutscher Tonsetzer* confirms that there will be much to say about Germany in the novel. There was, as we have seen, an allegorical dimension to *Berlin Alexanderplatz* and to *The Glass Bead Game*, both of which examined the nation's health from different angles. Mann goes further than they did and reveals in his title that the hero is to be a German figure with some claim to representing his fellow countrymen, thus adding another warning to his readers to be prepared for an investigation into the intellectual and cultural traditions of the nation.

A third area with which Mann will be concerned is the state of the creative arts in the modern world. Adrian is a composer, and his career reflects many of the difficulties faced by artists, writers and musicians alike, in the modern world. There has always been a tendency for the German *Bildungsroman* to concern itself with case studies of young men aspiring to be successful as artists, so much so that the *Bildungsroman* is often almost coterminous with its own sub-genre, the *Künstlerroman*. The word *Tonsetzer* indicates that the arts will form a major part of this novel, and that the creative artist will be seen as a barometer of his time.

The name *Leverkühn* points in the direction of Nietzsche. Although never named, Nietzsche is ever-present. He cannot be mentioned without decoding the allegory: Adrian's life is, on one of its levels, an imitation of the philosopher whose fertile imagination stirred the minds of Germany's intellectuals, poets and politicians during the first half of the twentieth century. The fifth centre of interest to emerge from the novel's subtitle is the 'friend', Adrian's biographer Serenus Zeitblom, whose relationship with his subject will be an important and complex one.

A gap of several years separates the date of Adrian Leverkühn's death (1940) from Zeitblom's biography, which is presented as having been compiled between 1943 and 1945. The novel moves forward towards a double climax: the fictional death of its protagonist and the real destruction of Germany, which is witnessed and reported almost incidentally by a narrator whose ostensible concern is merely to commit his friend's career to paper. But given the circumstances in which this is achieved, Zeitblom's warnings about Adrian's personal misadventures and impending tragedy take on a wider significance. His attitude is a mixture of devotion and horror, in which it is not difficult to see a reflection of Mann's own position while he wrote the book, torn between love of his native land and horror at the irreparable damage which Germany was wreaking upon herself and others. Mann began his first draft of *Doctor Faustus* on 23 May 1943, the day on which he has Serenus Zeitblom first put pen to paper.[3]

2. A DANGEROUS LIFE

Adrian Leverkühn was born in Thuringia, an area of central Germany which brought forth Martin Luther and Friedrich Nietzsche. His father Jonathan runs a farm and devotes his leisure hours to the pursuit of an eccentric 'speculative' interest in odd biological phenomena. Adrian attends school in Kaisersaschern, a fictitious amalgam of several venerable cathedral cities and Hanseatic settlements, which serves as a museum-piece of Germany's ancient traditions. Chapter 6 evokes the mystique, and especially the darker side of this ancient city:

> *Aber in der Luft war etwas hängengeblieben von der Verfassung des Menschengemütes in den letzten Jahrzehnten des fünfzehnten Jahrhunderts, Hysterie des ausgehenden Mittelalters, etwas von latenter seelischer Epidemie: ... – möge es gewagt klingen, aber man konnte sich denken, daß plötzlich eine Kinderzug-Bewegung, ein Sankt-Veits-Tanz, das visionär-kommunistische Predigen irgendeines 'Hänselein' mit Scheiterhaufen der Weltlichkeit,*

*Kreuzwunder-Erscheinungen und mystischem Herumziehen des
Volkes hier ausbräche ... Das Kennzeichen solcher altertümlich-
neurotischen Unterteuftheit und seelischen Geheim-Disposition
einer Stadt sind die vielen 'Originale', Sonderlinge und harmlos
Halb-Geisteskranken, die in ihren Mauern leben und gleichsam,
wie die alten Baulichkeiten, zum Ortsbilde gehören. (DF 49f.)*

(But there lingered on in the air something left over from the
mentality of the people who lived there in the latter decades
of the fifteenth century: the hysteria of the waning Middle
Ages, a kind of latent spiritual epidemic: ... – this may sound
far-fetched, but it was quite possible to imagine that there
would suddenly appear before one's eyes a children's crusade, a St Vitus's dance, some itinerant preacher of the 'Little
John' variety who would demand the burning of all one's
worldly possessions, or maybe a miraculous vision of the
true cross, accompanied by processions of people caught up
in some mystical trance ... The hallmark of this ancient
neurosis which undermined the town and revealed its innermost spiritual qualities is to be sought in its many 'originals'
– eccentrics and harmless half-wits who reside within its
walls and, like the ancient edifices, are an essential constituent of any panorama of the city.)

The picture of Kaisersaschern which is conveyed in the sixth
chapter of the novel is crucial for an understanding of Mann's
image of Germany. It is of a community in which the irrational
fervour of the late Middle Ages is lying quietly in wait for an
occasion on which to reassert itself. The pogroms of the twentieth
century are prefigured in carefully chosen references to the burning of possessions and to other excesses, memories of which are
indelibly etched into the cobblestones of the city's winding streets.

Adrian grows up despising all subjects other than music, and is
fascinated not by its harmonious properties but by its ambiguous
dependence on a combination of sensual appeal and mathematical precision. It is, in his words, *die Zweideutigkeit ... als System* (DF
63) ('systematised ambiguity'). On leaving school, he opts to
study theology, motivated more by intellectual arrogance than by
the fervour of a genuine devotion. At the University of Halle he is
exposed to two 'demonic' lecturers, the coarse Ehrenfried Kumpf
(Chapter 12) and the refined psychologist Eberward Schleppfuss
(Chapter 13). Like Luther, on whom he is modelled, Kumpf believes passionately in the physical existence of the devil, to whom
he applies many old-fashioned German euphemisms, *Deixel,*

Sankt Velten and other terms which imply an almost affectionate recognition of his adversary's presence (DF 133). One evening, Kumpf invites some of his students home to a meal and the inevitable happens: the Fiend appears to him in person, whereupon, in the absence of a more suitable missile, the outraged professor hurls a bread roll at his uninvited guest, emulating Luther, who is said to have put an inkpot to similar use. Adrian's other mentor, Schleppfuss, is, by contrast, chillingly cerebral in his wholesale condemnation of the female sex. He cites approvingly the tale of a young man who arranges for his girlfriend to be burnt at the stake as a witch in order that his sexual potency be restored to him. It comes as a relief to find Adrian changing courses and moving to Leipzig to study music in 1905.

His musical instruction began in Kaisersaschern, where Wendell Kretzschmar had acquainted him with some of the problems confronting musicians in the modern world.[4] Gradually, Adrian comes to realise that music has reached a dead end in this century, originality now having been replaced by the repetition, variation and parody of techniques pioneered during earlier generations. In his efforts to break out of this impasse, Adrian derives assistance from an unwholesome sensual experience described in Chapter 16. Having asked a sinister-looking tourist guide to recommend a restaurant in Leipzig, he is taken to a brothel. Here he finds himself surrounded by women clad in gauze-like garments, *Nymphen und Töchter der Wüste, ... Morphos, Glasflügler, Esmeralden ... in Tüll, Gaze und Glitzerwerk* (DF 191) ('Nymphs and daughters of the wilderness ... morphos, clear-winged insects and esmeraldas ... clad in tulle, gauze, and tinsel'), he observes, comparing these exotic females to the butterflies ('esmeraldas') of South America which had been the subject of his father's pseudo-scientific speculations.[5] Adrian escapes from this den of vice, not before an almond-eyed brunette dressed in a Spanish jacket has had time to brush his cheek with her bare arm. This 'brothel experience' proves fruitful insofar as Adrian now begins to compose in earnest, but within a year he has returned to the house of ill fame to seek out his wench 'Esmeralda', the source of his inspiration. She has had to leave the establishment as a result of an infection, and Adrian tracks her down to a similar venue in Pressburg, Austria-Hungary, and takes his pleasure with her, regardless of her well-meant warnings as to the likely consequences of their liaison. He contracts syphilis, and after two unsuccessful attempts to seek medication (Chapter 19), the disease takes its course unchecked.

Adrian Leverkühn's compositions, done in twelve-tone music according to the principle of the 'strict series' method (Chapter 22), become more mature as he refines his techniques. In 1911, on a visit to Palestrina (the site of some of Thomas Mann's earliest literary endeavours), Adrian records the appearance of a stranger whom he takes to be the devil. The visitor promises that the inspiration he seeks will come to him thr 'igh his illness, which he is now invited to view as a pact in which he has pledged his blood to the evil one. The terms of the pact dictate that his soul is forfeit and that during his lifetime he cannot enjoy 'the love that generates warmth' (*DF* 334).

On his return to Germany, Adrian withdraws to a remote farmhouse south of Munich, Haus Schweigestill in Pfeiffering, where he composes song-cycles, an opera, and various part-vocal, part-orchestral pieces. His carefully selected friends are described in detail. They include the impecunious Anglophile Rüdiger Schildknapp, the self-indulgent dandy Rudi Schwerdtfeger, Sixtus Kridwiss and his circle of pretentious intellectuals in Munich, the decadent sisters Clarissa and Ines Rodde, and sundry female admirers: Jeanette Scheurl, Meta Nackedey and Kunigunde Rosenstiel. Frau von Tolna, another benefactress, has an obscure affinity with Esmeralda.[6] The ancient-sounding names of these people, in whom Nietzschean traits often mingle with Teutonic primitivism, derive from contemporaries of Martin Luther.

The history of Adrian's personal relationships is marred by his cold detachment and accompanied by many portents: the sudden demise of Dr Erasmi, the arrest of Dr Zimbalist, the suicide of Clarissa Rodde, the disgrace of Baron von Gleichen-Russwurm. Adrian is seduced by his friend Rudi, whom he asks to propose to Marie Godeau on his behalf. Rudi woos her for himself, only to be shot by a jealous paramour. The Jewish impresario Saul Fitelberg attempts to persuade the recluse to settle in Paris (Chapter 37). His last love, a five-year-old boy, is snatched from him by a terrifying disease (Chapter 45). A visibly broken man, unable to conceal the symptoms of his malady, Adrian composes a counterblast to Beethoven's Ninth Symphony, *Dr. Fausti Weheklag* ('The Lament of Dr Faustus'), his last and greatest work. In 1930, having invited his friends to listen to extracts from it, he delivers a personal confession and reveals his 'diabolical' association to his incredulous entourage. At this point he collapses; the last ten years of his life are spent in a state of insanity, and eventually in paralysis. Zeitblom visits him in 1939, 'after the conquest of Poland', at which point all traces of his former brilliance have departed from the great man's countenance. The last page of the book brings together its personal and allegorical strands, when Serenus implores the Almighty to have mercy on his friend *and* on his country: *Ein einsamer alter Mann faltet die Hände und spricht: 'Gott sei eurer armen Seele gnädig, mein Freund, mein Vaterland'* (DF 672) ('A lonely old man folds his hands and speaks: "May God have mercy upon your soul in its misfortune, my friend, my fatherland"').

3. ADRIAN AND FAUSTUS

The title of the novel suggests that it is firmly based on the Faust tradition, and although these parallels are an important part of its overall design, they are not so obvious as to be self-explanatory. Adrian deviates in many respects from his literary prototype. He is not a restless striver or seeker after forbidden knowledge. He does not actively summon the devil for the purposes of entering into a compact with him. The novel does not warn against the perils of rejecting conventional theology (as the chapbook had done), nor does Mann use it to celebrate, with Goethe and his emulators, the creative powers of the imagination. Instead, Mann's intention seems to have been to revoke the spirit of optimism which Goethe is often assumed to have fostered in his play. *Doctor Faustus* revokes Goethe's *Faust* in the way in which Adrian 'takes back' Beethoven's Choral Symphony in the final work of his career. For this reason, Mann avoids direct references to Goethe in the novel and bases Leverkühn's 'Faustian' traits entirely on the sixteenth-century chapbook.[7]

Both Doctor Faustus and Adrian Leverkühn were born in Thuringia as the sons of peasants (H 11, DF 16f.); they are separated from their parents and looked after by wealthy relations in a nearby town, Faustus by a cousin, Leverkühn by an uncle (H 11, DF 47ff.). They both embark on theological studies, displaying a combination of intellectual brilliance and overweening pride, only to cast the Bible 'out of the door and under the table' (H 13, DF 176 f., 333) and pledge themselves to other causes, Faustus to magic, Adrian to music. Adrian remains fascinated by numbers, chords and the mathematical elements in music; a 'magic square' hangs by his piano (DF 127). Music had played a part when Faustus summoned the devil (H 15). Adrian has no need of an elaborate nocturnal ritual (H 14, DF 333) – he is guided by a 'messenger' to the brothel where he is welcomed 'as though he had long been expected' (DF 191). The contractual relationship with a woman who is paid for services rendered during a limited period of time reproduces the idea of a pact that remains in force for a set number of years.

Various significant events take place at similar points during the men's lives. Faustus is forcibly restrained from taking a wife (*H* 27–9), while Adrian is denied true love and frustrated in his marital designs (Chapter 42). Both men are warned about the torments which await them in hell; these will include exposure to extremes of heat and cold (*H* 41, *DF* 331). Faustus visits hell and other planets in the company of Mephostophilis; Adrian explores the oceans and outer space with an American professor, Capercailzie (*DF* 357–67). In the seventeenth year of the pact, Faustus resists attempts to convert him (*H* 110-14), while in 1923 (= 1906 + 17), Saul Fitelberg makes his unsuccessful bid to force Adrian out of his isolation.

Towards the end of his days, Faustus was said to have led a 'swinish and epicurean life', acting as a pimp (*H* 115–19), and Adrian enjoyed dubious relationships with the likes of Nackedey, Rosenstiel and Rudi, engineering Rudi's proposal to Marie in the capacity of a go-between. The shade of Helen of Troy is conjured up by Faustus in the twenty-third year of the pact in order that he may father a son on her (*H* 120). Adrian's 'last love' is the child Nepomuk Schneidewein, described as his 'son' (*DF* 660). Then, as his allotted days draw to a close, Faustus bewails his fate and implores others not to emulate him (*H* 124–32), while Adrian composes his lament and reveals his sins to his friends. As they meet their deaths, certain aspects of their last moments recall the Passion of Christ: Faustus holds a 'last supper', drinks conse-crated wine with his disciples, the students, and returns after his death (*H* 131–5). Adrian comes to resemble Christ and breaks down with arms outstretched, as if trying to embrace a piano – the pose is that of the crucifixion (*DF* 637, 663). Their stories are written down by their surviving assistants, Wagner and Zeitblom.

Although it is possible to read Adrian's biography without reference to any of these associations, there are many reasons why Mann wanted the traditions surrounding Faustus to assume a pivotal position in the narrative. During the previous 100 years, these traditions, especially Goethe's reworking of them, had come to be viewed as embodying a veritable map of the German soul and a blueprint of her national destiny. Commentaries such as the one published by Gustav von Loeper in 1870 hammered home the notion of Faust's identity with the spirit of the German nation. Oswald Spengler, the historian, went so far as to speak of the past 500 years of western civilisation as the 'Faustian Age' in his sensational morphology of history, *The Decline of the West*. It is against the background of these extravagant eulogies of the myth of Faustus that Mann's polemical intentions will become clear. He is intent on reversing the optimistic readings of the tradition, and on using the same material as the starting point for an investigation of the darker side of the German nation's supposed dynamism. Nor was he the first to do so; Wilhelm Böhm's study of the 'non-Faustian' aspects of the myth had appeared under the provocative title *Faust der Nichtfaustische* in 1933, and was, in due course, followed by other negative appraisals of the corpus of German Fausts. Mann's own son Klaus was probably the first German writer to use the material for an examination of the National Socialist ideology, in his novel *Mephisto* of 1935.

One question certain to be raised at this point concerns the extent to which Adrian himself is aware of the correspondences between his personal development and the traditional material which served as a model for his career. Were he totally unaware of the parallel, his life would serve as an example of the repetitiveness of history and recall the parallels which Döblin drew between Biberkopf, Job and other figures from the Bible. The four novelists considered in this study are all at pains to show the links between modern Germany and the often remote eras in which her present traditions are rooted. But Mann goes further in this respect than any of the other writers, implying that Adrian deliberately engineers his downfall by *posing* as a modern Faustus and orchestrating many of his misfortunes. From the time of his studies at Halle, he acts as though he were determined to see himself as a successor to the legendary magician, and repeatedly quotes key passages from the chapbook as though they applied to himself. He adopts the language of the sixteenth century, especially when revealing details of his sex-life, responds willingly to the lure of the occult, chooses to invest music with a diabolical significance, and refers to his 'brothel experience' as though it had been the result of a diabolical conspiracy. The uninvited guest who appears to him in Palestrina expresses himself in the language of the chapbook, whose content is already deeply graven on Adrian's mind. Rudi's treachery is clearly foreseen, indeed contrived, by the composer, as if to prove to the world that he is under the power of Satan. When Nepomuk dies (of entirely natural causes), Adrian tries hard to convince Serenus that his death was due to 'noxious influences' attributable to himself (*DF* 630).

It is not by any means clear why the composer should wish to project this unappealing image of himself to the outside world.[8]

Psychological and structural reasons could be cited. Mann does not dispense altogether with the principle of verisimilitude. It is a known fact that all human behaviour involves an element of role-playing and the selection and emulation of models for this purpose. What human beings like to think of as their own personal development is, to an extent, the result of a process of imitation. Many literary works show the effect of this basic human tendency, from *The Divine Comedy* and *Don Quixote* to *Hamlet* and *Moby Dick*. There are innumerable instances of voluntary and involuntary dissembling in literature: Faustus himself mimicked both the miracles and the Passion of Christ.[9] If one looks for realism in this, then it is not hard to identify factors such as escapism, hero-worship or feelings of inferiority as its causes. We have seen Franz Biberkopf struggle to organise his life according to an abstract 'model' of respectability as part of an escape mechanism; Hesse's 'Elder Brother' defended himself against regimentation by living as a Chinese recluse. Both Knecht and Grass's 'Author' create fictional biographies for themselves which then function as paradigms of human behaviour. No 'educational' novel would be possible without the influence of others, and this influence is the mainstay of education itself. To recognise the importance of such models, and eventually also to recognise their shortcomings and to abandon them, as Don Quixote and Franz Biberkopf do, is a frequent theme in literature.

Nowhere does this principle have greater validity than when it is applied to the figure of the artist. As an imitator by vocation, the creative artist is thrown back on the legacy of the past and obliged to study, appraise, select, adapt and develop the media that have been refined over the centuries. For all its revolutionary aspects, Adrian's music relies heavily on European traditions for its form and content. The harmonies may be original, but the forms he uses are conventional: the opera, the *Lied*, the oratorio. The content of his works is firmly rooted in literature; Adrian adapts writings of Dante, Shakespeare, Blake, Brentano, Verlaine and others in his compositions. It is understandable that, having immersed himself in these often visionary writings, he should start to fabricate a dream-world for himself, in which the more memorable experiences of his life take on a deeper significance. The vital constituents of his life coalesce in the figure of Faustus, who serves as an emblem of the search for an identity in life, and for the reliance of artistic activity on the traditions of the past. The culminating irony of the novel is that, while committed to the most radical innovations in music, Adrian Leverkühn should choose to base his private life on a story which is saturated in the superstition and demonology of the late Middle Ages. This is a question which must now be examined in the light of his national identity.

4. ADRIAN AND GERMANY

The story of Doctor Faustus is the most distinctive of all contributions to world literature in the German language. Long before Thomas Mann added his own name to the list, the original story had inspired countless continuations, imitations and parodies; some of the best known, after Goethe's (1790, 1808 and 1832), were written by Klinger (1791), Grabbe (1829), Lenau (1836) and Heine (1851). In all of these, Faust's German nationality is an important factor. As Grabbe's character puts it: *Nicht Faust wär ich, wenn ich kein Deutscher wäre* ('I should not be Faust, were I not a German'). Subsequent writers tended to make the same point in more overtly jingoistic terms. August Spiess speaks of *jenes Streben nach dem Hohen und Wahren, welches dem Deutschen vor den anderen Nationen eigen ist* ('the pursuit of the exalted and true, which characterises the Germans more than any other nation'). Alfred Rosenberg, the Nazi ideologue whom Hesse satirised as Professor Schwentchen, provided his own definition of what constitutes the 'Faustian': *eine nordische Heldensage, ein preußischer Marsch, eine Komposition Bachs*[10] ('a Norse saga, a Prussian march, a composition by Bach'). Such more or less popular sentiments mingled, in the early years of the century, with the theories of Oswald Spengler to create a basis for the propagandist use of the name of Faust as a byword suggesting the axiomatic distinctness and superiority of the German people. Mann's choice of subject must be viewed with this cult in mind. Had the magician of yore not had to serve as an emblem of German nationhood in this manner, he would not have been chosen as the pivot of Adrian's personal and intellectual development.

Having said this, there are many obstacles to the view that Adrian Leverkühn's outlook or behaviour are representative of the nation. He is in no sense a German chauvinist, and holds few, if any, political convictions. Haughty indifference and anti-German cynicism characterise his dealings with the rabid nationalists of Chapter 14. He uses few German textual sources in his music. His only opera is based on Shakespeare's *Love's Labours Lost*, which he insists on performing in English, despite the offer of a translation from Serenus, who construes his stubbornness on this point as a sign of his 'aversion to things German' (*seine Abneigung gegen das Deutschtum*, DF 221). In his song-cycles, he goes against the established *Lieder* tradition by selecting poems in English, French and Italian in preference to those by Germans. Only at the end of his life does he take up a major subject of German origin, which, like the Brentano poem *O lieb Mädel*, appeals to him on account of its biographical rather than national relevance.

Most of Adrian's companions have strong links with other countries. Wendell Kretzschmar, his first mentor in matters musical, was born in Pennsylvania. Professor Capercailzie, who reveals the mysteries of the universe to him, is an American scientist. Rüdiger Schildknapp is a fanatical Anglophile who slavishly imitates what he takes to be the British way of life, going to such extremes as to get off a bus in Italy if he discovers that there are Germans on board (*DF* 295). Esmeralda is far removed from the Nordic ideal of beauty. Her dark pigmentation, her Spanish jacket, her almond eyes combine to give her an air of foreignness that fits in with the name he gives her. Frau von Tolna is the widow of a Hungarian aristocrat. Marie Godeau is a Francophone Swiss. Nepomuk Schneidewein speaks with a Swiss accent. Even Serenus Zeitblom, in whom it would be tempting to see an incarnation of the German middle-class intelligentsia, does not conform to any stereotype: a great admirer of the Humanism of classical antiquity, he emerges as an early and clear-sighted critic of Fascism who carries his convictions to the point of resigning from his teaching post in 1934, the year in which Mann saw himself obliged to leave his native country.

The cosmopolitan aura that surrounds these events has its origins in several distinct circumstances, not least in the fact that the entire novel was written during its author's exile in the USA. A linguistic analysis reveals a high proportion of Anglicisms in the text.[11] *Doctor Faustus* inevitably reflects its author's preoccupations at the time of writing, his reading of American news magazines, for example (Chapter 27), and of Anglo-Saxon literature in general. Mann's commentary, *Die Entstehung des Doktor Faustus* ('The Genesis of *Doctor Faustus*'), is full of reminders of the influence of the American environment: it was a time when Mann would wake up speaking English, or, worse still, overcome by a craving for Coca-Cola. California could not be further removed from Kaisersaschern, and perhaps it is this sheer remoteness of his subject that forced Mann to adopt an indirect approach to his hero's German identity.

There is another side to Adrian's apparent interest in foreign cultures. That he should base his opera on Shakespeare is a reminder of the debt which successive German literary movements owed to the English dramatist. It was none other than Goethe who spoke of him as 'our Shakespeare', in the sense that he was the father of the new, informal culture which Goethe was helping to propagate in the eighteenth century. Adrian's journey to Italy is another reminder of Goethe, or of the 'educational visits' to Southern Europe undertaken by many subsequent artists from north of the Alps who later followed his example.

The problematic side to such reminiscences of Germany's greatest poet arises when one considers the effects that these activities have on Adrian. Shakespeare had provided Goethe with a model through whom he could appeal to German audiences and revitalise a dramatic tradition that had become over-dependent on alien traditions. Leverkühn, on the other hand, refuses to have his opera performed in German: his attitude to Shakespeare is diametrically opposed to Goethe's – he uses Shakespeare's English as a barrier between himself and the public. Nor does travel have the beneficial effect that it had on Goethe: far from broadening Adrian's horizons or helping him to achieve inner harmony, his journeys merely confirm his superstitions and permit him to fantasise about his damnation. Italy does not have a soothing influence on him, for he carries within him an incarnation of Kaisersaschern which haunts him in Palestrina. The childishly fanatical enthusiasm for things foreign as displayed by Rüdiger Schildknapp is not to be understood as an expression of broad-mindedness; it results from a withdrawn, whimsical and immature outlook on life. Even Zeitblom's much-vaunted 'Humanism' and 'Hellenism' are symptoms of an inner sterility, since he cannot put these values to any positive use in the present; like the scholars of Hesse's Castalia, he seems overburdened with knowledge, but, when it comes to seizing initiatives, he can at best observe but never influence the present.

Adrian's journeys do little to bring him closer to the mainstream of European cultural life; on the contrary, his travels invariably confirm him in his proud isolation from the human community. The Pressburg experience precludes a return to health and normality. Italy supplies an endorsement of the belief that the devil has him in his clutches. His plan to marry and settle in Paris with Marie Godeau is allowed to misfire because of the same, by now deeply ingrained, conviction. Just as each of his musical pieces is a milestone on the road to his personal damnation, each journey he undertakes is construed by him as further evidence of the devil's powers.

The prison-house which he systematically fashions for himself has a powerful influence over the composer's dealings with other people. He maintains a 'cold' detachment from his acquaintances, often forgetting, or pretending to forget, their first names and, like the bureaucrats of Castalia, refusing to address them in familiar terms. The German language, with its rigid distinction between formal and informal modes of address, serves him well in this respect. When he resolves to have *Love's Labours Lost* performed in its original language, he does so from a deep-seated unwillingness to communicate, as his friend is quick to recognise (*DF* 221). The composer's idiosyncrasies arise from this inbred tendency towards self-encapsulation which determines his unique, almost unintelligible epistolary style and his physical withdrawal to the remote Haus Schweigestill in the Bavarian countryside.

In all this, Mann inclines very much towards the satirical mode. Nowhere is this more obvious than in the protracted descriptions of Kaisersaschern in the sixth chapter. The 'Gothic' atmosphere of the city, where time seems to have stood still for the last 400 years, makes it seem the ideal breeding ground for a conspiracy with the dark legions of Satan. An evil *genius loci* watches over the city, and, beneath the visually quaint exterior and despite the burgeoning railway and other industries, an air of hysteria and brutality determines its true character. The local museum, ostensibly devoted to the 'cultural' history of the town, in fact houses a well-equipped torture chamber, an attraction worthy of mention before the municipal library with its charms from the Dark Ages (*DF* 48). Emperor Otto III, actually buried in Aachen, was laid to rest here and gave the place its eerie name ('Emperor's Ashes'). It should be noted that Otto's brief reign at the end of the tenth century was distinguished by two principal features: his personal antipathy towards his territories north of the Alps, and the fact that his contemporaries saw him as the last of the Holy Roman Emperors, which he would have been had the world come to an end in AD 1000, two years after his coronation. He is thus a doubly sinister patron for the city in which Adrian was brought up. The National Socialists had celebrated the millennium of Heinrich I and Otto I with great pomp in 1936, seeing them as the founders of their Reich; Thomas Mann is here inviting his countrymen to consider an alternative genealogy in the form of one of their less patriotic descendants.[12]

Walking through Kaisersaschern, it is easy to imagine some late medieval ritual taking place, the departure of a children's crusade, maybe, or a ranting fanatic commanding his followers to set fire to their chattels. At this point, Zeitblom interrupts himself and assures us that nowadays the police would not tolerate such behaviour, in the interests of maintaining order. And yet, perversely, in the interests of a new age and its new perception of order, the police did precisely that: they turned a blind eye to the outrages of the present, *Bücherverbrennungen und anderes, woran ich lieber mit Worten nicht rühren will* (DF 49) ('the burning of books and some other matters which I hesitate to mention by name'). A malignant cyclic process appears to be at work here, however much this may seem like a 'slap in the face' for the modern generation (*etwas … dem Geiste der Neuzeit ins Gesicht Schlagendes,* loc. cit.). It is perhaps as a defence mechanism that so many of the townspeople have retreated into a kind of self-imposed, thoroughly harmless insanity. Adrian's father, doting on his collection of nature's oddities, has the makings of one such slightly deranged recluse, and his son is patently an heir to the same tradition.

Another respect in which Adrian reflects his German patrimony is in his unquestioning devotion to art. The thought of taking up a practical career never enters his head. It was Madame de Staël who provided the Germans with the flattering epithet according to which they were 'a nation of poets and thinkers', and though neither a poet nor a philosopher himself, Adrian uses verse and mental calculations as the bedrocks of his music. In his quest for originality at all cost, he shares the ideals of German Romanticism. The term 'original', as applied to the cranks who inhabit Kaisersaschern, now acquires a new significance which puts post-Romantic art into an interesting new light. His pursuit of a new and unique methodology obliges Adrian to rely on his own personal experiences, but, because these experiences are banal and at times highly unedifying, they have to be represented through obscure, teasing symbols. Hence the prominence of secret codes, such as recurring sequences of notes representing Esmeralda's name, in his musical compositions. The ultimate legacy of the Romantic's search for novelty is the creation of cryptograms which act as barriers between the author and the general public and turn his work into a monologue with strongly autobiographical components.

Adrian may adhere to rigidly mathematical methods, but the Romantic streak is not the least of his personality traits. His identification with the past, his half-serious, half-ironic adoption of a Christian symbolism in which one feels he cannot or ought not to believe, his escapism in the face of social and political realities, his lingering addiction to an obsolete rhetoric, are all signs of a

Romantic mentality, albeit in its death-throes in a modern setting. The central experience of his life, the love of a diseased harlot, provides a mirror-image of the yearning nurtured by poets such as Novalis and Brentano for inaccessible sick, dead or immoral women.

That Thomas Mann's modern Faustus should be a composer of music rather than, as he was in most older versions, a scholar or a poet, is another by-product of the representative role which the author wishes him to play. Again, his national identity is the deciding factor. Modern Western music is, to a large extent, the creation of artists from within the German-speaking world, who, from the eighteenth century onwards, had a decisive effect in shaping our notions of harmony, tempo and other musical principles. In this, too, Adrian is patently a beneficiary of a well-established German tradition. There is again a dark side to his cultural heritage. Music is a paradoxical medium, at once sublimely spiritual and yet blatantly sensual, as Adrian acknowledges in his description of it as 'systematised ambiguity'. This ambiguity is elaborated on in Mann's essay *Deutschland und die Deutschen* ('Germany and the Germans') of 1945, where a parallel is drawn between the ambivalence of music and the ambivalence of the German character:

> *Es ist ein großer Fehler der Sage und des Gedichts, daß sie Faust nicht mit der Musik in Verbindung bringen. Er müßte musikalisch, müßte Musiker sein. Die Musik ist dämonisches Gebiet ... Sie ist christliche Kunst mit negativem Vorzeichen. Sie ist berechnetste Ordnung und chaosträchtige Wider-Vernunft zugleich, an beschwörenden, inkantativen Gesten reich, Zahlenzauber, die der Wirklichkeit fernste und zugleich die passionierteste der Künste, abstrakt und mystisch. Soll Faust der Repräsentant der deutschen Seele sein, so müßte er musikalisch sein; denn abstrakt und mystisch, das heißt musikalisch, ist das Verhältnis des Deutschen zur Welt, – das Verhältnis eines dämonisch angehauchten Professors, ungeschickt und dabei von dem hochmütigen Bewußtsein bestimmt, der Welt an 'Tiefe' überlegen zu sein.*[13]

(A major failing of the myth and its literary treatment is that they omit to establish a connection between Faust and *music*. He ought to be musical, ought to be a musician. Music is a demonic area ... It is an inverted form of Christian art. It is an ordered mathematical system and yet also a chaotic manifestation of the irrational, rich in evocative incantatory gestures and endowed with a magical numerology. Of all the arts, it is the one furthest removed from reality, but also the most impassioned. If Faust is to represent the German soul, he must be involved in music, for the relationship between the Germans and the world as a whole is both abstract and mystical – in a word, musical. It is that of a slightly demonic professor who, despite his clumsiness, is possessed of the arrogant conviction that he is superior to the rest of the world by virtue of his 'profundity'.)

Another sense in which music is relevant to the German question is that it has so often served as a safety valve for unfulfilled ambitions, consoling frustrations and distracting the underprivi- leged from their political and social disadvantages. The disen- chanted theologian in Knecht's fourth autobiography turns to music when he withdraws from public life (see p. 60, above). As Balzac had put it more than a century earlier, in a passage quoted by Mann in the above essay, *Les Allemands, s'ils ne savent pas jouer des grands instruments de la Liberté, savent jouer naturellement de tous les instruments de musique* ('The Germans may be unable to play the great instruments of Freedom, but they have a natural talent for playing every instrument in the orchestra').

The question as to whether belief in the devil is or is not a peculiarly German superstition is also raised by Thomas Mann. Martin Luther undoubtedly had a powerful influence in stimulat- ing belief in the physical proximity of a devil incarnate among his followers, as is shown by the sizeable corpus of tracts about devils and evil spirits that were printed in the sixteenth century. The chapbook about Doctor Faustus is merely the best-known exam- ple of a very extensive genre of so-called *Teufelbücher* ('devil books'). Mann does not hesitate when it comes to singling out the person whom he considers responsible for these deep-seated popular traditions:

> *Martin Luther, eine riesenhafte Inkarnation deutschen Wesens, war außerordentlich musikalisch. Ich liebe ihn nicht, das gestehe ich offen. Das Deutsche in Reinkultur, das Separatistisch- Antirömische, Anti-Europäische befremdet und ängstigt mich, auch wenn es als evangelische Freiheit und geistliche Emanzipation erscheint, und das spezifisch Lutherische, das Cholerisch-Grobianische, das Schimpfen, Speien und Wüten, das fürchterlich Robuste, verbunden mit zarter Gemütstiefe und dem massivsten Aberglauben an Dämonen, Incubi und Kielkröpfe, erregt meine instinktive Abneigung.*[14]

(Martin Luther, a towering incarnation of the German character, was exceptionally musical. I openly admit that he is
repugnant to me. His unadulterated Germanness, his anti-
Roman, anti-European separatism are, to my mind, unappealing and disturbing features, even when they present
themselves as evangelical freedom and religious emancipation. My instinctive revulsion is aroused by such specifically
Lutheran tendencies as his choleric vulgarity, his endless
abuse, expectoration and raging, his terrifying robustness,
combined with a tender depth of feeling and an unshakable
belief in all manner of demons, phantoms and hobgoblins.)

Adrian may have little in common with the founding father of the
Reformation, whose most direct descendant in the novel is evidently Professor Kumpf; but in his rigidly uncompromising separatism, in his all-or-nothing mentality, in his reluctance to make
concessions or to compromise, he, too, betrays something of the
Protestant ethic. The political dimension must not be ignored.
Mann adds: *Man hat die Politik die 'Kunst des Möglichen' genannt ...*
Ein solches auf Kompromiß beruhendes Fertigwerden mit dem Leben
erscheint dem Deutschen als Heuchelei[15] ('Politics has been described
as "the art of the possible" ... Any such coming to terms with life
on the basis of compromise is seen as hypocrisy by the Germans').
Again, there is a wider significance to Adrian's 'uncompromising'
insistence on the finality of his fall and damnation.

Finally, a set of figures will suffice to dispel any lingering
doubts as to Adrian Leverkühn's function as an allegory of modern Germany. The dates of his life were clearly chosen in such a
way as to fit in with several decisive political developments which
took place during the first half of the century. The most obvious of
these are set out below in tabular form:[16]

Year	German History	Adrian/Faustus
1905	First German intervention in Morocco (Tangier)	Adrian's brothel experience
1906	Algeciras Conference: Germany obtains concessions	Adrian contracts syphilis
1911	Second intervention in Morocco (Agadir)	The devil appears to Adrian
1914	Outbreak of the First World War	In the eighth year of the pact, Faustus visits hell
1918	Germany defeated	Adrian is taken seriously ill

1925 Treaty of Locarno	Adrian woos Marie Godeau
1930 Dissolution of Germany's last democratically elected parliament	Adrian collapses into insanity
1934 Thomas Mann emigrates	Serenus Zeitblom resigns
1939 Outbreak of the Second World War	Serenus pays a last visit to Adrian
1940 Western front opened	Adrian dies

In this model, the emphasis is on territorial aggrandisement. The attempted seizure of a foothold in North Africa marks the beginning of a quest for *Lebensraum* which involves the German Reich in conflicts with other nations that continue until the end of the Second World War. Adrian's private sexual fixation comes to represent a wider, more sinister 'conquest': the belated pursuit, initially undertaken by Wilhelmine Germany and continued under Hitler, of expansion in a world whose frontiers had, for better or worse, already been determined and defined. His personal immorality reflects his country's position within the existing community of nations.

It will be appreciated that these parallels provide the novel with a key that is in danger of appearing mechanistic and too obvious to be credible. Mann was certainly exposed to criticism on various fronts, some of which he was able to foresee. He was attacked for overdoing the parody as well as for ignoring Germany's positive contribution to European civilisation. Marxist critics felt that he had placed too much emphasis on reactionary figures like Martin Luther, and not enough on the revolutionary tradition that runs from Luther's contemporary Thomas Müntzer to Karl Marx.[17] More fundamental, perhaps, is the risk taken by Mann in flattering his German readers with an account of their 'demonic' patrimony, thereby reinforcing rather than counteracting the faults which he has so grippingly portrayed.

It must not be ignored that the inspiration behind this novel is satirical. Kaisersaschern does not exist, any more than Castalia does – or, we hope, ever will. Exaggeration of and extrapolation from reality are the tools of the satirist; objective analysis comes later. It could be argued that Thomas Mann's parody invalidates itself once it has been grasped. Adrian damns himself by willingly submitting to an antiquated literary model of human behaviour, and we would run the risk of following too closely in his footsteps were we to read *Doctor Faustus* as though it embodied more than a fiction of the German nation.

5. ADRIAN AND NIETZSCHE

In addition to the historical parallels considered above, the dates of Adrian's *curriculum vitae* show a correspondence with those of Friedrich Nietzsche. The events referred to are of a more intimate nature, and in order to appreciate the similarities, it is necessary to add approximately forty years to the philosopher's life.

Year	*Nietzsche's life*	*Year*	*Adrian's life*
1844	Nietzsche is born	1885	Adrian is born
1865	Enters Leipzig University	1905	Enters Leipzig University
1866	Brothel visit in Cologne	1906	Brothel visit in Pressburg
1882	Asks Paul Ree to propose to Lou Andrea Salomé for him	1925	Asks Rudi to propose to Marie Godeau for him
1889	Collapses into insanity	1930	Collapses into insanity
1900	Dies on 25 August	1940	Dies on 25 August

Adrian's surname, Leverkühn, provided the first indication of the importance that Nietzsche will assume in his story; to appreciate why the philosopher should rank beside the legendary Doctor Faustus as a principal constituent of Mann's 'myth of modern Germany' will require a few words of explanation. The addition of such data derived from life provides a welcome touch of realism in a story already rich in lifeless abstractions. Nietzsche is far closer and more real to the modern reader than Luther or Faustus; some of the problems which he faced are still with us today, and his life has been documented many times over by people who knew him well. There are times when Serenus quotes the philosopher's friends and acquaintances verbatim, giving his deliberations an added poignancy.

So important is Nietzsche to the structure of the novel that Mann spoke of it as his 'Nietzsche novel'.[18] This must be seen in the light of the philosopher's profound influence in shaping the minds of young writers in the first half of the twentieth century, when the impact of his work was as galvanising as it was unparalleled. Along with others of his generation, Mann was both attracted to and repelled by this revolutionary mastermind who dedicated his life to reshaping the values of modern Germany. While admiring the penetrating insight and verve with which Nietzsche had analysed and castigated the decadence of modern Western society with its enfeebled, sham morality, Mann was less impressed by the personal arrogance and elitism which the philosopher displayed. There was much that was positive in Nietzsche's writings. The parallels which he drew between psychology and morality were convincing enough, and the revitalisation of the German language effected by Nietzsche's lucid, often sparkling prose was to be welcomed, as was his concern for the arts; but Mann was less willing to accept his contention that pure instinct was somehow superior to the intellect, and that all moral values had become redundant. These reservations about Nietzsche find their way into various parts of the novel. Adrian shares Nietzsche's aloofness and arrogance, despising and shunning most features of modern German society. His 'coldness' and his 'laughter' may derive from the opening sections on the new 'Superman' from *Thus Spake Zarathustra*. There are other, less obvious reminiscences, such as Beissel's 'master' and 'slave' notes (Chapter 8), which reproduce the philosopher's distinction between 'master' and 'slave' morality. The narrator shows a tendency to imitate certain features of Nietzsche's literary style, and occasionally brings in his favourite words and phrases: *fragwürdig, dionysisch, zweisiedlerisch* (DF 29, 380, 295) ('questionable', 'Dionysian', 'like hermits who live in pairs').

This is still only a small part of an explanation. Nietzsche's peculiar sexual problems, especially as presented by Brann in his study of 1931,[19] assume a paradigmatic function in Mann's depiction of the vulnerability and, indeed, the immaturity of a man of great genius when it comes to establishing a satisfactory relationship with the opposite sex. Brann's theories concerning Nietzsche's latent homosexuality and idiosyncratic sexual proclivities are worked into the novel, so that an underlying thesis emerges, according to which the functioning of Adrian's sensuality has become impaired, much as happened to Josef Knecht in *The Glass Bead Game*, but in circumstances which are more fully reviewed in their psychological origins. Self-reliance has made the composer unable to sustain relationships with other people, especially women, to whose sensuality he responds with feelings of fear and of inferiority: this, at least, is how Brann presented Nietzsche to his readers. We can now appreciate why the strictly circumscribed 'contractual' relationship with Esmeralda proved so alluring, absolving Adrian of responsibility towards her, and why all other friendships with members of either sex tend to be based on a one-sided, uncritical adulation of his genius.

No account of Nietzsche's role would be complete without reference to the widely held view that he was responsible, however indirectly or unintentionally, for many of the ideas that later found their way into the ideology of the Third Reich. Some

authorities have attempted to establish a direct continuity of
thought from his ideas to those of the leading National Socialists;
Lukács spoke of Hitler as *der Testamentvollstrecker Nietzsches* ('the
executor of Nietzsche's will'), *Mein Kampf* has been examined in
the light of Nietzsche's individualism, and many historians
would go along with the view that, by creating a climate of
opinion that favoured the radical rethinking of conventional
morals, Nietzsche was unwittingly playing into the hands of those
who sought to destabilise and overturn the established political
order.[20] His fondness for brutal and bestial metaphors furnished
images which later demagogues adapted in order to justify
repressive policies and political aggression, and his castigation of
Jewish-Christian morality was vulgarised by a propaganda
machinery forever on the lookout for anti-Semitic material.

Finally – and this is where the novel transcends the level of
political allegory and parody – Nietzsche was himself a striking
example of the paradoxes of the human predicament. The refined
ideals which he advocated were in stark contrast to the misery of
his private life, much as Adrian's are. Nietzsche's ardent defence
of health and purity contrasted with his pitifully detailed accounts
of nauseous paroxysms and prolonged fits of vomiting and mi-
graine. A scourge of conventional morality, he devoted time to the
origination of a new religion incorporating many of Christ's
teachings in the form of a gospel of moral renewal and rebirth. A
brilliant psychologist, he repudiated the 'ascetic' ideals which he
himself had shown to be based on psychological principles. An
avowed affirmer of the will to live and a declared enemy of most
of its manifestations, Nietzsche shifted his ground in each successive book and pamphlet, sometimes praising, often denouncing
the great minds who had influenced him: Socrates, Goethe,
Schopenhauer and Wagner. A pianist and composer in his own
right, he partakes of that quintessential ambiguity which Mann
ascribes to the medium of music and to the German nation itself.
In this respect, the significance of *Doctor Faustus* goes far beyond
the already dated investigation of the German national character
that had served as its point of departure. The elusive ambiguity of
all experience is a theme which Adrian – the torn and contradictory genius – compels us to consider. What is true of him on a
narrow, personal level may also be of some relevance in other
areas that have no direct connection with the land which he
represents, as the example of Adrian's reluctant biographer,
Serenus Zeitblom, will show.

6. THE WEEPING TEACHER

Although Adrian Leverkühn bodies forth many tendencies indicative of the darker side of his nation's heritage, he inspires not loathing and contempt, but concern, sympathy and at times even admiration. That he should do so is due, to no small extent, to the attitude adopted by the man who retells his life, Serenus Zeitblom, a humble schoolmaster whose quasi-religious veneration of his friend and dog-like dependence on him come to figure as a major theme of the novel.[21] It will be seen that he is important not only as the sole purveyor of information about Adrian, but also as an independent participant in the action.

Serenus and Adrian are often viewed as contrasting with or complementing one another: Serenus is a Catholic, Adrian a Protestant, Serenus a self-conscious teacher of ancient languages, Adrian a bold creator of a new artistic medium, and so forth. Yet Mann may well have been thinking along quite different lines when he spoke of their inherent similarity, *das Geheimnis ihrer Identität* ('the secret of their identity') in his account of the genesis of the novel.[22] What he meant by the identity of these two figures has yet to be investigated. So regularly does Serenus occupy centre stage that it is clearly unwarrantable to reduce him to the role of a mere foil to his subject. We learn more about him than we do about Adrian: the name of his daughter, details of his wife's parentage, where and when he did his military service – right down to what was on the sandwiches which his wife prepared for the excursion to Oberammergau. His personality is revealed, indeed underlined, at every conceivable opportunity, until it becomes a source of irritation to the reader, who is deluged by repetitive references to his feelings of inadequacy, his jealous but ineffective concern for his friend, his constant sense of foreboding and horror. If Adrian is an emblem of a self-destructive Nietzschean vitalism, his friend seems determined to portray himself as a plodding rationalist unable to do more than to stand back and chronicle the cataclysmic effects of this attitude.

Serenus regularly presents himself as gauche and ungainly by issuing pedantic apologies for his defects as a narrator and as a person. He magnifies his failings by drawing attention to his limitations, apologising for the length of some of his chapters (*DF* 97), for using asterisks (*DF* 236), or for having to include a certain word in his text (*DF* 522). He gives obscure hints as to what is about to happen, only to ask our forgiveness for having done so (*DF* 238, 382).

What initially looks like an attitude of persistent self-denigration conceals a constantly shifting perspective; like the narrators we have considered so far, Serenus cannot easily be pinned down to a consistent point of view. There are times when he shows a 'motherly' concern for his friend (DF 186), or a sense of religious awe (DF 207). At other times he seems confused or full of disapproval; outright anger is also encountered (DF 253, 251, 196). This frequent change of emphasis, this perpetual sliding from certainty into doubt, from bitter disapprobation to an almost maniacal reverence for his subject, makes Serenus himself a figure of considerable fascination, as the dark glass in which Adrian's troubled personality is reflected and at times distorted. His reactions are often double-edged – *liebende Angst, in liebender Erschütterung, halb verärgert, halb teilnahmsvoll erschüttert* (DF 666, 350, 446) ('loving fear', 'in loving turmoil', 'half enraged, half shaken by feelings of sympathy') – which creates an impression of permanent uncertainty and equivocation.

There is a recurring feeling that he is a helpless spectator of some kind of gruesome horror film. His physical responses are listed; they reveal a deteriorating state of health as a not unnatural consequence of the events he is witnessing. Adrian's first written communication about his meeting with Esmeralda occasions what is graphically described as *ein leises Sichzusammenziehen meines Inneren* (DF 197) ('a quiet involuntary contraction inside me'), and it is not long before his hands begin to tremble and his knees to shake. *Wohl zittert die Hand mir beim Schreiben* (DF 206) ('My hand really trembles as I write') is a motif regularly associated with the narrator (DF 283, 299, 336, 503, 652); its full significance does not become clear until we learn that this trembling is caused not only by the story he is retelling but also by the air-raids on Munich which increase in intensity as he struggles to complete his narrative (DF 232). The realistic and allegorical strands come together effectively in this image: when Serenus trembles at the consequences of his friend's misadventures, the whole German nation trembles with him.

Tears frequently fill his eyes, and reading Adrian's posthumous manuscripts is apt to make him 'grow cold in the pit of his stomach' (DF 283). The words of Wagner's *Tristan and Isolde* move him to tears (DF 371), as does Adrian's farewell speech to his assembled contemporaries (DF 654). His knees tremble again when he undertakes his visits to his now benighted friend (DF 670).

These many signs of emotional behaviour contrast strikingly with the otherwise pedantic style which Serenus cultivates. He normally weighs each word with meticulous care and often laments his inadequate powers of communication. What he describes as *die Trockenheit und Steifigkeit meiner Natur* (DF 118) ('my congenital dryness and stiffness') is so often in evidence that one comes to grow wary of his insistent description of himself as 'the common man' (DF 296), 'the simple scholar and schoolman who is never very lively when making conversation' (DF 369), or 'the "good" man who never gives rise to emotions' (DF 442). The qualities which he most likes to emphasise are his good-naturedness (*Gutmütigkeit*, DF 380), his moderation and faith in humanism (DF 451f.), his wisdom and his lack of humour (DF 441, 118, 599).

Not all of this need be taken at its face value. The image of quiet sobriety clashes with his much-attested sentimentality and the jingoism that he displays during the First World War. His bourgeois 'goodness' is not borne out by his very offhand treatment of his 'dearly beloved' wife, Helene Ölhafen, who is but rarely favoured with his company and made to perform a thoroughly subservient role in his life. He may see himself as the antithesis of a Don Juan (DF 589), yet he admits to having had his own sordid affair with a cooper's daughter (DF 197f.), and suggests that he would not have been too embarrassed to know how to handle the situation that arose in Leipzig, had a similar temptation come his way: *Ich war niemals prüde und hätte ... schon gute Miene dazu zu machen gewußt* (DF 196) ('I have never been a prude and would have known how to put a brave face on it').

7. THE 'OTHER' GERMANY

The view to be considered here is whether this outwardly modest and decent narrator can be viewed as a representative of the 'better', or as his name suggests, the 'serene' side of the nation; whether, indeed, he stands for opposition to Fascism and for all those who would have prevented the catastrophe that befell Germany in 1933–45, had he been able to. There is certainly a wide gulf between his attitudes and those of his friend. His lack of humour is the reverse of the compulsive fits of laughter to which Adrian is prone, his stale marriage an antithesis to the devastatingly passionate affair with Esmeralda. Most aspects of their lives are illustrative of their differences, which could be conveniently summarised in such terms as the bourgeois versus the rootless genius, the mediocre versus the outstanding, reason versus energy, tradition versus innovation, classicism versus romanticism – a list of juxtapositions that could be prolonged almost indefinitely.

It would be tempting to suggest that there is something of Thomas Mann in the figure of the narrator. As we have seen, both men withdrew from the public life of the nation in 1934 and began their apocalyptic works on the same day in 1943. Both see themselves as educators. Like his creator, Serenus is a painstaking craftsman who enjoys experimenting with teasing motifs. Thus he claims that it was a mere accident, *Zufall* (DF 151), that Schleppfuss should happen to provide the subject of his thirteenth chapter, thereby drawing attention to the obvious significance of this detail. Apologies for his shortcomings, as well as the occasional protestation that he is not, of course, attempting to write a novel (DF 440), have the effect of disinforming the reader and blurring the distinction between fiction and reality. Additional tricks in which Mann indulges via the narrator include the special significance attached to chapters whose digits add up to seven.[23] In one important respect, it is evident that Mann was using Serenus to conduct a private battle against his detractors. One of their number, Walter Boehlich, had accused him of deserting his country, of not being present during the 'epoch of world history' that had just come to pass;[24] now Serenus argues that even when absent in the flesh, he was always present in spirit at his friend's side: *Aber heute ist seelische Tatsache, daß ich dabei gewesen bin, denn wer eine Geschichte erlebt und wieder erlebt hat, wie ich diese hier, den macht seine furchtbare Intimität mit ihr zum Augen-und Ohrenzeugen auch ihrer verborgenen Phasen* (DF 574) ('But today it is a psychological fact that I was present, for whoever lives through a story as often as I have lived through this one, becomes an eye- and ear-witness to its most hidden phases as a result of this terrifying sense of intimacy'). In this passage, Mann is defending himself against the charge that his dereliction of Germany, his acceptance of Czech and later American citizenship, had deprived him of the right to pronounce on matters affecting his country.

It would be unwise to overstress the parallels between Serenus and the author, if only because there is much in Adrian, too, to remind us of Thomas Mann. His strict methodology, his preoccupation with form, his concern about the cultural impasse that modern art has reached, the literary dimension of his creative work – these ideas are far from alien to Mann himself. To view Serenus as the 'good' and Adrian as the 'evil' German would be to misunderstand Mann's whole attitude to the crisis that led through Fascism to the Second World War. The essay *Germany and the Germans* was written in response to a set of opinions on the German national character which had recently been expressed by fellow-exile Bert Brecht, who viewed the rise of the Third Reich in a very different light from Mann. In Brecht's eyes, Hitler had risen to power aided by big business and discontented army officers, while the average German looked on aghast but was powerless to stop the process. The 'other' Germany was sound and upstanding; it comprised the overwhelming but silent majority – as much as ninety-nine per cent of her working-class citizens, Brecht argued.[25]

Thomas Mann suspected that there was a flaw in Brecht's model: support for National Socialism had been far greater than Brecht was prepared to admit, even among the supposedly sensible working populace. It was not his intention to show his readers a divided Germany, with Adrian taking the blame and Serenus representing the 'other' half in the guise of an innocent bystander. Mann is quite emphatic on this point:

> *Eines mag diese Geschichte uns zu Gemüte führen: daß es nicht zwei Deutschland gibt, ein böses und ein gutes, sondern nur eines, dem sein Bestes durch Teufelslist zum Bösen ausschlug. Das böse Deutschland, das ist das fehlgegangene gute, das gute im Unglück, in Schuld und Untergang. Darum ist es für einen deutsch geborenen Geist auch so unmöglich, das böse, schuldbeladene Deutschland ganz zu verleugnen und zu erklären: 'Ich bin das gute, das edle, das gerechte Deutschland im weißen Kleid, das böse überlasse ich euch zur Ausrottung.'*[26]

> (One fact is brought home to us by this historical development: that there are not two Germanies, one good and one evil, but only one, whose best qualities have been vitiated through the craft of the devil. The evil Germany is the good Germany gone astray, in its misfortune, its guilt and decline. Thus it is quite nonsensical for a native German mind to deny the evil, guilt-ridden Germany and to declare: 'I am the good, noble, and just Germany in a white robe, and I am handing over the evil Germany to you for extermination.')

These remarks oblige Mann's readers to concentrate on the similarities between the narrator and his subject, since they both reflect features which were conducive to their country's downfall. They do frequently display the same characteristics, such as a preoccupation with the outward form of their works, a love of rapturous speculation and a disdain for social and political realities. Self-centredness is not the least of their failings. Serenus may be a teacher, but, when he resigns his teaching post in protest in 1934, he is not making a political point (since his resignation is simply accepted) but retreating into isolation, much as Adrian had done from 1912 onwards. He may be a critic of the Fascist regime, but his protest is ineffective: his commitment to Humanism does not benefit humanity, just as the new harmonies of Adrian's music have no effect on harmony in the world at large. The futility of their devotion to aesthetic causes provides a major link between the composer and his biographer.

Even in his compulsive attachment to Adrian, his much-vaunted friendship, Serenus could be said to be mimicking the pact, since the relationship between them paralyses him and prevents him from living his life to the full. He is, in the end, destroyed by their friendship and faces the same form of emotional deprivation that affects Adrian: true love is denied to him. References to his spiritual exhaustion, loss of weight, conflicting responsibilities (*DF* 481, 470), to the fact that his life is acted out on the side, *mit halber Aufmerksamkeit, gleichsam mit der linken Hand* (*DF* 416) ('with divided attention, with my left hand, as it were'), suggest that Serenus is no freer than his friend. Adrian's inability to marry is counterpointed by the sham marriage in which Serenus is trapped; his 'good wife' is no more than an attentive domestic servant. The pursuit of Esmeralda has a low-key counterpart in a liaison with 'a girl of the people' which keeps him busy for a few months at Halle, giving him an opportunity to put his humanist theories into practice (*DF* 197); but in the end, neither man can surrender himself to a woman: their intellectualism, their disdain for the purely physical, are too strong. So Adrian must purchase his pleasure with a whore, while Serenus refers to his mistress as a mere 'thing' (loc. cit.). That our humanist should opt out of public life as a schoolmaster in 1934 shows how little he had learned from the story he is telling. He mimics Adrian in his unproductive, self-imposed isolation, assuming a position that is as paradoxical as it is pathetic: he deserts his pupils when their need of him is greatest, when his declared values need a spokesman and a champion. But far from offering support to the younger generation, he is not even able to restrain his two sons from rendering their services to their *Führer*, one in a civilian, the other in a military capacity (*DF* 16). In the end he looks back, a broken man, on a wasted life and one that is remarkably similar to that of the legendary doctor. In compiling his memoirs, he suffers his own private descent into hell. Not for nothing does he take his motto from an evocative scene depicting Dante's departure towards the underworld in the *Inferno*.

T. J. Reed distinguishes between an 'Apolline' Zeitblom and a 'Dionysian' Leverkühn,[27] a distinction which overlooks their

similarities. The novel warns against the Apolline serenity of the
former no less than against the creative sensuality of the latter.
Adrian is Apolline in his devotion to mathematical principles of
harmony and in his detachment from ordinary life, Dionysian in
his willing surrender to the devil, and the narrator is prey to his
own analogous dichotomies. If there is a single quality that determines Zeitblom's discourses, it is his love of paradoxes. He will
often pick out little inconsistencies and comment on them with the
help of a few well-honed oxymorons. The fashionable pundits of
Munich, typical products of what Hesse described as 'Feuilletonism', are derided as *Sprechliteraten* and as *stubenreine Bohème* (DF
271, 264) ('literary raconteurs', 'house-trained bohemians'). Sometimes Serenus will single out a word that possesses contradictory
levels of meaning and weigh them up, inviting the reader to
marvel at the bewildering duplicity of language:

> *'Bedenklich' ist ein vortreffliches Wort … Es fordert zugleich zum
> Eingehen und zum Vermeiden auf, jedenfalls also zu einem sehr
> vorsichtigen Eingehen, und steht im Doppellicht des
> Bedenkenswerten und der Anrüchigkeit einer Sache – und eines
> Menschen.* (DF 150)

> ('Questionable' is an excellent word … It encourages inspec-
> tion and avoidance, both at the same time, or at any rate
> demands a very cautious approach; it occupies a shadowy
> area somewhere half-way between what is worthy of con-
> sideration and what is disreputable about something – or
> some person.)

He never misses an opportunity to highlight the dualism of a
character: even Esmeralda, the 'witch', is praised for the 'higher
humanity' which she displays in warning Adrian about her infection:

> *Ich weiß es von Adrian: sie warnte ihn; und kommt nicht dies nicht
> einer wohltuenden Unterscheidung gleich zwischen der höheren
> Menschlichkeit des Geschöpfes und ihrem der Gosse verfallenen,
> zum elenden Gebrauchsgegenstand herabgesunkenen physischen
> Teil?* (DF 207)

> (I know this from Adrian: she warned him; does this not
> approximate to a refreshing distinction between the higher
> humanity of that creature and her fallen, physical side,
> which had degenerated into serving as a miserable utensil in
> the next best gutter?)

Each of Zeitblom's digressions focuses on some paradoxical antinomy: the 'mad monarch' Ludwig, the 'incestuous saint' Gregory, the identity of progress and reaction, and of aestheticism and barbarity (*DF* 569–73, 422–6, 489, 495). Here, there is a sense that the political theme is a mere fragment of a much wider phenomenon, of which the composer and his biographer are equally valid illustrations. The dualism which preoccupied Döblin, the 'yin' and 'yang' which pulled Knecht in opposite directions, determines the cultural milieu of Mann's Germany, and provides a force which sustains our two characters, while simultaneously working towards their destruction. Adrian's music is *both* great art and, in its relentless denial of freedom to individual notes, a prefiguration of Fascism. It is a music rich in improbable contrasts: one thinks of the mocking laughter of hellish hordes and the chorus of angelic children in his *Apocalypsis cum figuris*. The narrator imitates his subject in this respect as well: his prose is both brilliant and desultory, highly polished and yet bristling with non-sequiturs; in short, ideally attuned to his subject: it combines the exalted and the pedestrian, the bloom of poetic diction and the tongue-tied stuttering of the jaded civil servant. Only someone as deeply split as Adrian himself can tell his story without manoeuvring us into false pity or contempt: thus Serenus Zeitblom, the weeping teacher, the pathetic perfectionist, the platonic adulterer, emerges as the most appropriate, indeed as the only possible narrator of this life.

8. THE DEVIL AND HIS HABITAT

In a letter to Karl Kerényi of September 1945, Thomas Mann explains that the pact between Adrian and the devil would, as in the chapbook, provide the pivot around which the rest of the novel revolves:

> *Das Teufelsbündnis ist das General-Thema des Buches, das zwar in den Jahrzehnten von 1885 bis zu Hitlers Ankunft spielt, aber mit einem Fuß immer im deutschen 16. Jahrhundert steht.*[28]

(The pact with the devil is the underlying theme of the book which, while set in the decades from 1885 up to the advent of Hitler, has one foot firmly located in sixteenth-century Germany.)

This emphasis on the importance of the devil may strike the reader as misplaced. No pact is formally concluded, and the devil, who acted as the permanent companion-cum-servant in the sources about Faustus, keeps a low profile until the twenty-fifth chapter, the only section in which he appears. Mann therefore seems to have been at pains to excise him from the text and to have deprived it of what must have been the main area of interest to readers of earlier versions of the story: the interaction between the evil spirit and his human victim. The 'conjuring-up' of Mephistopheles, so important and protracted in Goethe's drama, is another casualty in Mann, where it is alluded to only briefly and retrospectively in the belated encounter when Adrian's visitor merely confirms that he had long ago entered into a pact 'with thy blood and promised thyself unto us' (DF 333).

While Mann may have dispensed with nocturnal rituals at crossroads, the devil is prefigured by many of the people whom Adrian meets during his formative years. Obvious examples include Professors Kumpf and Schleppfuss and the roguish Leipzig guide with his brass badge and diabolical laugh. But there are also other, less conspicuous parallels. Many of the composer's associates, even quite minor figures in the novel, are given features that remind us of some aspect of Hell or the devil, so that in the end everyone, from the stammering, spluttering Kretzschmar to the demented daughter of Adrian's Italian landlady, Signora Manardi, could be seen as a Satanic emissary. This diabolical identity extends to the animals as well: the dogs Luxl (diminutive of *Lucifer*) and Kaschperl (cf. Kumpf's *Kesperlin*), and one 'sulphurously yellow' cat belonging to Clarissa Rodde.

The conversation recorded as having taken place between the protagonist and his unnamed visitor in Palestrina stands out from the rest of the text in various ways. Structurally, it is the central section (the novel consisting of forty-seven chapters, two continuations and a postscript), and it is in dialogue form, like a scene from a play. The documentary trappings are no guarantee of authenticity: the devil avails himself of the same 'woodcut' style in which Adrian corresponds with his friend, suggesting that he is a projection, conscious or subconscious, of the composer's imagination, already predisposed towards a belief in the myth of Doctor Faustus. Several clues alert us to the artificiality of the experience. Adrian wakes up after the conversation with no clear recollection of how it ended. More significantly, the devil assumes the appearance and mannerisms of various key people he has met, thus proving himself to be an amalgam of the most important educative elements in the composer's life. There is nothing in what he says that Adrian does not already know or believe or wish to believe, long before the dialogue takes place.

Does Adrian himself believe that he has spoken to the devil?

The document passed on to Serenus contains no direct information on this point, but it is written on music paper, which gives it
the outward appearance of a creative work. In his answers,
Adrian vacillates between accepting and rejecting his visitor's
credentials and is not slow to charge him with the appropriation
of his own ideas. He puts it to him that the whole experience is a
hallucination brought on by an attack of fever (DF 315), to which
the devil counters that the fever has not produced him but merely
enhanced Adrian's ability to perceive him. The illness is a catalyst;
the visitor disputes that he has come into existence out of nothing.
Instead, he refers to the principle of mimicry, one of Jonathan
Leverkühn's hobby-horses, *Anpassung, Mimikry, du kennst das ja,
Mummenschanz und Vexierspiel der Mutter Natur, die immer die
Zunge im Mundwinkel hat* (DF 307 ('Adaptation, mimicry, thou
knowest them well, the masked ball and charade as staged by
Mother Nature, forever tongue in cheek'). Like the tropical *Hetaera
Esmeralda* that survives by imitating its environment, the Evil One,
by his own admission, gains power over his victims by copying
the features of their surroundings. He depends on the cultural
traditions of the community that believes in him. In this case it is,
of course, Kaisersaschern that supplies him with his most distinctive qualities, so that he can say of himself, *Wo ich bin, da ist
Kaisersaschern* (DF 304) ('Wherever I am, there is Kaisersaschern').
This could equally well be read the other way round, and will be
best understood in the light of another passage from *Germany and
the Germans*: *Wo der Hochmut des Intellektes sich mit seelischer
Altertümlichkeit und Gebundenheit gattet, da ist der Teufel*[29] ('Wherever intellectual arrogance is paired with old-fashioned, hidebound
spirituality – there lurks the devil'). It is not so much a question of
belief or disbelief in the devil as such; the point is to acknowledge
his origins and his cherished habitat: he is as 'real' as they are.

Adrian's dialogue with his visitor falls into four parts. It begins
with a general characterisation of the stranger which reveals certain parallels between the composer and his visitor: their coldness,
their roots in Kaisersaschern and the influence of Professor
Kumpf. The stranger comments on some of his victim's idiosyncrasies, such as his reluctance to use the familiar pronoun in
conversation. Having established his right to comment and criticise, he moves on to an analysis of three cardinal aspects of
Adrian's life, which are demarcated from each other by the three
different disguises which he assumes: the travelling actor or
pimp, the bespectacled musicologist, and finally the theologian in
the mould of Schleppfuss, complete with the latter's parted beard,

pointed teeth and unique lecturing style, which involves sitting sideways and gesticulating nervously at his audience with his tapered fingers.

The pimp, the musicologist, the theologian: these three personae adopted by the intruder provide successive images of the three areas which have the greatest bearing on Adrian's development: sexuality, art and religion. Chapter 25 must assume a central position within the book, since it is here that the main themes converge. In his capacity as a pimp, the devil confirms that Adrian has contracted syphilis, having taken his pleasure with Esmeralda in the belief that this experience would benefit the evolution of his talent. He is quick to establish a connection with his national character as a German, reminding Adrian that the sons of his country are reputed to lack a certain natural sparkle: *Begabt, aber lahm ist der Deutsche* ('The German is talented, but gauche'), so that even their great statesman Bismarck had to conclude that they need half a bottle of champagne to bring them up to scratch (DF 308). But it emerges that Adrian has miscalculated: pleasure alone is not sufficient to provide the necessary stimulus. Its after-effect, the disease which he catches from Esmeralda, will provide the catalyst which he desires.

The stranger changes his appearance, signifying a shift of perspective. He now turns to the crisis that faces modern music and gives his listener a run-down of the problems besetting today's composers: the absence of new methods, the shortage of patrons willing and able to commission new works, and widespread dissatisfaction with superficial ornamentation and playful virtuosity, predicting that from now on the mastery of abstruse techniques such as the solving of technical conundra will become all-important. The self-sufficient charm of pleasing sounds has become unacceptable. To find material that is in keeping with the demands of his time, Adrian will have to draw heavily on his tragic personal circumstances: *Zulässig ist allein noch der nicht fiktive ... Ausdruck des Leides in seinem realen Augenblick* (DF 323) ('The only form of expression still valid ... is uncontrived suffering as it is genuinely experienced'). This pinpoints the importance of the autobiographical component in Adrian's works, where his personal grief will regularly assume a key position. Here, the devil promises him success: he will break through the paralysing sterility of his age and, by 'daring to be barbaric', will return to a truer expression of religion than is found in the watered-down humanism of the present, devoid as it is of excesses, paradoxes, passion and adventure (loc. cit.).

Now, the visitor's appearance is transformed into a likeness of
Professor Schleppfuss, in which guise he answers the inevitable
question about the price that will be exacted in return for this
creativity. When he spoke of the 'new barbarism' of Adrian's
music, he was using a catchphrase with a political significance;
now, ominous words like *unterirdisch, Keller, dicke Mauern* (DF 328)
('underground', 'cellar', 'thick walls') are unpleasant reminders of
the methods used by the modern totalitarian state to enforce
obedience or dispose of the unwanted. Hell itself will embrace the
extremes of heat and cold, and the souls of the damned will rush
from one to the other, emitting howls of pain. Drily, the devil
observes the similarity between the plight of the damned and
Adrian's own predicament, torn as he is between irreconcilable
extremes. Hell, for Adrian Leverkühn, exists right here on earth.

9. THE THEOLOGY OF KAISERSASCHERN

This conversation has shown that Adrian is equipped with a clear
insight into his predicament and his prospects. It is remarkable
that he should subsequently do so little to break out of the situation in which he recognises himself to be trapped. Is he indeed
under some kind of curse, some inner paralysis that claims his
mind long before his body is stricken by the tertiary phase of his
illness? The phenomenon of paranormal suggestivity interested
Mann and was touched on in several of his earlier works, such as
The Magic Mountain and *Mario and the Magician*. Here, occult forces
are shown to be capable of gaining a powerful hold over people
whose minds and bodies are already afflicted by other forms of
decadence or disability. This is the cause of Adrian's weakness,
the passivity that prevents him from seeing his illness as a medical
rather than a moral problem: his venereal infection externalises
the ills that are deeply rooted in society. In its widest sense, the
novel explores the malaise, the decadence of early twentieth-
century culture, which finds a compelling metaphorical expression in the figure of the syphilitic artist, a theme which Mann is
known to have been considering as early as 1905. As the political
situation deteriorated for Germany and much of the rest of Europe during the 1930s, it became more pressing to examine the
reasons for this attack of collective insanity, and so Mann allowed
the theme to develop beyond an exploration of the aesthetic temperament and deliberately introduced parallel figures from a
wider social spectrum. Adrian holds the key to each individual
destiny; as the *Tonsetzer*, he provides the focal point for the mala-
dies of his contemporaries: the thinly-veiled barbarism of the

Kridwiss circle in Munich, Zeitblom's gutless sentimentality, the spiritual deracination and moral anarchy of the two Rodde sisters, Rudi's sham emotionalism and Rüdiger's callous opportunism. The extent of Germany's decline is highlighted by the insurance fraud perpetrated by Baron von Gleichen-Russwurm, the grandson of one of Germany's most respected and morally steadfast poets, Friedrich Schiller (*DF* 560).

It is no coincidence that Adrian's illness is closely bound up with his sexuality. An apparent biographical accident serves to illuminate a major social phenomenon; the composer is by no means the only character whose behaviour reflects a peculiar sexual disposition. Rudi's superficial charm and incorrigible flirtatiousness are decisive personality traits, Rüdiger exploits his wealthy patronesses, Serenus tries out his theoretical convictions on a barrel-maker's daughter, only to opt for the stability of a conventional marriage: in each case, their sexual conduct gives a reliable indication of their innermost personality. The Rodde sisters attempt to use marriage as a means of escaping from their drab, frustrating surroundings, but the darker forces of passion which they had hoped to curb are unleashed in the process and quickly exact a terrible revenge. Complex behavioural patterns are repeatedly traced back to sexual opportunism of one sort or another, and love turns out to be little more than a yielding of the body in exchange for tangible goods or services. Serenus admits that he was persuaded to enter into marriage for the sake of the 'peace and tranquillity' which it offered, as well as being motivated by a desire for an orderly integration into the community (*DF* 254, 15f.). Rudi seduces Adrian in order that the composer will dedicate a violin concerto to him; Rüdiger obtains expensive gifts and clothes from female admirers. The transactional nature of love, observed in its purest form in the visit to the brothel, is presented as a universal fact of life. Here, too, Adrian merely functions as a barometer of his environment.

That disaster should be visited upon him in the guise of a syphilitic infection cannot be fortuitous. The appearance of the disease at the beginning of the sixteenth century coincided with the Lutheran Reformation, already identified by Mann as a turning point in German history. Although they affected opposite extremes of life, the loftiest aspirations of the spirit and the basest of instincts, there is a sense in which these two cultural phenomena may be seen as related. The Reformation encouraged individualism in that it placed an obligation on people to make their own relationships with God, where previously they had relied upon an intermediary in the form of the Roman Church. We have seen that Mann blamed some of Germany's anti-European arrogance and her desire for cultural autarchy on Luther's separatist zeal. On a personal level, syphilis also has an isolating effect, introducing mistrust and suspicion into the community. Adrian attempts to turn the clock back by abandoning himself to a passion heedless of its consequences, but pays for his folly with his sanity and ultimately his life. The connection between his disease and the Reformation is made via the two physicians described in Chapter 19. The first of these is Dr Erasmi, whose name derives from that of the scholar Erasmus, who endeavoured, unsuccessfully, to mediate between the opposing factions at the beginning of the Reformation. Hopes fade for Adrian when Erasmi is found dead in mysterious circumstances. He now turns to Dr Zimbalist, whose name is associated with clashing brass 'cymbals' and whose tiny moustache is expressly likened to that of a face that was to play an important role in world history (*Attribut einer welthistorischen Maske*, DF 211). Mann uses the minor details of their names and appearances to mark out the beginning and the end of the disease that was paralysing Germany.

Music, as Walter Pater remarked, is the art towards whose condition all art constantly aspires, and perhaps for this reason it plays an important part in very many of Thomas Mann's novels and short stories, from *Little Herr Friedemann* and *Buddenbrooks* to *The Magic Mountain* and *Doctor Faustus*. Its methods are sufficiently close to those of the novelist for him to interpolate references to his own work, which he does by drawing parallels between verbal and musical composition. Kretzschmar speaks of the 'language' of music and substitutes words for musical notes when he describes a piano sonata (DF 72f.). Beethoven, we are told, used to compose in words. The letters of Esmeralda's name determine a melodic pattern in Adrian's music, and when he comes to write his *ensemble* of 1927, he says he had intended to write 'not a sonata, but a novel' (DF 603). So, although the musicological sections are the result of meticulous research, it would be wrong to view them as comments on music alone. They stand for all art, and for the relationship between the arts. Music is regularly based on literature or on some other art; here, a novel concerns itself with music, but in such a way that the effect is often ironic. To describe music, to put the effects of its rhythms and sounds into words, to pin a meaning onto its structure and its harmonies, is a task which must fail, since music shuns the apparent logic of verbal communication. When Serenus struggles to verbalise and to rationalise about his friend's compositions, he is pursuing an unattainable goal. The irony is further compounded by the circumstance that Adrian's music does not exist, despite superficial parallels with Berg and Schönberg.[30] It should also be noted that, when writing about his encounter with the devil, Adrian records the incident on music paper, so that again, the literary and musical media intertwine. The organisation of the twenty-fifth chapter is therefore part-musical and part-literary, music being represented by the staves on the paper and by the tripartite, sonata-like form with its interplay of questions and answers, while the dramatic element and the use of the Faust tradition derive from literary sources.

The third theme of the conversation in this chapter is that of religion. It has been noted that the 'devil' derives many of his features from the two professional theologians who were portrayed in Chapters 12 and 13. His coarse manner of speaking recalls Kumpf, his subtle reasonings stem from Schleppfuss. Adrian later admits that 'my study of the divinity was the clandestine origin of the pact' (*war mein Gottesstudium heimlich schon des Bündnisses Anfang*, DF 658). Here we find ourselves up against another paradox. The term 'theology' signifies the study of the divine (*theos*, god), and yet the two academic authorities here blamed for Adrian's voluntary pursuit of the devil have nothing to say about the creator; their whole attention seems to be riveted on the fiend. Kumpf's special field of inquiry is *die Hell und ihre Spelunck* (DF 133) ('Hell and ye darke chambers thereof'), a subject with which he identifies himself to the extent of imagining his arch-enemy hovering around his dinner-table at home. His career demonstrates how readily theology may degenerate into superstition and demonology. His first love was, we are told, not religion but literature (DF 131); this may have predisposed him towards the fantastic. But, in many respects, Kumpf and Schleppfuss are true to the demands of their vocation as theologians, recognising that it remains far easier to frighten the sinner by portraying punishments than it is to foster virtue by promising blessings and rewards. Having conveyed a real and horrifying picture of the devil as a tempter, Kumpf passes his student on to a colleague who identifies the area in which Adrian is most likely to confront temptation: in his own personal sexuality.

Eberward Schleppfuss is an example of a brand of extreme anti-feminism that is occasionally encountered in clerical circles. In the venerable tradition of Church Fathers like Tertullian (*De cultu mulierum*), he sees woman as the devil's portal, deriving the word *femina*, against all philological evidence to the contrary, from the

Latin roots *fides* and *minus*, and suggesting, on this tenuous basis, that women must be capable of 'less faith' than men. The Bible provides him with more ammunition of an equally spurious nature.

Vielmehr war es das Merkwürdige und tief Bezeichnende, daß ... der ganze Fluch der Fleischlichkeit und der Geschlechtssklaverei dem Weibe zugewälzt wurde, so daß es zu dem Spruch hatte kommen können: 'Ein schönes Weib ist wie ein goldner Reif in der Nase einer Sau.' ... Das Geschlecht war ihre Domäne, und wie hätte sie also, die femina *hieß, was teils von* fides, *teils von* minus, von *minderem Glauben* kam, nicht mit den unflätigen Geistern, die diesen Raum bevölkerten, auf schlimmvertrautem Fuße stehen, des Umgangs mit ihnen, der Hexerei, nicht ganz besonders verdächtig sein sollen?* (DF 143f.)

(It was, however, both remarkable and profoundly significant that ... the entire curse of our dependence on the flesh, our subservience to sexual needs, was the sole responsibility of the woman, which had given rise to the proverb: 'A beautiful woman is like a golden ring in the snout of a sow.' ... Sex was her domain, and why should not she who bore the name of *femina*, derived in part from *fides*, in part from *minus*, she who was *of less faith*, be guilty of a wickedly familiar interaction with the sordid spirits that inhabit this area, and, by associating with them, expose herself to the particular accusation of witchcraft?)

The biblical passage is subtly emended; Proverbs XI: 22 in fact makes reference to 'A beautiful but empty-headed woman ...'. There can no longer be any doubt as to how Adrian came by his fixed idea that a fleeting association with a fallen woman might cause him to be damned in all eternity; he is earlier described as having 'a religious disposition' (DF 62). But religious sentiment is easily perverted, as the 'hooked cross' adopted by Fascism itself demonstrates. Adrian learns a twofold lesson at the feet of his spiritual mentors at Halle: that the devil is real, and avails himself of sinister, underhand methods of temptation (Kumpf), and that women are his principal instrument of seduction (Schleppfuss). When, at the end of a year-long struggle to resist her attraction, he is finally united with Esmeralda, he cannot avoid seeing her as providing a direct link between himself and the powers of Hell. All he has done is to take theology – as it was communicated to him at university – to its logical conclusion, ignoring something which even Serenus knows very well: that theology is incompatible with logic (DF 124).

This, then, is the key to Adrian Leverkühn's strange and self-destructive conduct: his music is 'the music of Kaisersaschern' (DF 115), and so, too, is his sex-life. At his first encounter with Esmeralda, his attitude to women and to his own eroticism has already been predetermined by his two professors, with the result that he cannot do otherwise than view her from their rabidly biased perspective and react to her with their teachings at the back of his mind. Hence the fatal attraction of the forbidden; hence, too, the fear of binding involvement. There can no longer be any doubt that Schleppfuss *had* to be the subject of the thirteenth chapter of Adrian's life. Kaisersaschern (and this includes its nearby outpost Halle, and other places in which a typically Teutonic combination of arrogance and sentiment holds sway) is as monolithic and inflexible as Castalia, peopled by recluse-like monomaniacs oblivious to the damage caused by their age-old wisdom and doctrinal rigidity. Kaisersaschern is a fictional image of Germany, and for all its differences presents many close parallels with *The Glass Bead Game*, so much so that Thomas Mann himself referred to the novel as his *Glasperlenspiel mit schwarzen Perlen* ('Glass Bead Game with black beads'), in the dedication which he wrote in the copy that he sent to Hermann Hesse,[31] suggesting that his treatment of the subject was several degrees more pessimistic than his friend's.

10. PROGNOSIS

Is there, in the end, any hope for the victim and for the nation whose apparently fatal disease he has embodied? Adrian is comparable to the Fausts of the chapbook and Goethe's two-part drama in that he commits grave transgressions in both mind and body, but Goethe's Faust is saved, and the author of the sixteenth-century story does not prejudge Faustus, who ends up wandering around aimlessly after his death, presumably waiting for the Last Judgement. But for our twentieth-century Faustus, the outlook seems devoid of hope: the final glimpse is of a living corpse, vegetating away in his room, unable to recognise his erstwhile admirers while the nation plunges ever deeper into disaster. The novel ends with the protracted agonies of Leverkühn, Zeitblom and the country which they both represent.

It is not easy to see how things could have been different: 1945 was the 'Year Zero', the year of the *Kahlschlag* ('complete clearance') for German literature, much as it was for the old Reich. Thomas Mann himself refers to this novel as *das Buch des Endes*[32] ('the book of the end'), fearing that there would be no new beginning after the war, that Germany would have to remain permanently occupied by foreign armies and perhaps partitioned into a series of purely agrarian states, as would have happened had the Morgenthau Plan of 1943 been implemented. Her culture would be dead for many years to come, partly because of the widespread burning of books by modern authors that had taken place from 1933 onwards, partly also because of the moral *impasse* which Adorno had in mind when he spoke of the impossibility of writing poetry after Auschwitz. Also, there is a veiled auto-biographical layer in the novel, to which Mann alluded when he spoke of it as *ein Lebensbuch von fast sträflicher Schonungslosigkeit, eine sonderbare Art von übertragener Autobiographie* [33] ('an almost criminally outspoken account of a life; a strange species of metaphorical autobiography'). Not only did Mann see himself as guilty of sharing many of Adrian's characteristic faults (a rigid compositional technique, a sense of alienation from ordinary life, vestigial leanings towards homoeroticism), but he also seems to have been firmly convinced that he would die in 1945. As he explains in *The Genesis of Doctor Faustus*, his mother had died at the age of seventy, and, given his interest in meaningful numbers, it seemed plausible that he would, too. In this respect, there is another personal element in Adrian's relentless progress towards the inevitable: sickness, paralysis and insanity become the symbols of the darker side of his creative gifts, fitting punishments for the hubris of the genius. Goethe may have tried to present the figure of the poet as the darling of the gods in poems such as 'Ganymed' and other celebrations of the creative imagination, but Mann suggests an alternative genealogy when he depicts the artist as the instrument of an omnipresent, all-corrupting force.

At the very end, however, Mann – like Döblin and Hesse before him – rises above the starkly pessimistic level of his narrative and drops hints that Adrian's death may not have been in vain and that, by extrapolation, there may be hope for a better Germany in the future. There is a suggestion that Serenus has at least been able to obtain insights into the causes of some of the horrors he has chronicled, and that his knowledge will be passed on to future readers with benefit. He is, at the end of his tale, still capable of prayer, still capable of hope. Adrian's music lives on. Serenus sees his biographical compilation as a 'provisional' labour (*DF* 7), encouraging his readers to share his hope that the day will come when his friend will receive the recognition he deserves. The prospect of true glory, of immortality as trail-blazing composer, is not quite beyond his reach in the new postwar order. When it

18. GW vol. 11, p. 166.
19. Brann, 1978, esp. pp. 209–13.
20. *Der Spiegel* 24/1981, pp. 156–84; Pütz, 1975, pp. 102–4.
21. See Durrani, 1985.
22. GW vol. 11, p. 204.
23. Henning, 1966, p. 51.
24. Hasselbach, 1978, p. 11.
25. Brecht, 1943.
26. GW vol. 11, p. 1146.
27. Reed, 1976, p. 396.
28. Kerényi, 1960, p. 123.
29. GW vol. 11, p. 1131.
30. Brode, 1973, p. 458f.
31. Presentation copy for Hermann Hesse, Deutsches Literaturarchiv, Marbach.
32. GW vol. 11, p. 162.
33. Ibid., p. 681.
34. Ibid., p. 294.

CHAPTER FOUR

Günter Grass: *The Flounder* (1977)

Eine Zeit ist immer ein Durcheinander verschiedener Zeitalter,
ist durch große Abschnitte hindurch undurchgoren, schlecht
gebacken, trägt Rückstände anderer Kräfte, Keime neuer in sich.
Ist eine Symbiose vieler Seelen; die führende sucht sich die andern
einzuverleiben. Jetzt ist zuerst da die eigentlich abgelöste Kraft, die
Äußerung des letzten Wirkens des Gesellschaftstriebes, das hoch
entwickelte Humanistische, Mönchische. Dann das Ländliche.
(Alfred Döblin: 'The Spirit of the Naturalistic Age')

(Each epoch is always a confused amalgam of different ages,
and remains over long stretches of time unleavened, half-
baked, carrying within itself the residual leftovers of spent
forces along with the seeds of new ones. It is a symbiosis of
many spirits, the strongest trying to swallow up the others.
At present we are dominated by a force that has already
been overtaken by events: the last workings of social con-
straint, a highly developed Humanism and Monasticism.
Then, the rural impulse).

1. POSTWAR *ENFANT TERRIBLE*

A persistent theme in the German novel of the twentieth century
has been our inherent dualism and the clashes which it produces
with social organisations that demand a steady commitment to
fixed principles which are intolerant of modification. Döblin had
tried, in 1929, to portray an individual struggling to overcome this
unfavourable heritage; Franz Biberkopf, the 'thinking beaver',
begins by relying, over-confidently and arrogantly, on a plan
which ignores the fundamental division within him. He is nearly
destroyed by the consequences of his own foolhardy dependence
on unsuitable friends and by the naive pride which he takes in his
sexual conquests. At the last moment, the author pulls him back
from the brink, sounds his 'fanfares', but places him in a limbo
from which he can only watch as his fellow-men march forward

towards an uncertain future. It is as though Döblin the political thinker was unable to endorse the optimism of a text which Döblin the artist had produced. Neither were Hesse and Mann, who, during the two troubled decades that followed, portrayed exceptionally talented, potentially brilliant creative artists who were being torn apart by their divided personalities. The spiritual divisions which destroyed Knecht and Leverkühn could be attributed to a conflict between the powers of human reason and sensuality; in both cases, they were manifestly aggravated by a rigidly conservative and intolerant social background.

Castalia and Kaisersaschern are symbols of Germany as their authors saw her: monolithic, inveterately old-fashioned, proud of her ancient spirituality and wisdom, intellectually uncompromising and inflexible. *The Glass Bead Game* and *Doctor Faustus* complement one another in several respects. Hesse examines the workings of an impersonal system that presses young men of promise into the service of a rigidly top-heavy bureaucracy; Mann shows us an outstandingly talented composer who is unable to overcome his own personal enslavement to ethnically determined patterns of thought. The three novelists considered so far register their numerous reservations about specific authorities which they see as failing to prepare people for the realities of life. These include the legal and penal systems and the police in *Berlin Alexanderplatz*; the schools, academies and official boards in *The Glass Bead Game*, and the universities, churches and literary salons in *Doctor Faustus*. In each book, a frustrating alliance appears to operate between organisations whose declared aim it is to improve the lot of the individual, and repressive forces which restrain him from achieving his potential in life. Solutions are occasionally glimpsed from afar: in the as yet untested conversion of Franz, the promise of young Tito, and in the lingering silence after the last note of Adrian's music has faded, although such hopes diminish in credibility, given the irony with which they are introduced by unreliable narrators.

Nowhere do the protagonists of these novels reveal their vulnerability more conspicuously than in their attitudes to their bodies and to the physical side of their existence. Franz blindly pursues pleasure and, for all his dependence on female companions, persists in treating women as mere objects. He may dissociate himself from the 'white slavery' arrangement with Reinhold, but his attempt to engineer an exhibition of Mieze for the benefit of his old antagonist shows how little he has learned in this respect. In Castalia, Knecht is obliged to suppress his sexuality, having been taught to view scholarship as all-important and marriage as little more than a curiosity. There are signs that a spartan and studious lifestyle and the total absence of women among the scholars may have inclined him towards homoerotic attachments. Adrian Leverkühn combines Franz's animal sensuality in his pursuit of Esmeralda and surrender to Rudi with Knecht's remote intellectualism and disdainful detachment from large areas of human activity. Nietzsche had argued that all creative life resulted from an amalgam of dark passion (the 'Dionysian' force) and sublime self-control (the 'Apolline'); but, in their different ways, Biberkopf, Knecht and Leverkühn have to abandon the struggle to reconcile the two extremes. Freud taught that distinctive behavioural patterns could be related to sexual factors; the three novels bear this doctrine out in some detail. The time has come to justify the inclusion of Günter Grass among a group of writers who, as the beneficiaries of an increasing interest in philosophy and psychology at the turn of this century, distinguished themselves as observers of the many social and political factors which have shaped the distinctive character of modern Germany.

On the face of it, Grass may well seem to have less in common with the at times laboured moralism of Hesse or with Mann's history of ideas than he has with the kaleidoscopic and often unstructured fiction of Döblin. From the time of his meteoric rise to fame in 1958, he has enjoyed the reputation of being, in the minds of many, at best a cynical 'angry young man' in a specifically German mould, and at worst an unprincipled scandalmonger and muck-raker. Several protracted court cases during the 1960s dealt with matters such as whether publishers were at liberty to refer to him as *Verfasser übelster pornographischer Ferkeleien* ('author of swinish pornographic excesses of the worst kind') in print.[1] Many of the early verdicts on Grass on both sides of the Atlantic were phrased along similar lines:

> Here is one long, crazy, unalleviated nightmare, void of any beauty or sanity. If you can stick with it and stomach it, you will, perhaps, find it a brilliant artistic experience ... It groans with obscure symbolisms, is rotten with perverted eroticisms, and is revolting in its numerous blasphemies of the Catholic Church.[2]

Some critics went so far as to suggest that *The Tin Drum* was fundamentally hostile to interpretation; many agreed with the poet Enzensberger, who denied that there was any moral purpose behind the novel and concluded his review of it with a quotation

from Shakespeare that does not hold out much hope to the would-be exegete: 'It is a tale told by an idiot, full of sound and fury, signifying nothing'.[3]
Gradually, opinions such as these began to be reversed, not least because it was becoming increasingly difficult to ignore the many signs of Grass's obvious commitment to social and political causes and the role which he played as an active supporter of the German Social Democratic Party. Research undertaken in Britain and elsewhere did much to support the view that Grass is a serious and consistently committed author rather than a mere buffoon or deliberate iconoclast. In a concise defence of his works, Grass invokes the role of the two thieves in the Bible:

> *In meinen drei Prosawerken ... war ich bemüht, die Wirklichkeit einer ganzen Epoche, mit ihren Widersprüchen und Absurditäten in ihrer kleinbürgerlichen Enge und mit ihrem überdimensionalen Verbrechen, in literarischer Form darzustellen. Die Realität, als das Rohmaterial des Schriftstellers, läßt sich nicht teilen; nur wer sie ganz einfängt und ihre Schattenseiten nicht ausspart, verdient es, Schriftsteller genannt zu werden ... Es bleibt erstaunlich, daß immer wieder darauf hingewiesen werden muß, inwieweit die Position des Lästerers im Alten wie Neuen Testament verankert ist. Ich erinnere an den einen Schächer am Kreuz; durch seine Gegenposition erst wird die Position des anderen Schächers deutlich.*[4]

(In my three prose works [prior to 1968] I endeavoured to present an entire epoch as it really was in a literary form, paying attention to its contradictions and its absurdities, to its lower middle-class limitations and its all-encompassing crimes. Reality, the raw material of the novelist, is indivisible, and only one who is able to capture it in its totality, without omitting the darker side, deserves to be remembered as a writer ... It is astonishing that one is constantly obliged to stress how deeply the role of the blasphemer is rooted in the Old and New Testaments alike. I refer to the wicked thief on the cross: thanks only to his opposition the attitude of the other thief is brought out.)

There could hardly be a more cogent defence of the novelist's rightful concern with the evil that exists side by side with the good in this world. Simply by perceiving and depicting it, the writer makes a distinction between right and wrong, as the Evangelist had done in his account of the crucifixion. Grass, no less than Döblin, whom he acknowledged as his mentor,[5] is painfully aware of the unresolvable dualism of the human condition; his characters suffer its torments as Hesse's and Mann's had done, prompting *Der Spiegel* to speak of him as 'the Thomas Mann of the 1970s'.[6] The man once stigmatised as a reckless blasphemer now stands accused of peddling a hotchpotch of outdated philosophies and of lacking a coherent point of view. There are, of course, those who would like us to see him as a harmless purveyor of schoolboy anecdotes, as witness the following review of *The Flounder*:

> *Grass, der Ideologien scheinbar ungerührt in seinem großen Kochtopf zu einem blasenwerfenden Brei verkocht, verbreitet dann noch (aus epischer Not und Notwendigkeit?) den wohligen Stallgeruch und Küchendampf von der guten alten Zeit, wo ein dicker Arsch, ein lauter Furz, ein satter Rülpser mehr sagen als alle Argumente.[7]*

(Grass, who boils down what seem like undiluted ideologies in one gigantic cauldron until they resemble a bubbling broth, proceeds then (following the rules or constraints of the epic writer?) to put about the homely odours of the stable-yard and the steamy kitchen in order to recall those good old days when a fat bum, a deafening fart and a satisfied burp convey a great deal more than any rational arguments.)

At the other extreme, the man who was once hailed by George Steiner as 'the active conscience of Germany' is often dismissed as a tedious moralist subscribing to bourgeois liberal views favourable to the establishment. Thus Gertrude Cepl-Kaufmann voiced her scepticism about Grass's 'strong attachment to the past as he had personally experienced it', a factor which she held responsible for his woolly avoidance of political ideologies, *seine mangelnde politische Potenz und seine mangelnde historische Perspektive*[8] ('his political impotence and his lack of a historical perspective').

The shock-vibrations of the 1960s have lost much of their impetus; comparisons with Thomas Mann, and the appearance, in 1987, of a ten-volume annotated edition of his works, have transformed the *enfant terrible* of yesteryear into something resembling a postwar classic given to constructing sweeping cultural analogies. Among his contemporaries, he remains the foremost member of a peculiarly German tradition in fiction, as is perhaps best evidenced by *The Flounder*, a satirical history of one corner of the German nation which complements the earlier examples to perfection. Instead of basing his investigations on the philosophy, art or religion of the land, Grass, being Grass, begins by scrutinising the cooking-pots and examining the condition of the stale linen in the bed-chamber.

2. DANZIG

The precise depiction of a specific locality was of great importance in the three novels discussed above. Berlin, Castalia and Kaisersaschern had a representative function that went far beyond the author's need to supply a topographical backdrop. Berlin was the throbbing centre of the nation, and yet also a modern Babylon and a battleground for the forces of good and evil, and in their different ways both Castalia and Kaisersaschern provided suitable scenarios for an investigation of particular aspects of the German character. The city of Danzig, whose history Grass relates in *The Flounder*, shares the sweeping symbolic function attaching to the other localities, while differing from them in a number of important respects. Danzig had already provided the setting for many of Grass's previous novels. His first three major prose works, *The Tin Drum, Cat and Mouse* and *Dog Years* are now commonly referred to as 'The Danzig Trilogy', and there are cross-references between these texts and *The Flounder*, where Oskar of *The Tin Drum* is repeatedly mentioned (F 255, 529). Many of the historical figures from *The Flounder* had put in episodic appearances in earlier works.

The city in which Grass had spent the first seventeen years of his life is obviously rich in personal associations and memories which he was to recall from his later perspective as an exile. So abundant and varied were the lives of its people that the single suburb Langfuhr took on a universal representativeness as an area into which all human experience could be projected:

> *Es war einmal eine Stadt,*
> *die hatte neben den Vororten Ohra, Schidlitz, Oliva, Emaus, Sankt Albrecht, Schellmühl und dem Hafenvorort Neufahrwasser einen Vorort, der hieß Langfuhr. Langfuhr war so groß und so klein, daß alles, was sich auf dieser Welt ereignet oder ereignen könnte, sich auch in Langfuhr ereignete oder hätte ereignen können.*[9]

(Once upon a time there was a town which possessed, along with the suburbs of Ohra, Schidlitz, Oliva, Emaus, St Albrecht, Schellmühl and the port of Neufahrwasser, a suburb by the name of Langfuhr. Langfuhr was so large and so small that everything that happens or could happen in this world had happened or could have happened in Langfuhr.)

Then, there is the historical dimension. Over a considerable period, the city itself occupied a political and cultural vacuum halfway between Germany and Poland. This is reflected in its neutrality as a 'Free City' in the period between 1920 and 1939, during which it was nominally detached both from the old German Reich and from the newly constituted Polish Republic. The tensions that led to the outbreak of the Second World War were discernible with exceptional clarity in this frontier post, which claimed a German-speaking majority of ninety-three per cent in the city proper, and where the National Socialists attained higher figures in the elections of 1933 than they did in Germany itself (50.03 per cent as opposed to 43.9 per cent). 'Danzig was a German microcosm', writes the historian Hans Leonhardt in his inquiry into the manner in which developments in that city were to fore-shadow later events in the Reich.[10] It was here that the first shots of the war were fired, an event recalled in the 'Polish Post Office' section of *The Tin Drum*. His native city provided Grass with a basis for an investigation into the history and character of the German people: it could almost be described as a ready-made, authentic Kaisersaschern.

Yet it always was a frontier post. Inhabited, prior to 1945, by a mixture of nations, dominated by Germans who in some of their traditions were closer to Warsaw than to Berlin, it was throughout its history a meeting-place of East and West. Nowhere are the complexities of its status investigated with greater sensitivity than in *The Flounder*, where it emerges as an intersection of ancient trade-routes and as a melting-pot of ideas that arrived there from all over Europe. But a high price was exacted for this cosmo-politanism; since the arrival of the Teutonic Knights in the area at the beginning of the fourteenth century, it served as a pawn in the political machinations of Germans, Poles, French, Russians and other parties with interests in that part of the continent. It is not fortuitous, but inevitable, that many of the characters whom Grass puts before us are riven by paradoxical forces and exposed to unresolved conflicts. The legacies of Hanseatic merchant-adven-turers, Slav peasants, Latin missionaries, ancient Baltic idolaters and many other social and religious groupings overlay one an-other and provide the intellectual and moral ferment of ideas and influences that is at the forefront of the novel. The indigenous people of the area, the Cassubians, have affinities with many cultures, although, sedentary and peace-loving, they tended to be the losers in the repeated struggles for supremacy that were acted out between Germans and Slavs on their territory. From the start,

Grass has shown us people who are divided against themselves: Mahlke in *Cat and Mouse*, combines a practical 'Teutonic' tenacity with a lofty 'Polish' idealism, symbolised by the screwdriver and the religious medallion which he wears round his neck. A ruthless soldier, and yet also an unswerving devotee of the Virgin Mary, he destroys himself when he discovers that the world will not allow him to pursue his conflicting ideals with impunity. The many social and cultural tensions present beneath its surface allow Danzig to figure as a suitable 'hot-house' location within which the human predicament can be presented with exceptional clarity.

The city as portrayed in the Danzig Trilogy no longer exists. The Free City of the interwar years is gone, flattened by Allied pattern-bombing, German sabotage and Russian artillery fire during the last days of the war. The centre has been reconstructed, but many of the inhabitants, including Grass himself, have been resettled. Under a different name, Gdańsk continues to occupy an important and controversial position on the world stage; but, as Grass shows in the ninth month of *The Flounder*, its problems are those of the Polish state. The paradise and the hell of his youth have been transformed and are now as inaccessible as Kaisersaschern or Castalia. Like Joyce, Grass is writing from the perspective of an exile who, while free to return to his native city, can only do so as a tourist or, latterly, as a celebrity. In some respects, therefore, Danzig has become a Garden of Eden, lending itself to artistic variations on the Fall of Man and to lamentations for an innocence lost.

The characters who people the microcosm of Danzig are frequently divided against themselves. Oskar Matzerath of *The Tin Drum* is able to describe himself both as Jesus and as Satan at different points in the narrative. Pilenz plays the part of Evangelist and of Judas to Mahlke, who distinguishes himself both as a life-saver and as a ruthless killer. The drum itself is an object whose beats featured at the end of *Berlin Alexanderplatz*; the connotations that could be attached to it are ambiguous in the extreme. Like the cerebral and yet intensely passionate music created by Adrian Leverkühn, it evokes discipline and chaos at the same time. The regular beats of the drum suggest the self-control and coordination of marching men, and yet its bursts of noise recall the primeval environment of the jungle, abandonment to passion, and the dissolution of identity. These contrasting signals are underlined by its colours, white and red, in which innocence and sin, purity and passion are juxtaposed.

If there are parallels in respect of method with earlier novelists of the twentieth century, there are also sharp contrasts between Grass and his senior colleague among postwar West German writers, Heinrich Böll. In comparison with Böll, Grass appears to prefer open endings and to invest his characters with positive and despicable qualities at the same time. Böll inclines more obviously towards idealism, and usually steers his readers in the direction of approval or condemnation of the various figures in his novels. The conflict tends to be between good and evil characters rather than, as in Grass, between good and evil forces within the same character. This crucial distinction will help to account for the perspective through which Grass views historical developments in *The Flounder*.

It should now be possible to appreciate why so many of Grass's early reviewers and critics reacted unfavourably or even despairingly to what they were reading, concluding that his novels were unreceptive to interpretation. The image of robust naivety could all too easily be mistaken for uncaring complacency, the open endings construed as gestures of capitulation in the face of an inimical life-force. Many readers have responded to the frankly sexual passages as though the author fully endorsed what he was describing, viewed lust as inevitably triumphing over love, and agreed that the brute in man would always defeat the idealist in an unequal competition. But far from being an insensitive cynic out to shatter our lingering hopes and ideologies, Grass is touched by the pessimism of one who sees life as a succession of essentially similar blunders. His political speeches showed him to be in agreement with the programme of cautious reform initiated by the Federal Republic's Social Democratic Party under Willy Brandt; more recently, he has been heard deprecating the haste with which the former German Democratic Republic was swallowed up by its wealthier neighbour. In politics as in all other walks of life, not least in culinary matters, slow and scrupulous preparations are called for. When Grass's characters pursue vain, wrong-headed ideals, as Mahlke did in *Cat and Mouse*, we are shown why and made to see their aberrations in the context of a society whose actions have been precipitate and whose care for the vulnerable is inadequate. This brings him a good deal closer to veteran moralists than to the purveyors of pornographic thrills; and when Grass justified the inclusion of scurrilous episodes in his novels with the words *weil sonst mein Buch niemand kauft*[11] ('because otherwise no-one would buy my book'), he was merely doing what many a preacher has done from the time of Bishop

Alcuin onwards. The racy passages, to which so many armchair moralists have objected,[12] are a time-honoured means of enticing the reader to swallow what will turn out to be an exceedingly bitter pill.

3. PAST AND PRESENT

Almost every novelist assumes an alien personality and becomes, temporarily, a member of another community or a citizen of a bygone age. This can involve identification with a remote epoch or culture. Hermann Hesse admits that he pictured himself as a Rainmaker in the Stone Age: *Oft habe ich Ninon erzählt, als sie mich fragte, was ich denn vor 20 000 Jahren gewesen sei, daß ich damals Wettermacher war. Um es ihr noch klarer zu machen, und auch aus anderen Gründen, habe ich im letzten Jahr die Sache aufgeschrieben*[13] ('Whenever Ninon [Hesse's wife] asked me what I was up to 20,000 years ago, I would tell her that I was a weather-maker. To show her exactly what I meant, as well as for other reasons, I committed the matter to paper during the past year').

All authors considered in this study have been inclined to view the present in terms of the past. This involved projecting their heroes not merely into one, but into a series of parallel lives in the past. Biberkopf was directly compared to Job and Isaac, and in a more general sense to Adam after the Fall. Knecht portrayed himself as a shaman, a hermit and an Indian Prince. The words cited above show just how closely Hesse identified himself with the idealised portraits which are incorporated into *The Glass Bead Game* as the fruits of its hero's researches. He was demonstrably given to inventing images of himself as he might have been during some earlier period of history. That he should have written down the first of Knecht's literary exercises to illustrate one such affinity for the benefit of his wife shows a remarkable similarity between his methods and those of Günter Grass. Also, Adrian Leverkühn was motivated by a not dissimilar desire for an anchor-figure in the past, though in his case the person he chose to emulate became a fiendish snare for him rather than a salutary means of escaping from an oppressive present.

As was noted earlier (p. 101, above), the search for models is one of the most fundamental preoccupations of the human race and the basis of all education. The artist mimics this search for several distinct reasons: in order to find material for artistic creations, and out of a desire to enter into the minds and personalities of the figures that inhabit the evolving works. Historical drama has long served as a means of opening up discussions about the practices and malpractices of the present. Just how deeply embedded and complex these reverberations can be has been shown in recent studies of Shakespeare; Greenblatt's investigations of *King Lear* and the methods of the sixteenth-century exorcists reveal a decisive influence not merely on the background, but on the literary structure of the drama.[14] Often, topics of great interest and relevance could not be discussed openly for fear of censorship; historical drama and fiction provided convenient routes for such matters to be aired, albeit indirectly.

Biberkopf, Knecht and Leverkühn are figures who exist in a particular relationship to the past, ironically, humorously and tragically imitating historical personalities or other literary characters. What distinguishes them from earlier literary figures of whom the same is true (Don Quixote) is that they do not follow a single model, but manage to relive the careers of many different people simultaneously; Adrian imitates Faustus, Nietzsche, Alban Berg and many others. The antecedents of each modern 'hero' are so prolific that anyone wishing to pursue each of the individual parallels will be lost in a welter of information. The modern fictional 'character' as an identifiable and immutable unit does not exist.

The Flounder results from a controlled experiment to demonstrate the chaotic fragmentation of the traditional fictional character. Grass begins by putting forward a modern unnamed 'Author' who invents fictional biographies for himself, much as Hesse had done via Knecht, for the purpose of keeping his wife, codenamed Ilsebill, entertained during her nine-month pregnancy. Each of these lives is set in a specific historic epoch, with copious references to authentic figures, places and dates. The book was diligently researched over a period of five years, and many of its sources have now been identified.[15] The initial intention appears to have been to focus on nine periods, beginning in the Neolithic and winding up with the emergence of Socialism at the turn of this century, in such a way that each era would coincide with a separate month of Ilsebill's pregnancy. Towards the end of his work, it seems Grass decided to incorporate a further two periods, making a total of eleven rather than nine epochs. The resulting imbalance was not unwelcome, as it breaks up the mechanistic scheme and introduces an element of uncertainty: this is no attempt to fit history into a straitjacket, as Vico and Spengler had done. Each period is presided over by a single female figure, the 'Cook', whose story is related by one or several male observers, the 'Episodic Narrators', with whom the narrator temporarily identifies himself.

Month	Period	Cook	Narrator(s)
1	Neolithic	Aua 2211 BC	Edek
1	Iron Age (Migrations)	Wigga AD 221	Edek
1	Early Middle Ages	Mestwina d. 997	Adalbert of Prague
2	High Middle Ages	St Dorothy of Montau	Albrecht Slichting
3	Reformation	Margarete Rusch 1498–1585	Jakob Hegge and others
4	Thirty Years' War	Agnes Kurbiella 1619–89	Anton Möller Martin Opitz
5	Seven Years' War	Amanda Woyke 1734–1806	August Romeike
6	Napoleonic Wars	Sophie Rotzoll 1784–1849	Friedrich Bartholdy
7	Socialism	Lena Stubbe 1848–1942	Friedrich Otto Stobbe Otto Friedrich Stubbe
8	Emancipation	Sibylle Miehlau 1929–62	Author
9	Communism	Maria Kuczorra b. 1949	Author

These episodes intertwine with sequences illustrating the deteriorating marital relationship between the Author and Ilsebill, his travels during (and after) the period of writing, and a large number of poems, some of which comment on the action or explain the narrative method adopted by the Author. Attention regularly returns to the activities of a group of feminist activists, and especially to their trial of an omniscient Flounder, a mythical creature regarded as having encouraged the male sex in its destructive tendencies throughout history (see pp. 162–9, below).

The word *Geschichte* signifies both 'a story' and 'a history'; the two concepts merge with one another as the Author embarks on his exploratory forays into the early epochs with which we still have much in common. Here, 'his story' is refashioned into 'her story': the book combines the fruits of painstaking scholarly re-

search with a vibrant, at times riotous, fantasy.[16] It is not possible
to ask whether the 'factual' items are 'mounted' onto the tales of
domestic life, or vice versa; fact and fiction flow into one another
in such a way as to expose the artificiality of our conventional
distinctions between them. The past is inseparable from the
present:

> *Wir sind immer nur zeitweilig gegenwärtig. Uns nagelt kein*
> *Datum. Wir sind nicht von heute. Auf unserem Papier findet das*
> *meiste gleichzeitig statt.* (F 144)

> (We are always at best temporarily present. No dates nail us
> down. We are not of today. On our paper, most events take
> place simultaneously.)

4. A HISTORY OF COOKERY AND COPULATION

James Usher, sometime Archbishop of Armagh, calculated that
the world had been created at 9 a.m. on 23 October 4004 BC. Somewhat more modestly, but with equal assurance, Grass begins his
history of Danzig on 3 May 2211 BC. The book surveys a timespan
of 4,185 years, from the day the Flounder is trapped by the first
male Edek until he befriends Maria Kuczorra in September 1974
on the same stretch of Baltic coastline.

History begins in the Age of Aua, the benign triple-breasted
mother goddess. This is the earthly paradise in which all are
abundantly provided for: *Immer war Stillzeit* (F 13) ('It was always
feeding-time'). Three bounteous breasts represent contentment
and plenty, as well as a numerical triumph over the dichotomies
that will beset all future generations (F 8). As instruments of social
control, they are effective in a manner unmatched by any subsequent generation:

> *Auas Herrschaft war milde: die Steinzeitfrauen legten sich,*
> *nachdem sie ihre Säuglinge gestillt hatten, ihre Steinzeitmänner*
> *an die Brust, bis sie nicht mehr rumzappelten und fixe Ideen*
> *ausschwitzten, sondern still dösig wurden: brauchbar für allerlei.*
> *So wurden wir allemann satt. Nie wieder, als später Zukunft*
> *anbrach, sind wir so satt geworden.* (F 13)

> (Aua's reign was benevolent. After suckling their infants,
> the Stone Age women would put their Stone Age men to the
> breast, until they stopped fidgeting and sweating out
> obsessional ideas, and became calm and sleepy: ready for all
> manner of things.
> That's how we all had our fill, every single one of us.

Never again, when sometime later the future burst upon us, did we have it quite so good.)

This atmosphere of universal contentment recalls the Garden of Eden. The individual has yet to be discovered: all men are Edeks, all women are called Aua. Society is matriarchal: the menfolk are kept in ignorance of potentially dangerous knowledge, including all numbers greater than three and the uses of fire other than for cooking. The idyll is shattered when one of the Edeks catches the mythical Flounder,[17] who introduces him to the hitherto proscribed secrets of science; the men now take up metalworking in preference to cookery, and relations between the sexes deteriorate.

The result is an uneasy equilibrium, until a neighbouring tribe of 'Ludeks' arrives on the scene and hostilities begin to flare up. Rather than opt for open warfare, the women invite them to a meal: *Nicht Krieg wurde erklärt, sondern zu Tisch wurde gebeten* (F 74) ('There was no declaration of war, but instead, an invitation to sit down at table'). The men come to blows with one another, but all-out war is frustrated by a timely understanding among the womenfolk. The storm-clouds of future conflicts are not far off; once the men recognise their destructive potential, the conflicts will be on an incomparably larger scale.

When 111 generations have elapsed, the third breast has atrophied and the hunters have become sedentary farmers. Wigga encourages the cultivation of root-crops. The Golden Age has given way to bitter drudgery. Now the Germanic Goths, *Goitschen*, are in the offing, proud, literate, socially organised and equipped with their own futile democracy: *Stundenlange Thingsitzungen hielten sie ab. Jeder widersprach jedem* (F 88) ('Public assemblies lasted for hours on end. Everybody contradicted everybody else'). The feckless but good-natured aboriginals view these intruders as a master-race. Twentieth-century frictions are adumbrated: the local people of the Baltic, dreaming their immortal daydreams, are about to be overrun by the more efficient Goths (*Goitschen* rhymes with *Deutschen*) with their love of mental puzzles, duels, the acquisition of honour, organisation. But Wigga again uses the dietary weapon as an instrument of social control. By feeding the famished but carnivorous Goths a pottage prepared from unpalatable manna-grass seeds, she persuades them to strike camp and journey southwards in search of something more tasty. Their migrations will lead to great things, but people of the Baltic are left to enjoy several uneventful centuries.

A major confrontation during the tenth century proves less easy to head off. Bishop Adalbert arrives in the area to convert the heathens. Grass presents him as a dour ideologue and determined agitator for his cause. That is, until his cook, the local pagan priestess Mestwina, falls in love with him and determines to try her hand at converting the converter. An amber love-charm dropped into his soup produces astonishing results:

> *Immer wieder und noch einmal drang der Asket mit seinem gar nicht mehr bußfertigen Werkzeug in ihr Fleisch. Ganz nach Art der Pomorschen, doch mit mehr Glaubenseifer und dialektischem Widerspruch, erschöpfte er sich in ihr. Dabei murmelte er sein Kirchenlatein, als wollte er den Heiligen Geist nach neuer Methode ergießen* ... (F 98f.)

(Time and time again the ascetic penetrated her flesh with an impediment inappropriate to the task of doing penance. Just as the Pomorshians would have done it, albeit with greater religious zeal and dialectical contradictions, he spent himself within her, all the while muttering his Church Latin as though he had devised a new means of pouring forth the Holy Spirit ...)

The paradoxical tensions of mind and body keep each other in check; the fish-god Ryb and the (triple-breasted) Virgin Mary are venerated side by side in rituals composed of ancient incantations as well as Christian litanies. Only when the Bishop resolves to upset this delicate compromise by banning the cult of the fish does Mestwina make him pay for his 'dialectical contradictions'. Ignoring his 'pious greeting' (F 101), she batters him to death with a cast-iron spoon.

With the arrival of Christianity, the women's official role as social regulators diminishes, yielding to a 'progressive' male vitality. Domination by men will last until well into the twentieth century, as is acknowledged in the novels by Döblin, Mann and Hesse. Adrian Leverkühn's experiences could be summed up in the present narrator's words: *als wir zwangsgetauft ... wurden, vermehrte sich nur die Sünde* (F 124) ('the only thing that increased after the compulsory baptism was our sinfulness'). The Flounder is quick to align himself with the new religion, recognising that 'the absolute supremacy of the women could not have been overthrown without the assistance of the Christian religion' (F 153). The rite of marriage strengthens the position of the male, but women are left with some power due to the importance of 'fasting and feasting' in the Church calendar. Dorothea Swarze, the later

St Dorothy of Montau, demonstrates how a medieval woman could rebel against the yoke of marriage, using the articles of the new faith as her deadliest weapons. Her doting husband must suffer her transports, her pious versifying, her monotonous Lenten cuisine; eight of their nine children die of neglect, a three-year-old falling into a cauldron of boiling soup unobserved, while her mother kneels in ecstasy on a bed of dried peas (F 146). Pilgrimages lead to financial ruin. She has, inevitably, reinterpreted the faith: Jesus is the object of her lust, her public seizures are an embarrassment to the community. To pacify her opponents, the Church suggests burning her as a witch, but eventually opts for canonisation, as the Teutonic Knights are in urgent need of a local saint to encourage them in their bloody work in the East.

If Dorothea was the first woman to have rebelled against the paternalistic institution of marriage, the sixteenth-century Abbess Margarete Rusch, alias 'Fat Gret', is a rebel of a very different kind. Hers is the 'third month' of the Author's cerebral pregnancy, during which the vital parts of the new organism are formed. *Doctor Faustus* argued that the Reformation was the turning point in German history, marking the beginning of a preoccupation with spirituality and a rabidly doctrinal intolerance: Grass invests the sixteenth century with a similar significance, while viewing the same period from his own characteristic perspective.

Fat Gret stands between the opposing forces and reconciles enemies by ensuring their physical contentment. Her ideological position remains as uncertain as it is irrelevant. No-one can tell whether she supports the patricians or the artisans, the Hanseatic League or the Polish Crown, the Pope or the Reformers. At a time when the Church of Christ had split and bloody battles were fought over the form of the communion, Gret resolved such matters in her own way:

> *So hat Äbtissin Margarete Rusch die todernste Streitfrage ihres Jahrhunderts, wie nun Brot und Wein, das Abendmahl zu reichen sei, auf ihre Weise, also bettgerecht beantwortet ... Da erhob sich nicht die Frage: Dieses ist tatsächlich oder bedeutet nur Fleisch und Blut ... Ach wäre doch dieser Hausbrauch für Papisten und Lutheraner, für Mennoniten und Calvinisten praktische Religion geworden.* (F 244)

(Thus Abbess Margarete Rusch solved the deadly serious question preoccupying her century, the question of how to share out the bread and wine of the Eucharist, in a characteristic manner appropriate to her bed ... There, the question did not arise: Is this really bread and wine or only a sign and symbol thereof ... Would that this domestic practice had been adopted as a religious ritual for Papists and Lutherans, for Mennonites and Calvinists.)

The technically detailed description of Gret's *Bettmessen* ('masses held in bed') has been described as prurient, the sort of thing written mainly to entertain a *Stammtisch* of highbrow voyeurs.[18] But it is no less valid to argue that Grass is merely contrasting different types of obscenity. Given the bigotry of the iconoclasts, the armies of Calixtines and Utraquists who killed each other like flies in defence of their creeds, Gret is not perverting Christian dogma so much as delivering a satirical counterblast to the endless and painful controversy over the outward forms of Christian ritual. Her bedtime operations are described as *die Urform der Nächstenliebe* (F 238) ('loving one's neighbour in the original form'), and provide an antithesis to the Reformer's programme. Like Luther, Gret embarks on her reforming career in 1517. Again, there are parallels with the present. Comparing her posterior to 'two collective farms' (loc. cit.), Grass celebrates the body as the last bastion that holds out against the ideologues: *Da traut sich die Ideologie nicht hin. Den kriegt sie nicht in den Griff. Dem kann sie keine Idee ablesen. Schlechtgemacht wird er deshalb* (F 239) ('No ideology dare approach it. They can't get a hold on it. They can't abstract ideas from it. That's why it is abused'). In the debate on the relative merits of mind and body, the third month, vital to the development of the child's own body, vividly illustrates the disastrous consequences of an official preoccupation with ideology.

Margarete 'laughs in the face of her century' (F 17); Agnes Kurbiella survives by dint of sheer self-abasement, as the pail into which her contemporaries disgorge their misery. Seventeenth-century Germany was torn apart by the Thirty Years' War, which saw the continuation of sectarian strife in the aftermath of the Reformation. But in the ensuing fragmentation, there came the beginnings of a recognisably German style in the arts, which explains why Grass places Agnes in the service of a poet and a painter, Martin Opitz and Anton Möller. The chapter *Von der Last böser Zeit* ('On the Burden of a Wicked Age') is another striking invention with implications for the present. Here, an imaginary meeting takes place between two eminent literati: the aging Opitz, physically broken by illness and worn out by unsuccessful diplomatic machinations, and the teenage rebel Andreas Gryphius, the archetypal 'angry young man', come, ostensibly, to pay his respects to the established doyen of poetry.[19]

Their encounter is surrounded by many hilarious paradoxes. Gryphius, the very picture of boyish vitality, writes poems in which even the most fleeting pleasure is condemned as an unpardonable vanity. Opitz rebukes him for going too far: human endeavour cannot be dismissed as 'straw, dust, ashes and wind'. Gryphius hits back at the older man for his political opportunism, his service to dubious princes, his willingness to act as a double agent for the Poles and the Swedes. Opitz can defend himself on the grounds that *ihn trüge keine Partei, sondern der Wunsch nach Duldung jeglichen Glaubens* (F 286) ('he was not motivated by party allegiances, but by a longing for the tolerance of every creed'). As in the previous month, political ambivalence is treated as preferable to radicalism, indeed as the true prerequisite to peace. Before Gryphius can answer, Agnes serves dinner, and the man who recently castigated all sensual pleasures tucks into the bland but wholesome meal with apparent gusto.[20]

The pacifying effect of Agnes on the burnt-out men of genius is beyond doubt. Of all the women we have met so far, she is the first to be capable of true love in the modern sense, an invention for which the Flounder claims the credit. But while he had intended it to help break down the old matriarchal system (F 308) and to enhance the cause of male dominance, the result is not as envisaged. The object of the girl's love is neither Opitz nor Möller, but a Swedish cavalry ensign who raped her and killed her parents. Grass reveals a fundamental flaw in the constructive theory of love by showing it to be as paradoxical as it is unpredictable, striking at random, like rain (F 317).

The Thirty Years' War resulted from unresolved conflicts arising out of the partial Reformation of German-speaking Europe. It is another turning point in the fortunes of the nation, leading, initially, to a great increase in the number of independent city-states, bishoprics and petty principalities, whose rivalries were to bring untold strife and carnage to the country. Amanda Woyke experiences the rise of Prussia under Frederick the Great and the devastating effects of the Seven Years' War, fought largely on German soil as a civil war between Prussia and Austria, after an unprovoked attack by Prussia on Saxony. As in previous epochs, a clear distinction is drawn between the woman with her soup kitchen and potato plantation, and the men who sabotage her humanitarian work with their ruthless military operations. In a face-to-face meeting with her monarch, Amanda pleads in vain that he abandon his *Schlagtotschlachten* in favour of *Kartoffelschlachten* (F 362) ('lethal battles', 'potato battles'), the aim of which would be to cover Brandenburg and Pomerania with potato plantations, in order to win a victory, not over other men but over hunger and disease. Frederick – in whom the Nazis saw their most immediate predecessor – cuts a pathetic and lonely figure, listening to Amanda's motherly advice but refusing to act upon it. The similarities between the women of different generations are underlined by their bonds of kinship. Sophie Rotzoll is Amanda's granddaughter, and the war in her lifetime begins with the French Revolution. Her adolescent friend Friedrich Bartholdy is swept away on the tide of revolutionary idealism, sports the tricolour and joins a group of would-be democrats, for which he is sentenced to life imprisonment at the age of seventeen. Governments come and governments go; Napoleon arrives in Danzig in 1807, but his erstwhile supporter must vegetate in the fortress of Graudenz for thirty-eight years, while Sophie remains devoted to him, and partial to the fly agaric they used to gather in their childhood. Her greatest moment comes when she tries to eliminate the unpopular French governor Rapp with a combination of lethal toadstools. But like the 1944 attempt on Hitler's life, her plans misfire and she must wait another twenty-three years before her loved one is freed and they can start gathering mushrooms and hallucinogenic toadstools together again. The implication is that freedom can still only be experienced under narcosis; in the aftermath of the French Revolution the enjoyment of political liberties is still an untimely illusion. Hope beckons for the future: the foetus will be viable from the seventh month onwards.

Bartholdy dies in 1848, the year in which another, more successful revolutionary tide swept across Europe, unseating old tyrants, establishing parliamentary assemblies in Germany for the first time, and setting the seal on the future unification of the country. Also, Lena Stubbe is born in 1848; she survives until 1942, the year in which the Reich's fortunes were permanently reversed with the encircling of the German Sixth Army at Stalingrad. As was observed in *Doctor Faustus*, biographical dates are chosen for their historical significance. Lena's lifespan corresponds to Germany's at times misdirected struggle for unity, expansion and status among the dominant nations of the world. It is punctuated by the deaths of her two husbands, Stobbe and Stubbe, in 1870 and 1914, felled in action during the first weeks of the Franco-Prussian and First World Wars. Both men are loud-mouthed petty tyrants and impotent alcoholics, who eke out their miserable *Säuferdasein* and *Maulheldentum* (F 476) ('drunkard's life', 'loud-mouthed chauvinism') until they are slain in the conflicts which they help to cause. Pathetic figures they may be, but they effectively represent those very forces that propelled Germany and many other European nations towards wars of hitherto unknown brutality: vulgar, misinformed jingoism triggered off by economic misery and sexual frustration. Their names, Friedrich Otto Stobbe and Otto Friedrich Stubbe, in which the first names of the Holy Roman Emperors clash with an undistinguished surname, underline the repetitiveness of history during the period of industrialisation, expansionism and would-be colonialism. Again, it is the Flounder who encourages them to seek glory on the battlefield in order to escape from female domination, *Wollsocken-Bratkartoffel-Nähkästchen-Weiberkram* ('woollen socks', 'fried potatoes', 'sewing-boxes', 'women's junk'), and Grass makes no secret of his feelings when he describes the First World War as 'this masterpiece of European masculinity' (F 483).

Lena tolerates this behaviour because she recognises that her husbands' blows are 'failed caresses' (F 476). When Stubbe tries to hang himself, she saves him and concocts a 'nail and rope' soup that protects against suicidal depression. But as a mere woman she, too, is passed over by the great men of history. The socialist leader August Bebel, ironically one of the first to define the role of women in socialism,[21] refuses to supply an introduction to her *Proletarian Cookery Book* for fear of exposing himself to ridicule. The underlying thesis of the book is fundamental to *The Flounder* as a whole: that 'the palate must be enlightened along with the brain' (F 513).

Like so many of her female predecessors, Lena Stubbe dies as a victim of violence, beaten to death by a common criminal in the concentration camp at Stutthof while serving soup to Jewish and Ukrainian prisoners. As in Grass's earlier novels, the horrors of the war are portrayed effectively, but only by indirect means. He does not show violence in the actual theatre of war, but its causes and effects off the battlefield. The seventh month reaches its conclusion with a catalogue of inhumane acts: *das vergiftete Blut, der ausgehungerte Leib, das verbrannte Fleisch, das erstickte Lachen, der Rumpf ohne Kopf, die erschlagene Fürsorge* (F 530f.) ('the poisoned blood, the starved body, the burnt flesh, the strangled laugh, the torso without a head, the battered provider'). The violence done to the body over the centuries could not be more starkly presented. The Flounder, as the presumed originator of the theories that led to these brutal acts, now turns on his protégé, warning him that he has gone too far. The book must end here, and he refuses to accept responsibility for anything that happens from now on. But the

Author insists: he will not relinquish his role as a witness now. He must move forward with time itself, through two world wars and into the present, as Grass has always insisted on doing in his major novels.

5. FATHER'S DAY

'Imprisoned in Günter Grass's new and corpulent book', writes D. J. Enright of *Dog Years*, 'a thinner but very considerable novel is struggling to get out.'[22] Opinions are divided as to whether the eighth month represents the climax or the nadir of the Author's creative pregnancy. G. P. Butler dismisses it as a 'hymn of hate' entirely in keeping with the interests of that 'footloose yet uxorious satyr' who provided the previous chapters. Rolf Michaelis, writing in *Die Zeit*, complains of repetitions and of gratuitous film-like effects. He registers a deterioration of the command of language, *Sprachverfall*, and chides Grass for donning the garb of fashionable slang in order to pass himself off as a trendy youth: *Grass schminkt sich bis in den Jugend-Jargon auf jung.*[23] When the shock had worn off, other critics began to treat Billy's tragic death more positively and to see it in the context of the rest of the novel: as one of three endings, and as a warning to our excessively liberated feminists not to follow blindly in the footsteps of the men. Reddick notes that the 'search for emancipation turned into a permanent process of systematised violence'.[24] The cautionary undercurrent of this fable-within-the-fable is unmistakable, and it seems pointless to regret its inclusion without first inquiring into its significance and its relationship with the other episodes.

At the end of the seventh month, the Flounder protests that whatever happened after Lena Stubbe was no concern of his. The great despots of the twentieth century are mentioned by name, but he is quick to dissociate himself from their activities:

> *Ihr könnt mir Alexander und Cäsar, die Hohenstaufen und die Deutschherren, auch noch Napoleon und den zweiten Wilhelm anlasten, aber nicht diesen Hitler und diesen Stalin. Die liegen außer meiner Verantwortung.* (F 532)

> (You can blame me for Alexander and Caesar, the Hohenstaufen Emperors and Kaiser Wilhelm, but not for this Hitler and this Stalin. They are beyond my responsibility.)

Although the Author immediately rejects this disclaimer, he does not appear to implicate the fish in any of the ensuing events. The names of Hitler and Stalin are mentioned almost by accident in the eighth month (F 563f.). But since the Author has declared his intention of proving the Flounder wrong on this point, the Father's Day narrative must be considered with the Flounder's role in mind. The story relates the murder of Sibylle Miehlau ('Billy'), who, despite a somewhat strained relationship with her three lesbian friends Fränki, Siggi and Mäxchen, accompanies them on an outing to the forests near Berlin to celebrate Father's Day among crowds of beer-swigging men. The occasion coincides with Ascension Day, the feast day which marks Christ's final departure from this world; the setting recalls that of Mieze's murder by Reinhold in *Berlin Alexanderplatz*. The celebrations depicted here are in the form of a secularised Church festival. The cult of the open air, the importance attached to physical strength and feats of endurance, the forced camaraderie that leads to a ruthless intolerance of outsiders suggest that what happens here on the shores of Lake Grunewald is a blueprint for a fascist society. Even the headgear worn by the participants seems to consist mainly of helmets left over from the recent world wars (F 536). Christianity, an instrument of oppression from the time of Mestwina onwards, supplies the initial rhetorical pathos, *Hier laßt uns Hütten bauen* (F 540) ('Here let us build tabernacles', cf. Luke IX: 33). But this linguistic veneer soon acquires a political dimension as the language of religious tradition degenerates into something more reminiscent of recent demagoguery.

Jadoch, ein Volk von Brüdern, wie es im Lied heißt, Männer zuhauf. Alles was Mann ist, feiert am Himmelfahrtstag den Himmelhochvater, den Übersollvater. Und auch die Jungs auf ihren geputzten Motorrädern – 'Ja, ihr, da drüben am anderen Ufer!' – die noch nicht wissen, wohin mit der Kraft, die sich in Leder geschmissen haben: schwarze Engel, mit Nieten beschlagen, wirklich wie Filmfiguren, die lässig federn und immer die richtige Witterung haben. Schlanke, auf Lauer stehende Hechte. Und einer bläst auf der mitgebrachten Trompete angriffige Signale. Ja, laßt uns Vatertag feiern ... (F 540)

(Yessir, a nation of brothers, as the song goes, men in their millions. Let all good men and true celebrate the Father-as-high-as-Heaven, the super-productive Father on this Ascension Day. Even the lads on their polished motorbikes – 'Yes, you chaps over there on the other bank!' – the ones who are bursting with energy, decked out in leather: black angels with metal studs, just like the movies, casually swaying on their machines, they have a nose for where it's at. Sleek as wolves, forever on the lookout. One of them has brought a

trumpet along and is making aggressive noises. Well then,
let's celebrate Father's Day ...)

The images are powerful ones. The 'angels' in their steel-studded
black leather jackets, dog-like in their elasticity and their keen
sense of smell, recall the famous speech in which Hitler exhorted
German youth to be *flink wie Windhunde, zäh wie Leder, hart wie
Kruppstahl*[25] ('as nimble as whippets, as tough as leather and as
hard as Krupp's steel'). Their fondness for black leather and steel
should render them suspect to any reader with a historical perspective. The trumpet is another uncomfortable reminder of the
past: a link with the exterminating angels of the Apocalypse, and
also with trumpeter Meyn of *The Tin Drum*.

The communal apotheosis of the perfect father leads directly to
a demand for an equally perfect son, a desire articulated by the
feminists, with the help of echoes from Nietzsche (*Übersohn*, F 575)
and the Bible, *Ich werde mir einen Sohn zeugen ... Der soll Emanuel
heißen* (F 556) ('I shall sire a son unto myself ... His name shall be
called Emanuel'). This is not a gratuitous biblical reminiscence but
the logical conclusion of a ritual which by this point has acquired
its own momentum.

The victim of the resulting excesses is partly responsible for
what happens. By treating the half-baked adolescent Mäxchen as
a child, she provokes a spirit of rebellion in the others which is to
culminate in the girl's preposterous assertion *Ich, Maximilian, bin
das neue Geschlecht* (loc. cit.) ('I, Maximilian, am the new sex').
Echoes of Christ's passion recur during the ensuing rape: the
instrument with which it is effected is bizarrely likened to the
transub-stantiated host (F 574), the ritual itself to a crucifixion (*ein
bißchen kreuzigen*, loc. cit.). But then, as a result of the violation,
Billy triumphs over her former *Zwiespältigkeit* (F 546) ('divided-
ness'), and begins to see things 'differently, in a new light, clearer
than before' (F 576).

On one level, the gruesome events of Father's Day function as a
warning against the false camaraderie of the mass rally, the spon-
taneous demonstration and the popular festival (*Volksfest*), in
which destructive forces lurk just below the surface. Biberkopf's
reluctance to join in with other groups at the end of *Berlin
Alexanderplatz* makes a similar point. Here, Billy remains an outsider and a loner, treated as such both by her ideologically radical
friends and by the gang of brutal bike-boys. But her ordeal is more
than just another manifestation of gratuitous violence; there are
many indications that she provides the vital link between the past
and the present. Her name is a virtual anagram of Ilsebill, but it

also emphasises the prophetic, sibylline gifts that the earlier 'cooks' (Dorothea, Gret and Lena) possessed. Like Sigismund Markus of *The Tin Drum*, whose initials she shares, she is an outsider who is divided between her identity as a lesbian and as a heterosexual (Markus was a convert, divided between Judaism and Christianity). She is a ready-made scapegoat whose 'passion' is put before us in a ritual enacted with the assistance of Christian symbolism and against the familiar backdrop of a secularised Church festival (Markus dies during the run-up to Christmas, Billy on Ascension Day: their deaths are associated with the advent and with the departure of the Saviour).

The relatively recent institution of Father's Day represents a crude modern attempt to cash in on the commercial potential already enjoyed by the much older and well-established festival of Mother's Day. That an excursion in honour of the male principle should end in a rape and a murder provides further evidence of the futility of imposing the model of one gender upon the other. What unfolds in this chapter are the visible consequences of a blinkered commitment to *one* of the antithetical principles that govern our lives, without concern for the other. Grass is suggesting that whether male or female, mind or body, each is unviable on its own and requires harmonious integration with the other, as the earlier histories have demonstrated. Despite the unattractive image of the lesbian foursome, he is not using this chapter to deride homosexuality, any more than the earlier novelists were when they introduced the theme to hint at inner imbalances in their characters (Franz, Knecht, Adrian). Billy's companions are ridiculed and condemned, not on account of their private sexual orientation, but because they are unable to devise a more appropriate means of self-expression than to ape the sex they claim to despise, adopting men's names and brashly addressing each other as 'lads'. The opening pages of 'Father's Day' have already provided a graphic inventory of an unappetising, resolutely male society, represented by the kind of people who take part in these mass outings: *Skatbrüder und Briefmarkensammler, verbitterte Rentner, entnervte Familienväter, Ladenschwengel und picklige Lehrlinge* (F 534) ('Skat-playing chums, stamp-collectors, embittered pensioners, dads heading for nervous breakdowns, shop assistants and spotty apprentices'). All their activities are as unappealing as their appearance and their accoutrements: an old man with a handkerchief tied round his bald head attaches leeches to his spindly legs, etc. (F 555). It becomes difficult to understand why the supposedly liberated women should, paradoxically, view the fathering of a son as the crowning achievement of the day. Yet they do, and so does Ilsebill when considering the outcome of her own pregnancy: she, too, will call him Emanuel (F 608). An explanation of sorts emerges from the context: aspirations latent in the (male-oriented) Christian scriptures and in the Nietzschean cult of the Superman are seen to have played a part in conditioning the women's fantasies.

We have already had several opportunities to observe the powerful effect which Nietzsche's tracts and Christian sentimentality have had on the mind of modern Germany, most particularly in Mann's *Doctor Faustus*. Via Adrian Leverkühn, Mann showed his country succumbing to the demonic lure of a misrepresented Christianity in combination with an arrogant Nietzschean counter-morality. Such were some of the catalysts which helped to isolate Adrian/Germany from the community of nations. In *The Flounder*, there is a suggestion that such tendencies linger on beneath the surface and are visible with exceptional clarity in the enclave of Berlin shortly after the building of the Berlin Wall.

For Thomas Mann, it was his fellow-countrymen's unrelenting preoccupation with philosophy and theology, with music and literature, which predisposed them to submit to the seductive words of their leaders and blinded them to the social and political realities of their time. Grass shows us the German nation from the opposite angle. People's minds are befuddled by an over-indulgence in food and drink, hastily prepared (barbecued) and gormandised, leaving them contentedly oblivious of the violence which they harbour in their midst. The atmosphere is resolutely Germanic; leisure activities like *Skat* and *Kegeln* ('cards', 'bowling'), cow-bells and beer-bottles set the scene for some typically Teutonic frivolity. The trees among which the revellers foregather are unmistakably 'Prussian'. Then there are the students, who are assumed to belong to traditional duelling fraternities with nationalistic names like Teutonia and Germania. The tense political situation prevailing at the time is contrasted with the people's frivolity: 'Morale was high. The weather couldn't have been better ... The political situation as tense as ever: one year after the Wall went up' (F 537). The question of German unity is raised several times in passing, then dropped again (F 543, 553).

The sorry state of the Federal Republic emerges most clearly from the picture which Grass paints of the student societies, whose grandiose names contrast with the pathetic condition into which their members have drunk themselves:

> *Ich weiß nicht, ob die studierten Säufer sich einer sogenannten*
> *schlagenden Verbindung zurechneten, ob ihre Korporation*
> *Teutonia, Saxonia, Thuringia, Rhenania, Fresia oder nur schlicht*
> *Germania hieß. Ich habe auch keine Lust, in einschlägiger*
> *Literatur nachzulesen, welche Aufgaben, Pflichten und Rechte*
> *Burschen und Füchse haben. Schmisse von Mensurenschlagen*
> *hatten die Bengel keine.* (F 560)

(I do not know if these scholarly inebriates considered themselves to be members of any so-called fighting fraternity, or
whether their association was called Teutonia, Saxonia,
Thuringia, Rhenania, Fresia, or just simply Germania. Nor
do I have any desire to consult the relevant literature about
the tasks, duties and rights of freshers and seniors. None of
these so-and-sos bore any duelling scars).

The students were placed into this collection of self-preoccupied
chauvinists by design, as a comment on the degeneracy of the up-
and-coming generation. Too soft to continue with their traditional
duels, they now spend their time challenging each other to drinking contests. There is an antithetical relationship between the
intoxicated intelligentsia and the scavenging motorcyclists: *Die*
Saxonen quatschten dumm; die Schwarzgelederten sagten kein Wort
(loc. cit.) ('The Saxons chattered away stupidly; the black-leather
boys didn't breathe a word'). When the crisis comes and Billy is
violated, the students are too far gone to be of any use; again their
stupor is contrasted with the vigilance of the bike-boys:

> *Kein Blick der bebrillten und nichtbebrillten Korpsstudenten*
> *konnte sich irgendwas abgewinnen. Die hingen viel zu besoffen in*
> *ihrem Wichs, um Anteil nehmen zu können. Nur die Schwarz-*
> *gelederten auf ihren Maschinen waren Zeugen ...* (F 573)

(Neither the bespectacled nor the unbespectacled members
of the student corps caught a glimpse of what was going
on. Decked out in their regalia, they were too plastered
to take any interest. The black-leather boys were the only
witnesses ...)

The contrast is between instinct and intellect: *War es Instinkt, war es*
Erkenntnis (F 561) ('Was it instinct, was it knowledge?'). The
students, representatives of the latent intellectual power of the
nation,[26] are too easily lulled into an indifferent stupor; the bikers
on their powerful machines embody brute force in an unholy
alliance with modern technology. There could be no more telling
image of the precarious position of the nation, whose intellectual

life is paralysed as a result of her material well-being, while brutal forces lurk on the fringes, combining the watchful agility of the beast of prey with the destructive power of the modern machine. Billy, the 'sibyl' of the past, the 'Ilsebill' of the present, is caught in the crossfire. Her death is no random instance of a few hooligans running amuck, but a meticulously choreographed set-piece demonstrating the eruption of violence in a community whose values have been thrown into confusion by an ill-balanced combination of half-forgotten moral principles, physical over-indulgence, gender alienation and the cult of the strong man, the hero, the father-figure. What began as an innocent-looking excuse for a celebration degenerates into a cult of the ego and the primitive life-force, in which there is no place for compromise, no place for the uncommitted outsider. For this reason – along with many others, such as his extensive previous attempts to trace the aetiology of German Fascism – Grass may have felt that he could dispense with a separate chapter on the years of Nazi rule; what he says here about the Federal Republic at the peak of her economic miracle, symbolised in an extreme form by the 'hot-house' enclave of West Berlin, serves to reawaken vivid memories of the sins of the past as well as expose dangers for the present and future.

6. LIFE GOES ON

Das Buch geht weiter und die Geschichte auch (F 532) ('The book goes on and so does history'), remarks the Author at the end of the seventh month, tacitly acknowledging that history unfolds before us like the pages of a volume. One generation merges into another, and each mirrors, explains, distorts its antecedents. At first sight, there may be little to connect the Father's Day orgy in Berlin with the riots that took place eight years later at the Lenin Shipyard of Danzig/Gdańsk. Both episodes centre on a murder, but the details point towards an ironic antithesis rather than to a logical progression. Closer to one another in time than any of the preceding epochs had been, the Grunewald incident and the shooting of strikers in the Polish shipyard seem to take place in different worlds. Placing Maria Kuczorra immediately after Sibylle Miehlau enables Grass to contrast Germany's extravagant affluence with the plight of her eastern neighbours.

The formula 'Life goes on' recurs when Jan Ludkowski is shot (F 600). He had also been participating in a mass gathering, attended by people from all over the area. The atmosphere seemed 'cheerful', *heiter* (F 598), and there is some singing. But the conspicuous over-consumption of the lakeside picnickers contrasts sharply with the hefty price increases that have been imposed on the Polish workers. Billy was assaulted while the organs of the state preferred to 'look the other way' (*wir wollen hier nix gesehen haben*, F 542), while Jan is shot by militiamen acting on orders from above: both receive their lethal injuries in the stomach.

There is again a political dimension to Jan's death. It occurs during a nominal thaw in relations between East and West, not long after the treaty of normalisation signed by the German and Polish governments in 1970, a development of which Grass, a staunch supporter of Brandt's *Ostpolitik*, took a positive view. But what have such treaties done for the ordinary citizens? he asks. Political accords are abstract and intangible; what matters to the people is, as always, the supply, quality, and price of their daily bread.

> *Man rede so viel über den Vorrang der nationalen Aufgaben. In den Zeitungen stehe nur noch Erhabenes über die Größe der geschichtlichen Stunde. Über den Konsum stehe nichts geschrieben. Das alles seien Zeichen schlimmer Art. 'Die setzen die Preise rauf', sagte Maria zu Jan.* (F 595)

(There was a great deal of talk about the priority of the national aims. The newspapers were full of lofty phrases about the great historical moment that had come. Not a word about the consumer. All the signs were very disturbing. 'They're going to put up the prices', said Maria to Jan.)

There is a striking difference between Maria Kuczorra and the 'cooks' of the first seven months, for in this account it is Maria who, along with the other women of the city, manoeuvres the men into a confrontation with the militia. No good can come of this. Naively trusting what has been drummed into her at school, she refuses to believe that Capitalism and Communism are capable of applying the same methods: *Das sei einem schon in der Schule beigebracht worden ... Wenn sich das im Kapitalismus so zugetragen habe, dürfe sowas im Kommunismus nicht passieren* (loc. cit.) ('That's what they taught us at school ... If that kind of thing happens under Capitalism, then it mustn't be allowed to happen under Communism'). Grass, by contrast, is only too well aware of the analogies between the two systems: the noises in the shipyards are the same, as are the bosses' priorities (F 636f., 239). But Maria believes that she knows better, and, in a flagrant breach of the pacifism displayed by all of the seven cooks up to Lena Stubbe, organises the men, pushing her own docile Jan into militant activity: *Und wenn es den Männern an Mumm fehle, werde es Aufgabe der*

Frauen sein, ihren Männern Dampf zu machen (F 596) ('And if the men have run out of oomph, then it is up to the women to get them going again'). Something of the uncompromising, aggressive feminism of the eighth month lives on in her. She, too, is a beneficiary of the postwar reversal of roles illustrated in its most extreme form in the Father's Day episode. The bitter results of this abandoning of a traditionally pacific role soon become apparent. Jan Ludkowski is a poet and a dreamer, given to fanciful speculations about Hamlet and ancient Polish folk-heroes. He is pushed into the firing line by an over-ambitious girlfriend: *Sie wollte sich unbedingt verbessern* (F 592) ('She wanted to better herself at all costs'). The historical comparisons in which Jan immerses himself are nothing less than an acknowledgement of the perverse repetitiveness of history to which Maria, by contrast, seems blind. There is a marked affinity between Jan and Hamlet, another disconsolate victim of his own theoretical insights, which is underlined when Jan suggests ideas for a continuation of Shakespeare's play.

Maria now has to pay a high price for her mistake. Prematurely aged, she is 'turned to stone', forgets how to laugh, and is reduced to a pitiful, embittered existence. The final copulatory act in which she engages with the Author on the seashore is devoid of pleasure, engineered perfunctorily as it is by Maria herself.[27] That she should at this point seek and obtain the advice of the Flounder does not augur well for the future. There are indications that she is in his clutches already: she has abandoned her children and put down a deposit on a car (F 643f.). Repeated warnings suggest that, where the Flounder is involved, things will take a nasty turn: *Ach Butt! Dein Märchen geht böse aus* (F 641) ('O Flounder! Your tale will end badly'). An examination of the mythical flatfish is long overdue.

7. THE TURBOT'S TALE

When it became known that Grass was about to publish a volume called *The Turbot*, a German angler's magazine put in an urgent request for a review copy – the first of many misunderstandings concerning the role of the fish in the novel.[28] Far from detailing procedures for catching it, the best advice appears to be: leave well alone.

The author's illustration on the cover depicts a huge fish without scales, covered in characteristic barnacle-like tubercles: a *Steinbutt* or turbot. They weigh up to forty kilogrammes and are regarded by connoisseurs as a great delicacy, unlike their distant cousin, the pedestrian flounder, a mere titch by comparison. We shall follow Ralph Manheim and demote the creature, since his role in folk-mythology is of greater concern than his dimensions or his flavour.[29] In his present capacity, he derives from Grimm's collection of folk-tales, the *Kinder- und Hausmärchen* of 1812, where he features in a story entitled *Von dem Fischer un syner Fru* ('Concerning the Fisherman and his Wife').

Most editions reproduce the story in a Low German dialect, suggesting that it originated somewhere along the North Sea coast, but it was first written down by Philipp Otto Runge in Pomerania. It therefore fits in well with the overall design of the novel, representing as it does the popular mythology of the people of the Danzig area, as well as folk wisdom in a more general sense. Variants of the story have been found in many parts of the world.[30] The story concerns an impoverished fisherman who catches a turbot, which he agrees to set free when he learns that it was an enchanted prince. His wife Ilsebill is furious and makes him summon the fish again and ask for a favour. Reluctantly, he asks for a proper little hut to replace the 'chamber-pot' which they have hitherto inhabited. The hut appears. Ilsebill complains that it is too small. The fish is summoned again, and in quick succession provides the couple with a stone cottage and a castle. He is later persuaded to make Ilsebill King, Emperor and finally Pope. Each time the reluctant fisherman goes down to the shore, the sea becomes rougher. When his wife has become Pope, he is relieved, since there is nothing left for her to aspire to; but Ilsebill has set her sights on becoming God.

> 'Now then, what does she want this time?' asked the Flounder.
> 'Alas', he said, 'she wants to be God Almighty.'
> 'Go to her, then, she's back in the chamber-pot.'
> And there they remain to this very day.

Grass does not favour long compound titles for his novels. The subtitle 'A celebration of life, food and sex' was created for the Anglo-Saxon market in the hope that it would boost sales figures. That Grass was thinking along quite different lines is shown by his own suggestion for a suitable subtitle: *Ein Märchen* ('A fable'). It is a term easily misunderstood:

> *Der Begriff Märchen ist bei uns mit so viel Lieblichkeit und Anheimelndem und Vorgefaßtem besetzt, daß ich diese Formbezeichnung nicht benutzen konnte, es sei denn, ich hätte in Kauf genommen, daß man sich mehr über diese Begriffsbestimmung als über das Buch ausgelassen hätte.*

> *Ich habe die Märchenform, das 'Es-war-einmal-Erzählen' von*
> *Anfang an benutzt, von der 'Blechtrommel' angefangen, und halte*
> *auch diese spezifisch deutsche Form des Erzählens für eine der*
> *Grundlagen unserer Literatur.*[31]

(The notion of a fable sparks off so many associations in this
country – cosiness, homely delights, and other preconceived
ideas – that I felt I could not describe the form of the book in
this way without running the risk of provoking more comment on the choice of this label than on the book itself.

From the time of *The Tin Drum*, I have always availed
myself of the structure of the folk-tale and of narrative methods along the lines of 'Once upon a time ...'. I regard this
typically German form of story-telling as one of the foundations of our literature.)

Undoubtedly, something of the original fable lingers on in the
completed novel, where the Author invents story after story, and
the book is eventually dedicated to the child Helene Grass. The
poems which punctuate it also emphasise its affinity with the
German Romantic tradition, an influence to which Grass himself
drew attention at a reading of his work in Cologne.[32] The formula
'Once upon a time' recurs (F 51, 532), as does the term *Märchen* – a
kind of cross between a story, a fable and a fairy-tale: *Nur das
Märchen ist wirklich* (F 418) ('Only the fable is real'). The Author's
always semi-fanciful reconstructions of his own experiences show
the necessary intertwining of fact and fiction: the 'writer's work-
shop' aspect is not the least of this novel's concerns. Folk-tales
tend to resemble one another to the point of being variations on
the same theme, and so Grass can use the *Märchen* as a symbol of
the repetitiveness and the ambiguity of experience. Nothing can
be pinned down. The oral tradition which has existed in Europe
until recently proves that there is no single truth, and no single
falsehood either, when it comes to explaining what happened in
history:

> *Und auch die Geschichte vom Butt ist so überkommen. Jedesmal*
> *wurde sie anders wirklich erzählt ... Jenes Märchen ... war als*
> *letzte Fassung druckfertig und eindeutig gemacht worden,*
> *während das ungedruckte Erzählen immer die nächste, die ganz*
> *anders verlaufende, die allerneueste Geschichte meint.* (F 345f.)

(That is how the story of the flounder has been handed
down. Each time it was told truthfully in a different way ...
That story ... finally became unambiguous and printable in

its final version, while stories that are not printed go on developing in a different way each time they are told and are always brand new.)

The entire novel may be described as a sustained attempt to show the operations of this principle.

Grass had already experimented with the method of mounting a recognisable folk-tale onto an allegory of modern history in the 'Faith Hope Love' section of *The Tin Drum*. This technique takes a more ambitious form in *The Flounder*. Here the fish is no pale, atavistic reminiscence of the wisdom of an earlier generation, but an ever-present participant who, like the 'devil' in *Doctor Faustus*, has a decisive effect on the central character, the Author. The popular myth of the fisherman and his wife furnishes Grass with a convenient analogy of many aspects of modern German history as he perceives it. Initially, it presupposes that history follows a linear course, resulting from an inborn desire for progress. Husband and wife enjoy a rapid improvement in their standard of living as a result of the woman's demands for greater comfort and higher status. This is the 'economic miracle' in a nutshell, and a model of all progress: demand stimulates production, which in turn fuels new demands.

In the end, however, the apparently well-oiled, stable system collapses, not only because demands become excessive, but also because the woman is trapped by the relentless mechanism which she has set in motion. Like the sorcerer's apprentice, she cannot stop the cycle. She gets no real satisfaction from the speedy gratification of her whims and must immediately formulate new desires, each of which is less reasonable than the previous one. Progress is not an end in itself; in the long term it is futile and explosive. At the end of the story, the 'linear' pattern proves to have been deceptive: history is not linear, but cyclic. A new model has been put in the place of the old one.

Each cycle is contained in a larger one. Ilsebill's repetitious demands, her continuing insistence that their benefactor will be able to provide more and ever more, her husband's appeals to her and his journeys down to the seashore, involve constant repetition from which there is seemingly no escape. 'Life goes on'; there are no grounds to hope that a lesson has been learned at the end. The doctrine of 'eternal recurrence' which has preoccupied German philosophers (Schopenhauer saw it as a curse, Nietzsche as an incentive) is here presented uncritically as the framework of our existence. Progress, for humankind, is like that of a snail in its spiral shell, to use another much-favoured motif in Grass's

writings and drawings: imperceptibly slow and necessarily repetitive. There is no qualitative difference between St Dorothy's
endless pilgrimages and the modern Ilsebill's package holidays to
the Caribbean, or between the grievances of the fourteenth-cen-
tury artisan in the Hanseatic port or his present-day equivalent in
the Polish dockyards. The smaller cycles are held together within
a larger unit, and we are under the permanent threat of a return to
the beginning. A reversal has already occurred by the time the
novel ends; the book was written between 1972 and 1977, and
bears the traces of the oil crisis of 1973 (F 474), as well as showing
concern about the contrasts between rich and poor nations in the
'Calcutta' section. The first poem spells it out:

> *Ich schreibe über den Überfluß ...*
> *Ich schreibe über den Hunger ...*
> *Über den Ekel vor vollem Teller ...*
> *Tiefkühltruhen, wie ihnen geschah,*
> *als Strom nicht mehr kam.*
> *Über uns alle am leergegessenen Tisch*
> *werde ich schreiben;*
> *Auch über dich und mich und die Gräte im Hals.*
> (F 11f.)

> (I write of affluence ...
> I write of hunger ...
> Of nausea before a plate full of food ...
> Chest freezers, and what became of them
> when the power dried up.
> Of us all, sat round the empty table,
> I shall write;
> of you and me and the bones that stick in our throats.)

The narratives converge on a potential catastrophe, foreseen more
directly in Grass's later novel, *The Rat*. In *The Flounder*, the ending
may still seem to leave the question open, but it possesses no less
of an apocalyptic potential than the three earlier novels with their
powerful portents of doom (the Whore of Babylon, the Last Glass
Bead Player, and Adrian's descent into Hell).

Another area of overlap with the folk-tale is in the depiction of
an ongoing battle between the sexes. Human development results
from never-ending conflict between man and woman, whose interests are polarised and irreconcilable. Such progress as there is
does not result from constructive cooperation, but, almost by
accident, from a headlong collision between males and females on

the perennial battleground where all important issues are fought
out. At times the man is appetitive, the woman restraining
(months 1–7; the 'alternative truth' of F 407–18), at times it is the
other way round (the folk-tale; months 8 and 9; Ilsebill and the
Author). Trivial domestic issues may thus have far-reaching, even
devastating consequences (Dorothea's antipathy towards her
husband provides the Church with a saint; boredom and frustration at home lead to the First World War).

The insatiable Ilsebill of the legend is more than just a disobedi-
ent wife: she is a traitor to her own sex, and in this respect she
anticipates the eighth and ninth months of the novel. Not content
to possess palaces and mansions as a queen or empress, she insists
on a change of gender along with everything else. This is no
positive demolition of barriers (as it might have been if she were
actually seen ruling wisely) but a blind craze for power, which the
fisherman's wife can only imagine in terms of male stereotypes.
Hers is an entirely wrong-headed attitude to emancipation, and
one that foreshadows the precipitous efforts by Maria, the lesbi-
ans and Ilsebill to hijack a ready-made role model from their
erstwhile oppressors.

In all this, the Flounder plays the subordinate part of an oblig-
ing, at times somewhat Mephistophelian servant who provides
what he is asked to supply and then silently observes the ensuing
battle between sense and sensuality. He partakes of the divine in
his limitless ability and willingness to fulfil every request, but in
tempting and ensnaring the appetitive mortals he has something
of the devil within him. In the novel, he remains ambiguous, seen
variously as God (F 80, 385f.), Jesus (F 157) and Satan (F 101). Time
and time again, he presses his seductively progressive advice on
the menfolk, arousing them from their acceptance of matriarchal
society, persuading them to devise new orders and 'enforcing
Apolline Reason' (F 55). He stands for pure theory, supporting
everything from Bronze Age trade to Marxian socialism. But his
plans are made to miscarry by the men's foibles and the women's
resourcefulness. In any contest between pure theory and the unpredictable realities of life, theory must suffer a resounding defeat. The Flounder exemplifies not the strength but the limitations
of Pure Reason when applied to the endless, unpredictable flux of
life.

The eponymous fish is seen in two contexts within the novel: as
the instigator of male opposition to all forms of feminine assert-
iveness, and as the defender who is on trial for his chauvinist
principles which have harmed the human race in the past. It is

necessary to distinguish between these two roles. The *Feminal* treats him as a whipping-boy for everything that went wrong in history. Try as he may to exculpate himself with the help of his considerable powers of rhetoric, he remains a convenient peg onto which the women can hang their own not inconsiderable grievances and prejudices. In this respect, he is a concrete image of *their* narrow view of the past, 'psychologically rather than physically real'.[33] To blame him is like blaming God, or the devil, for one's own mistakes; the *Feminal* is acting in the tradition of Adrian Leverkühn when it shifts responsibility onto a convenient scapegoat. Historical inquiry, Grass is suggesting, must not take the form of a law court where everyone is so eager to apportion blame, to reduce complex issues to a simple matter of right and wrong, that the ever-elusive human factor is ignored.

The irony of the situation is heightened further. The Flounder proves unexpectedly cooperative, more than willing to provide the tribunal with self-incriminating evidence. After all, it seems he wanted to be caught by them in the first place. Ultimately he is of their invention, so it is hardly surprising that the women should find him so malleable. Moreover, it is soon revealed that there are modern equivalents of each historical woman sitting on the bench: the feminists are, in effect, judging themselves, however much they try to deny this. As an emblem of an intangible, hypothetical *Weltgeist* (F 478), the Flounder can remain contentedly oblivious of the carnival atmosphere that builds up in and around the disused suburban cinema where his case is heard. The idea of a cinema as a law court reminds us again of the many distortions of past events that are regularly put out by the media for the benefit of today's armchair historians. The mood here is close to that of a circus, and the rise and fall of inane splinter groups mirror human folly as revealed in media events such as show trials and the televising of parliamentary debates.

Yet the light-hearted tone does not prevail throughout. The Flounder does accept that women have been second-class citizens in the past and that men have failed to accord them a fair share of their power. That he should support their quest for greater influence is to be welcomed, but his sudden and total switch from the cause of one gender to that of the other smacks of the one-sided approach that caused strife and frustration in the past. The *flatfish* is by nature a one-sided animal, and it is therefore an excellent symbol of the either-or mentality on which so many ideologies have come to grief, Christian sectarianism no less than twentieth-century chauvinism. As an advocate of sudden changes and radical breaks, he gets his deserts when the hyper-emancipated feminists capture him and put him on trial. His philosophy accords well with their perspective. The reader will by now have abandoned the book or come to agree that it is not a question of supporting one sex or the other, pursuing one goal to the exclusion of all else, but of 'the one and the other together' (F 412), a perspective which our flatfish is congenitally unable to appreciate.

8. DATES AND DATA

If the events of the past elude clear-cut evaluation, there are, as every schoolchild knows, a reassuring quantity of dates and numbers that can be verified and committed to memory. The factual stratum was, it transpires, part of the original conception of the work: *Eigentlich wollte ich ... nicht Geschichten erzählen, sondern Zahlen nennen und den kaschubischen Legendensumpf statistisch trockenlegen* (F 343) ('My intention was not to tell stories ... so much as to reel off numbers and to drain the swamp of Cassubian legends with the aid of statistics'). Grass may not have been true to this programme, but there remains a very considerable amount of factual material in the novel – another respect in which it resembles *Berlin Alexanderplatz*. We do not, in the end, find out 'how many peasants were reduced to serfdom by the end of the Thirty Years' War' or at what age their children were put to work in the fields (loc. cit.); but key dates and figures are put before the reader on almost every page. The result is not so much 'a cookery book interspersed with stories'[34] as 'a history book interspersed with recipes'. Many sources can be identified, and the evidence suggests that Grass subjected them to careful scrutiny.[35]

What he says about Dorothea von Montau yields important information about how Grass manipulates the historical documents on which so many of his episodes are based. The main source for this character is Johannes Marienwerder's biography *Das Leben der seligen Dorothea von Preußen* ('The Life of the Blessed Dorothea of Prussia'), possibly consulted in Franz Hipler's late nineteenth-century modernised version.[36] This volume is of immense importance in that it was the first book in the German language ever to be printed in Prussia, as well as being one of the most detailed attempts at a psychological study of an individual from the late Middle Ages. It also paints, as McFarland has shown, an unusually detailed picture of ordinary domestic life at the time.[37] Here we read of Dorothea's indifference to the pleasures of the palate, a central concern of her husband in the *vita* as in the novel: *Viele Jahre hindurch pflegte sie des Tages nur einmal zu essen gar mäßig, Fasten- oder Milchspeise, nicht Fleisch* (M 423) ('For may years she would eat but once a day, Lenten fare or dairy foods in moderation, but no meat'). Grass accurately records the day on which the source states that she was immured: 2 May 1393. Marienwerder has her return from her pilgrimage to Rome on 'the last Sunday before Whitsun' (M 412); Grass refers to the occasion differently but no less accurately as 'the Sunday after Ascension Day', probably on account of the symbolic function of Ascension Day in the eighth month. While such dates are regularly reproduced with precision, it is in his interpretation of these episodes that Grass parts company with his informant. Agreeing that Dorothea had a tendency to laugh out loud in church, Grass cannot share the constructive explanation which Marienwerder provides:

> *Sie konnte mitunter ihre überfließende Freude, Wonne und Jubiliren nicht verbergen, sondern sie äußerte dieselben vor den Menschen in der Kirche mit Lachen und Gebärden, mit Lauten und Worten; sie konnte sich nicht halten.* (M 390)

(There were times when she could not conceal her overflowing joy, pleasure and jubilation, but expressed them in the presence of people in the church with laughter and gestures, noises and words; she could not stop herself.)

Grass adopts the point of view of the townsfolk towards their odd contemporary:

> *Zu oft und zu störend falle die auch sonst auffallende Dorothea während der Messe in Ekstase. Sie verhöhne durch Kichern und prustendes Lachen die heilige Wandlung ... Man höre sie schreien und eher lüstern als fromm nach dem Herrn Jesus rufen ... Frech trete die Sünde verkleidet als Büßerin auf.* (F 176f.)

(Too frequent and too disruptive were the many ecstatic fits by which that generally very striking Dorothea was struck down during mass. Her giggling and her ostentatious laughter were seen as mockery of the holy transubstantiation ... She could be heard shrieking and calling for the Lord Jesus in lewd rather than pious tones ... Brazenly, sin had reared its head in the guise of a penitent.)

Again and again, Grass supplies his alternative readings and emendations to the chronicles. Dorothea's husband is not allowed to die of natural causes at the convenient moment (M 390), but is bought off by the Church and allows himself to be pronounced dead in return for a new abode and identity, much to his satisfaction (F 188). The ironic asides allow themselves to be interpreted in many ways, as anti-religious slander, as vicarious attacks on the Author's (or author's?) wife, or as part of a comic investigation of a certain type of neurosis. Ultimately, the speculation about Dorothea's true character is a comment on the impossibility of writing history other than in the form of the *Märchen*. The proximity of good and evil, spirit and sensuality, is seen with exceptional clarity in the well-documented life of this controversial saint, who by an extraordinary coincidence was canonised just six weeks before the publication of *The Flounder*.

For all its paradoxes and uncertainties, the novel is crammed with factual-looking data, much as Döblin's survey of modern Berlin had been. The reader is subjected to a barrage of figures, many of which may seem to be of little overall consequence. Thus Wigga succeeds Aua after 111 generations, while Romeike participates in twenty-three battles and sustains nine war-wounds in seven years. A total of thirteen pairs of spectacles are broken in the course of the book, and on Father's Day the emergency services are called out 112 times to deal with eighty-seven injuries, of which nineteen are serious and one is fatal. Dates are called up with uncanny precision, as if they had been stored in a computer: the Flounder is caught on 3 May 2211 BC, Gryphius visits Opitz on 2 September 1636, Lena Stubbe dies on 4 December 1942. Historical events are pinned down: King Przemyslaw of Poland is assassinated on 6 February 1296, the Teutonic Knights seize Danzig on 14 November 1308, Vasco da Gama reaches Calicut on 28 March 1498, Stefan Batory is feasted in Danzig on 12 December 1577, and Friedrich Bartholdy proclaims the city a republic on 17 April 1797. As far as can be ascertained, these figures are usually accurate to within a few days.[38]

Leaving aside the possibility that there may be a cryptic significance in some of these numbers, as has been argued with regard to Grass's earlier novels and to 'Father's Day',[39] it is worth noting the sharp contrast between the apparently scientific precision of the numerical data and the imaginative fabulising that was necessary to produce the episodic narratives. We must not assume that Grass either knows or believes that Adalbert was slain with a cast-iron spoon rather than with a wooden oar, still less that the notorious iconoclast Jakob Hegge, on whose escape from Danzig in 1526 most historians waste few words, was helped on his way by a painful though expedient testectomy. What is relevant here is the tension between the improbable adventures created by the Author in his guise as a Rabelaisian raconteur, and the stark, impersonal factuality of the figures which the same Author is given to citing. The non-specialist reader has no option but to accept these numbers, the more so since dates of treaties and battles and other 'key events' are fed to us at school as the very stuff of history. But in his attempts to persuade us to adopt a fresh attitude to the past, Grass deliberately oscillates between verifiable data and outrageously speculative fantasy. The end result of this procedure is to generate a unique image of the human condition.

The facts and figures that are so liberally put before us do not open any meaningful doors to the past, however authentic they may be. The train carrying Lena Stubbe to Bebel's funeral in Switzerland arrives in Zurich 'punctually at 15.29 hours' (F 521); such information is patently irrelevant. The conjecture that it was possible, back in 1913, to foresee Socialism polarising into Communism and National Socialism is more interesting than all the railway timetables of the period. The 'facts' with their intrinsic promise of certitude stand out, ironically, not as an aid but as an impediment to an understanding of the issues. Grass uses his feigned dependence on dates and data to stress the severe limitations of conventional learning. For all his erudition, the unpredictable, purely human factor is what most concerns the novelist, who acknowledges our paradoxical reliance on both fact and fantasy. While presenting himself, like Döblin before him, as the all-knowing *poeta doctus* who has every fact at his fingertips, Grass simultaneously reveals the limitations of our knowledge of the world. Information about the number of people who sustained injuries on Father's Day is as irrelevant to Billy as the statistics of 1927 were to Mieze or the laws of Newton to Ida. As if to underline his scepticism about the value of temporal coordinates, Grass withholds other information which might interest his readers. The vital dates of Ilsebill's pregnancy are not provided, nor are those of any of the Author's own activities during this period. The year in question is identifiable only with reference to Willy Brandt's resignation and Poland's defeat of Chile in the World Cup (F 516–522, 633).

There is another thread that runs through the novel as if in counterpoint to the confident recital of dates. Grass rarely misses an opportunity to convey authorial diffidence in the midst of these facts and figures. The stories are, by the author's admission, 'invented', and, while citing dates with computer-like accuracy,

he admits to being unsure about many day-to-day events. There is uncertainty about how many geese Gret prepared for a given occasion ('nine or eleven', F 342) or how many crows witnessed Billy's humiliation ('seven, eleven', F 553). The Author cannot even make up his mind as to whether this is a biography of nine or eleven cooks! The figures on their own are, as always, devoid of significance. A few contradictions are also slipped in to illustrate the point: on page 539 Billy is said to have been raped by 'three or five' Russians in her youth, and four pages later this has become 'five or seven'. A personal story always changes in the process of telling, and so does the stuff of history. In the present novel, it remains uncertain whether Father's Day is set in 1962 or 1963.

9. DICHOTOMIES AND DESTRUCTION

It will be observed that nearly all numbers mentioned in the casual fashion outlined above are odd rather than even. Seven 'black angels' violate Billy, nine or eleven turbots are consumed by the vengeful feminists, thirteen pairs of glasses are smashed. Rarely does the Author mention an even number of items. It is the role accorded to the 'third breast' in the context of the bountiful Aua that determines his preference in this direction. The number three holds within it a promise of the impossible: *wenn ich ins Leere greife, meine ich die dritte Brust* (F 9) ('when I reach out into the void, I mean the third breast'). It holds out a hope of superabundance (F 8). The range of meanings encapsulated within this number include the Trinity and the 'third', alternative, political party of the present (F 9, 24). When he harks back to the Golden Age of the triple-breasted mother-goddess, Grass is voicing a yearning for something so perfect that it cannot be attained: the elusive world of contentment that transcends inner divisions. Readers of *The Tin Drum* will remember that Oskar stopped growing at the age of three, thereby becoming three times wiser than anybody else (*der Dreimalkluge*). Inflation has meantime taken its toll: the Flounder is *neunmalklug* (F 18) ('nine times wiser than the rest'), and an especial importance attaches to the numbers 33, 101 and 111.

The promise of release from our dichotomies is not fulfilled: the ending is open, with the female characters merging into one in a world still governed by a duplicitous flatfish. Even the otherwise open-minded, anti-Aristotelian Romantics cannot transcend their either-or mentality when selecting *Märchen* for an anthology. Only occasionally, and then dimly and from a distance, Grass envisages the possibility of a triumph: in the world of myths and in the figure of 'Lud', who accompanies the episodic narrators on their journeys through time (F 584–9).[40] Lud, Ludek, Ludewik, Ludrichkait and the others originated as a tribute to Grass's deceased friend Ludwig Gabriel Schreiber, and became the novel's principal opponent of the narrow mentality that can only see things in terms of hostile oppositions, theses and antitheses: *Als Lud ... christlich wurde, hat er nie den Schmerz des Gekreuzigten, immer dreieinig das Prinzip dargestellt* (F 585) ('When Lud ... became a Christian, he never portrayed the suffering of the crucified, only the triune principle'). It is in this figure that we come as close as anywhere to the definition of those qualities that permit a muted celebration of life: *Wir sangen bis in die Nacht und waren verzweifelt. Wir hielten an unserem Traum fest* (F 589) ('We sang well into the night in our despair. We held on to our dream'). But like his model, the fictional Luds are dead (Ludkowski), abroad (Ludwig Skröver), elusive (Axel Ludström), offering little comfort for the present: *Wie mir Lud fehlt* (F 588) ('How I miss Lud').

It is left to none other than the Flounder to hold out a glimmer of hope at the end, in his sensibly self-critical address to the women of the *Feminal* (F 611–7), in which he advises the total rejection of those values which mankind (and latterly womankind) have been pursuing. Here, the crusading spirit, which elsewhere in the novel lies deeply embedded within the ironic sketches of human folly, comes to the fore in an unadulterated, direct manner. In an impassioned, inevitably misunderstood, diatribe, comparable in many ways to Adrian's *Oratio ad Studios*, the Flounder inveighs against himself as the representative of our blind faith in abstract principles. Now he derides those very ideas which he had peddled to the menfolk of many generations: *die Größe der Nation, die Reinheit dieser oder jener Idee, die Ehre Gottes, den unsterblichen Ruhm, das Vaterland* (F 612) ('national grandeur', 'the sublimity of this or that idea', 'the glory of God', 'everlasting fame', 'the fatherland'). The outcome of ideologies based on these notions is to be seen in the arms race, which provides the greatest threat the world has ever known:

> *Welche Vernunft waltet, wenn ein Gutteil Lohn des Arbeiterfleißes in immer perfektere Vernichtungstechnologien investiert wird? Welcher säkularisierte Teufel putzt das Feindbild so blank, daß sich die Menschen mitten im erklärten Frieden ächzend unter der Rüstungslast gegenüberstehen: Auge in Auge, verblendet, todsicher? Immer noch Beelzebub? Der sogenannte Todestrieb? Oder neuerdings ich, der Butt aus dem Märchen?* (F 612 f.)

(What sense governs a world in which a sizeable proportion of the wages of hard-working people is invested in the increasingly refined technology of mass destruction? What secularised devil created so glaring an image of the enemy that even in a declared state of peace human beings face each other groaning under the weight of their accumulated weaponry: eye to eye and yet unseeing, in deadly certainty? Still Beelzebub? Or latterly I myself, the Flounder, born of the folk-tale?)

Now, the omniscient fish is prepared to equate himself with the devil, if only to make humankind acknowledge the folly of its continuing commitment to organised violence. As if in some morality play, not unlike the Doctor Faustus of earlier traditions, he steps out of his role and addresses his audience, and us, the readers, directly. Here, in these five pages, is the stark message embodied within the superficially ribald stories. Violence must be identified and exposed for what it is, wherever it lurks, especially when it is insidiously present in our midst:

> *Man besuche nur Schützenbälle, man sehe bübischen Zweikämpfen zu, finde in Fußballstadien Vergnügen oder mische sich auf Himmelfahrt, wenn hier, in Berlin, lauthals Vatertag gefeiert wird, in die Menge: diese gestaute, auf Anlässe lauernde Aggression. Diese Brunst, eindringlich und zerstörend.* (F 614)

(One need only visit the amateur marksmen's parties, watch youngsters fighting, sample the delights of the football stadium or join the crowds right here in Berlin in their noisy celebration of Father's Day: so much pent-up aggression waiting for the right moment. The rutting instinct, penetrating and destructive.)

The Flounder encourages his female accusers to learn from the mistakes of the past. First, though, they are rebuked for accepting the decisions of their menfolk too readily. In Germany, they should have spoken out against the policy of rearmament that was imposed upon the nation before the ruins of the last war had been demolished (F 617). Along with many other writers, Grass is deeply resentful of the way in which Chancellor Konrad Adenauer backtracked on his own undertaking never to let Germans bear arms again. But worse was to come. Female politicians began to enter the arena of world affairs. Golda Meir and Indira Gandhi are mentioned by name, and another political figure might have been added, had *The Flounder* been published three years later than it was. These women proved to be no better than the males, remaining trapped, as they did, *im logischen Streckbett des männlichen Geschichtsverständnisses* (loc. cit.) ('in the logical straitjacket of a masculine perception of history'). The powerful social and political subtext of the events of the eighth month is brought home in this impassioned valediction.

The women of the *Feminal* take no heed of what has been said. They are more interested in devising punishments for the scapegoat that they have apprehended than in hearing him recant; they seem unable to listen to, let alone learn from him. They point at him and mutter *Da! Da!* (F 622) ('There! There!'), as the children do to the Black Cook in *The Tin Drum* and as Professor Kumpf had done when he believed he had seen the devil. To recoil in horror is so much more convenient than to acknowledge and learn from one's own aberrations.

10. DIET AND DEATH

The festive banquet, *das Buttessen*, at which turbot is ceremoniously consumed by the ladies of the tribunal, marks a return to a theme about which little has so far been said, despite its prominence in the novel and in Grass's work as a whole. The *erzählendes Kochbuch* ('cookery-book interspersed with stories') promised in *From the Diary of a Snail* is submerged in an avalanche of historical fact-cum-speculation, narrational digression and cautionary didacticism. Yet Grass was quite unambiguous about his intention to provide a 'history of eating', in which he would portray 'guests and people as animals that know how to cook, the process of eating, waste'.[41] The relationship between the ideological and culinary history in this book is important and will provide material for a few concluding observations.[42]

One of the strengths of any novel is its ability to extend its readers' awareness of the neglected or misunderstood contingencies of their lives. Döblin had done this in a remarkable manner by bombarding the reader with minute, atomic items of information that pass almost subliminally through our minds. Grass opens up other areas of experience that have played a part in shaping the modern world, while at the same time challenging the apparent authenticity of written documents. While he was working on *The Flounder*, he came to realise that the early 'sources' on which historians rely are a kind of 'unacknowledged fiction' (*nicht zugegebene Fiktion*). He was able to claim, in conversation with Heinz Ludwig Arnold, that he could invent more reliable data than what has come down to us in written or traditional form from the Middle Ages:

... das [ist] alles entweder kirchliche oder fürstliche Schreiberei jeweils zu dieser oder jener Position, und damit arbeiten die Historiker. Die Löcher dazwischen sind für den Schriftsteller interessant. Ich sehe mich in der Lage, genauere Fakten zu erfinden als die, die uns als angeblich authentisch überliefert worden sind.[43]

(... that is all just scribal work done at the behest of the Church or the princes in order to justify one position or another, yet the historians make use of it. The holes in between are what interests the novelist. I see myself as being able to invent more reliable factual data than that which has been handed down to us as though it were authentic.)

Minor changes in the nation's diet are just such 'factual data' to which little time is devoted in the classroom despite its decisive influence on world affairs. The substitution of the potato in place of millet as the staple diet of north-eastern Europe in the eighteenth century marks a historical watershed that has received less attention than, say, the campaigns of Frederick the Great, still seen in some quarters as one of modern Germany's greatest national figures. The colonialist interests of the Portuguese were stimulated by an increasing demand for pepper and other spices. From the dawn of history, a close link has existed between what we eat and what we are, as Feuerbach and Lévi-Strauss have indicated in different ways. In Grass's simplified model, the wholesome diet of the Neolithic brought with it tranquillity; in the Iron Age, root crops tied people to the soil, while dependence on meat encouraged migration. Cheap imports of herring and beer sparked off social unrest during the Middle Ages. Personalities are shaped by particular foodstuffs: Fat Gret's humour and ebullience derive at least in part from her devotion to spices, while the Baroque poets' detestation of worldly pleasures is a direct consequence of the bland Schonkost ('invalid's fare') which is forever on their menu. Battles are fought with the 'food weapon', as Wigga shows, religions are supported or weakened by the same means (Dorothea, Mestwina). When the rice crops of Bengal were diverted to sustain Allied troops in the Far East in 1943, 2,000,000 civilians perished: another piece of 'alternative history' that Grass would like to see recorded and debated, perhaps in the form of a film, if hunger can be filmed (F 214).[44]

The significance of the culinary stratum does not end here. Our total dependence on an uninterrupted supply of nourishment is the curse and the boon of human existence: a reminder of mortality and yet also a link with men and women of all nationalities and epochs. Grass would like to envisage his readers experimenting with some of the recipes in order to increase their empathy with the historical figures,[45] thus achieving a kind of secular communion with bygone characters. He is by no means the first writer to emphasise the connection between eating habits and personality. Franz celebrates a sexual conquest with two fillets of veal, and succumbs to the lure of 'fruit' when he joins the gang of robbers. Frequent meals highlight his sensuality; the abattoir chapter of *Berlin Alexanderplatz* contains reflections on the nature of the human animal. The 'spiritual' republic of Castalia enforces a frugal diet, banning meat and alcohol in its cultivation of an image of clean living. In *Doctor Faustus*, food ranks beside sexuality as the province of evil: Kumpf makes the connection by throwing food at the devil, and Adrian is introduced to Esmeralda in response to his inquiry about a restaurant. Far from 'celebrating' our dependence on food, many authors use the festive meal as a prelude to a disaster. As a literary motif, therefore, the feast is a well-established portent of doom in such disparate works as *The Odyssey*, *Macbeth* and *Biedermann and the Fire-Raisers*. The biblical 'Last Supper' is a familiar example. Grass has always been conscious of the sinister side of our sustenance: the death of Oskar's mother in *The Tin Drum* and Mahlke's insatiable greed in *Cat and Mouse* are two instances of its fatal consequences. Tooth decay, a symptom of our addiction to the pleasures of the palate, is the central motif of *Local Anaesthetic*. In *The Flounder*, there is no shortage of figures for whom eating has lethal consequences. Abbot Jeschke is fed to death, Adalbert of Prague is slain by his cook, Sophie's toadstools kill six men, Billy is murdered at a picnic, Jan is shot in a stomach still full of pork and cabbage. While promising life, our diet also precipitates death: it furnishes yet another ready-made symbol of ambiguity.

For all its potency as a signal of doom, Grass does not conclude the novel, as he might have done, on a tragic note. There is less pessimism here than in his next novel, *The Rat*. His characters are neither celebrated nor condemned. The sustained emphasis on cookery and consumption is not least an acknowledgement of the continuity of the drama of life and an acceptance of the essential sameness of its participants. Dishes containing the local cheese, *Glumse*, recur throughout history, and herrings are eaten by everyone. When the city is invaded, whether by generals or by missionaries, the vanquished are made to cook for the victors, allowing for a rapid assimilation. The result is a close bond between people: *Schließlich sind wir Kaschuben alle über ein paar*

Feldwege miteinander verwandt (F 591) ('After all, we Cassubians are all related to each other via the odd gooseberry bush').

This inter-relatedness of all and sundry is borne out by the many ties of kinship that link the novel's characters with one another: Amanda Woyke is Sophie's grandmother, and Billy is Lena Stubbe's great-granddaughter (F 362, 545). Ulla Witzlaff is a reincarnation of Margarete Rusch, as well as a descendant of the old woman who told the tale of the Flounder to Runge. She is also related to the poet Wiclaw or Wizlav of Rügen, who first brought a specifically German literary culture to the shores of the Baltic; Jan Ludkowski is especially knowledgeable about him (F 271, 594).[46]

Grass does not see the past as a closed book, but as present within our midst. The Lutheran pastor of a Berlin Church is *der Hegge von heute* (F 271) ('[Preacher] Hegge of today'). Slichting's comments on the medieval flagellants read like a wise old man's reflections on the degeneracy of popular culture in the 1970s:

> *Damals war das Geißeln so etwas wie Kiffen. Besonders die hochgotische Jugend, zu der ich mich nicht mehr zählen konnte, suchte den wärmenden Gestank der Flagellantenhorden, ihren der Litanei hörigen Schlagrhythmus, ihren in alle Höllen verstiegenen Angsträusche, ihre Gruppenekstasen und gemeinschaftlichen Erleuchtungen.* (F 137f.)

(The flagellations current in those days were not so very different from smoking pot. The gilded High Gothic youth, of whom I was no longer a member, were particularly receptive to the warm stench of the hordes of flagellants, to their beat rhythms deriving from the litany, to the *angst*-ridden hallucinations that sent them off into every imaginable hell, to their group ecstasies and public visions.)

The aspirations of the shipyard workers today are no different from those of the medieval artisans; only 'the patricians have different names' (F 140). Similarly, the great idealists from St Augustine to Ernst Bloch have much in common, be they Catholic or Communist systematisers (F 168). It is a short step indeed from here to the recognition that we all 'live on' in one another; Grass's ploy of fragmenting a far from perfect modern man, complete with his many hang-ups, the Author,[47] into the episodic narrators is less of a confusing literary device than a statement of belief in the brother- and sisterhood of the human race which ought (but still all too often fails) to assist us in transcending the dichotomies which brought much misery to the divided prewar heroes portrayed by Döblin, Hesse and Mann.

NOTES

1. For an account of the trials, see Arnold and Görtz, 1971, pp. 265–327.
2. Several such reviews are cited in Loschütz, 1968, 13–26. The passage quoted is by McGovern, cited by Leonard, 1974, p. 97.
3. Loschütz, 1968, p. 11f.
4. *WA* vol. 9, p. 318.
5. Ibid., pp. 236–55.
6. 18/1979, p. 184.
7. Karasek, 1977, p. 104.
8. Cepl-Kaufmann, 1975, pp. 14, 112.
9. *WA* vol. 3, pp. 519, 838–40.
10. Leonhardt, 1942, esp. pp. 41, 46.
11. Arnold and Görtz, 1971, p. 307.
12. One such was Witte, 1974/5.
13. Michels, 1973, p. 87.
14. Greenblatt, 1988.
15. *WA* vol. 5, p. 659.
16. Ibid., p. 654.
17. *Der Butt* actually denotes a 'turbot'; see p. 162, below.
18. Butler, 1979, p. 27.
19. Opitz and Gryphius were both in the Danzig area in 1636; it is unlikely that they will have met (Flemming, 1965, p. 27). Möller had died in 1611 when Opitz was fourteen; Agnes could not have served both men at the same time.
20. Gryphius, in whom some see a portrait of Böll, retains his ambiguity in Grass's next novel, *The Meeting at Telgte*.
21. Bebel, 1879; for Grass's use of this figure in the context of the debate about political revisionism, see Tudor, 1988, pp. 141–9.
22. Enright, 1965, p. 8.
23. Butler, 1979, p. 28f; Michaelis, 1977, p. 30.
24. Neuhaus, 1979, p. 142; Thomas, 1979/80, p. 84; *WA* 657; Reddick, 1983, p. 150.
25. This speech is also referred to in *Cat and Mouse*, *WA* vol. 3, p. 53, 870n.
26. Grass is often heard criticising German students for their lack of political initiative; see *WA* vol. 9, p. 197.
27. White, 1990, p. 131.
28. Raddatz, 1977, p. 892.
29. Manheim, tr. Grass, 1978, points out that Webster's Dictionary defines *Flounder* as 'in a broad sense any flatfish'.
30. See Bolte and Polívka, 1912, pp. 138–42; Röllecke, 1978.
31. Interview in *Die Zeit*, 12 August 1977, p. 30.
32. Neuhaus, 1979 , p. 137.
33. Thomas, 1979/80, p. 76.
34. *Ein erzählendes Kochbuch*, Arnold, 1978, p. 30; n. 41, below.
35. See Mews, 1983, pp. 163–78; McFarland, 1990, pp. 69–96.
36. Marienwerder, 1892, henceforth м.
37. McFarland, 1990, pp. 81–90.
38. The Teutonic Knights entered Danzig as reported on 14 November 1308, but Przemyslaw was assassinated on 8 February 1296 and Batory made peace with Danzig on 16 December 1577 (see *The Cambridge History of Poland from the Origins to Sobieski*, 1950, pp. 117, 112, 291). Vasco arrived in Calicut around 20 May 1498. Bartholdy's 'rebellion' took place on 13 April 1797 (see Keyser, 1921, p. 163).
39. Harscheidt, 1975; Reddick, 1983, p. 153f.
40. Brode, 1979, p. 195; Neuhaus, 1979, p. 144.

41. *WA* vol. 4, p. 437.
42. See also Phelan, 1990.
43. Arnold, 1978, p. 31.
44. Grass and his informant are evidently unaware of Satyajit Ray's treatment of the subject in his much-acclaimed film *Distant Thunder* of 1973.
45. Arnold, 1978, p. 28.
46. Ulla is probably a cryptic tribute to Grass's second wife; see Brode, 1979, p. 189.
47. It is difficult to take a positive view of the Author's immaturity and voyeurism; see White, 1990, p. 131. For this reason, it would seem unwise to distinguish between 'Günter' and 'Grass' elements in the narrators, as Forster, 1980, does.

Summary and Conclusion

Der Schriftsteller und der Dichter, nochmals gesagt, sind aber eine besondere Art Wissenschaftler und stehen daher fest auf der Erde. Sie haben aus Gründen ihrer Wissenschaft mehr Zugang zur Realität und zu mehr Realität Zugang als sehr viele andere, denen ihr bißchen Politisieren, Geschäftemachen und Handeln als einzige Realität vorkommt.
(Alfred Döblin: 'The Historical Novel and Ourselves')

(I repeat that the writer and the poet are a distinct type of scientist and therefore have their feet firmly on the ground. Because of the science they practise, they have more access to reality and have access to more reality than the vast majority of people who assume that the small world of their politics, commerce and action is the only reality there is.)

Literature, as Kafka observed in 1911, may be seen as the 'diary-keeping of a nation', and there are good reasons for considering major novels and other literary texts as expressions of specific national identities.[1] The terms *Bildungsroman* and *Entwicklungsroman* are used to characterise a German contribution to the novel as a literary form; both imply a pedagogic objective which manifests itself in the gradual evolution of its hero's personality. As early as 1916, Thomas Mann foresaw that a political component would gradually come to replace the 'romantic, apolitical individualism' that had arisen out of late eighteenth-century idealism and had hitherto determined the ethos of such novels. As Germany underwent a process of democratisation, its literature would be determined less by the old ideal of *Humanität* – a respect for the individual cultivated by the German neo-Classicists Lessing, Goethe, Schiller and their contemporaries –, and more by the intellectual, politically and socially radical aspirations which were the by-products of the First World War. A significant concomitant of this process was, as Mann correctly predicted, the subversion of the older humanitarian values and their replacement in the novel by mere parody:

> *Welches war denn aber von jeher das Mittel und Werkzeug aller Zersetzung? Es war der Intellekt. Und welches war immer die Kunstform, in die der Instinktwille zu intellektualistischer Zersetzung sich mit Vorliebe, ja mit Notwendigkeit kleidete? Es war immer die Parodie.*[2]

(And what has always been the means and the instrument of all subversion? It was the intellect. And what has always been the artistic form chosen by preference, indeed by necessity, by the intellect in its desire to subvert? It was always parody).

Although each novel considered in this study shows an individual undergoing an educational process, the old formula of the *Bildungsroman* is modified to such an extent that it would not be inappropriate to speak of a 'subversion' of the tradition. Hesse and Mann provide portraits of talented individuals through intermediaries who, for all their limitations, succeed in giving elaborate accounts of their subject's career, focusing especially on the teaching he receives and its effect on his progress through life. Yet, from the outset, neither Knecht nor Leverkühn stands much chance of integration into their respective societies. As men of artistic temperament, they display signs of hypersensitivity and an extreme single-mindedness. Yet this is not the main obstacle to their development. They inhabit worlds in which lip-service is paid to lofty humanitarian ideals, but where the individual has few if any active democratic rights. These men appear to be emotionally frigid, cold-hearted, arrogant recluses. Incapable of achieving stability in an environment that accords them little scope for self-expression, they come across as tormented, cerebral outsiders whose failure to attain recognition and fulfilment may be taken as implied criticism of the culture which produced them.

Döblin and Grass owe a less obvious debt to this tradition, but pursue their pedagogic aims with equal rigour. Here, too, there is a central individual, Franz Biberkopf and the Author of Grass's narratives, whose activities are examined over a period of one year and a half. The novels may break off with their protagonists still intact, but by the end they have both sustained a defeat. Biberkopf has had to abandon his erstwhile attempts to be integrated into a world which wooed him with the false promise of 'respectability' after his release from prison. As the novel reaches its conclusion, he is exposed to new, more serious dangers, and feels threatened by the sound of marching men pressing forward past him towards their ominous rallies. Neither Döblin nor his readers could have foreseen the full significance of this chilling but, for the moment at least, indecisive conclusion. The novelist's assurance that he was sounding fanfares on behalf of his redeemed character was premature.

The Flounder is another tale of defeat. It investigates the breakdown of the Author's marriage to Ilsebill, recording the final phase in their relationship, from the conception of a child in obviously strained circumstances in the first chapter to an act of adultery on the Baltic sea-coast several months after the child has been born. Although this book also ends openly, with an acceptance of the eternal pull of the feminine, the outlook for the future contains little promise for humankind. The shooting of Jan during the last 'month' and the Flounder's deadly earnest warnings about the perils of rearmament are indications that humanity has yet to learn its lesson from history; much space is given, at the end, to the dissembling guises adopted by violence in our midst, where it lurks skin-deep even in an outwardly tranquil and prosperous world. Billy is murdered close to the spot where Mieze met her death thirty-five years earlier, and we have to conclude that the level of violence latent within society shows no sign of diminishing.

Much has been said about the psychological burdens which the four protagonists must bear. An almost mechanical division between rational man and sensual man, Apolline serenity and Dionysian subservience to pure instinct, appears to characterise their interaction with their environment. There are times when the Anglo-Saxon reader will be reminded of the forced symbolism of *Doctor Jekyll and Mr Hyde* or *The Picture of Dorian Gray*; the struggle to reconcile carnal and spiritual energies is not the least of these novels' concerns, in which the images of the 'twin poles' of existence and the ever-elusive 'bridge' between them recur with some frequency. Grass's Author may serve as an emblem of these divisions: his sexual dependence on Ilsebill and her many substitutes represents one extreme of his personality, which is determined at the other by a frenetically compulsive intellectual inquiry into the labyrinthine course of history. The imbalance between the physical and the ideal is an important structural principle affecting the German novel, and it will be appropriate to reconsider it in the light of the intellectual evolution of the modern nation.

From the period of Weimar Classicism (c. 1800) onwards, many of the German-speaking poets and thinkers gave prolonged consideration to the polarity of human nature, tending to see the world as a battleground where an unending conflict between opposing forces is in progress. This conflict could be observed in every area of human endeavour, from personal morality and interpersonal relationships to the products of the imagination and philosophic constructs. Many examples can be cited; they range from Faust's awareness of his two souls and his ensuing pact with the devil to Kant's distinction between 'pure' and 'practical' Reason, Schiller's theory of 'naive' and 'sentimental' poetry, Schopenhauer's view of the roles of the 'will' and the 'idea' in shaping our world, and Nietzsche's analysis of man's 'Apolline' and 'Dionysian' tendencies. Schematic distinctions of this kind are, it goes without saying, not the prerogative of Germany but common to the intellectual traditions of many nations, deriving as they do from the twin sources of Aristotelian logic and Christian discrimination between the absolutes of good and evil. But an awareness of the 'dualism' of the human condition seems to come across more strongly and more conspicuously in the fiction of Germany, for reasons which it may now be possible to identify. The notion of a Faustian pact with the devil in which noble and base aspirations vie with one another in the human soul has, as we have seen, commended itself to successive generations as an apt symbol of the nation's destiny, however emphatically Goethe and other writers may have warned their compatriots against subscribing to this all-too-narrow model of human behaviour. It proved easier to recall, and to sympathise with, Faust's anguished lament about his two warring souls than to endorse the conciliatory message of the angelic figures who bear his remains aloft at the conclusion of the play.

On a political level, too, German-speaking Europe has been beset by divisions to a greater extent than most other Western states – another factor that will have played its part in validating the dichotomous model. Sectarian strife tore Germany apart in the sixteenth and seventeenth centuries, and, although this has long ceased to be a burning issue, the lasting legacy, enforced by the carnage of a civil war in the eighteenth century, the Seven Years' War, has been a deep sense of mutual distrust between the 'Prussian' North and solidly Catholic areas like the Rhineland and Bavaria. Such sentiments have lingered on well into the twentieth century. The geographical position which Germany occupies in Europe today is partly responsible for perpetuating the construct: located halfway between the rational and pragmatic West and the soulful, mystic East, Germany stands at the crossroads, not only of trade-routes, but also of ideologies. Her postwar division into two differently constituted states can be attributed to inner tensions as well as to strategic planning on the part of the occupying powers. Even today, many of Germany's foremost writers and political commentators continue to express their reservations about the process of unification, and not a few would prefer to see a political endorsement of the separate nationhood of East and West Germany.[3]

Tendencies of this·kind assisted the evolution of a national literature in which man is all too often depicted as being torn apart by a lethal combination of incompatible ideals. From Schiller's Wallenstein and Kleist's Michael Kohlhaas, via the Romantic *Doppelgänger*, down to Hesse's antithetical pair, Narcissus and Goldmund, and Brecht's Good Person of Sezuan, the heroes of German fiction and drama have tended to display irreconcilable ambiguities which may have underlined their fictional origins as well as endowing them with an intriguing air of mystery. The early German film industry exploited this cultural heritage to the full, turning out innumerable fantasy-pieces peopled by schizophrenics and other 'marginal' characters teetering on the borderline between normality and insanity, or robot-like 'doubles' who combined human emotions with mechanically precise actions. Research has shown how strongly the entire modern film industry has been influenced by such paradigmatic works as *The Student of Prague* (1913), *The Golem* (1915), *Homunculus* (1916) and *The Cabinet of Doctor Caligari* (1920).[4]

It is a short step from the literary investigation of the divided or deranged personality to a more general, not infrequently satirical inquiry into the fortunes of a nation conscious of its internal schisms. The reader may be surprised to discover that many such works turn out to be set in an indeterminate limbo rather than to be located in any recognisable province of Germany, but there are good reasons why this should be so. For much of her history, the German-speaking world lacked political cohesion and possessed no cultural centre comparable to Paris or London. To locate a novel with any claim to general representativeness in Cologne or Munich would be to invite criticism on the grounds of a regional bias. Only Döblin, writing before the Second World War, could use Berlin as a recognisable cipher for the entire country. Even there, his characters are the product of a specific environment and their behaviour will perhaps be felt to be as unrepresentative as their idiom is unfamiliar in the southern *Länder*. The later novelists chose their settings with great care, determinedly avoiding the charge of narrow provincialism or local patriotism. Hence the geographically neutral sites of Kaisersaschern – a German city that has affinities with Aachen, Naumburg, Lübeck and other ancient cultural centres – and Castalia, the utopian province, apparently oriented towards the future, while concealing within its confines a wealth of information about the present. Danzig is another elusive, half-real, half-fantastic location in which historians have discerned a 'German microcosm'.[5] No longer accessible, it is vividly evoked and yet unreal at the same time: a fitting foundation for a case history of Germany's bygone and present ills.

In all this, the elements of simplification and satire can be discerned. The imaginary city or province in the manner of Swift's Lilliput or Butler's Erewhon readily lends itself to the indirect criticism of an entire community, as do the reminiscences of legends, myths and folk-tales which are repeatedly worked into each of these novels. The narrator of *Berlin Alexanderplatz* supplies pithy summaries of his narrative at the beginning of each book. Nursery rhymes and biblical extracts punctuate the story as if to illustrate or underscore its didactic import. Hesse uses a ponderously scrupulous chronicler to describe a country dedicated to an imaginary game based, of all things, on the manipulation of glass beads on wires. Mann asks us to believe that a uniquely talented composer of avant-garde music is under the illusion that he has clandestinely concluded a pact with the devil, just as a legendary sorcerer is reputed to have done at the very beginning of the modern age. Grass depicts an omniscient fish who is credited with having influenced the cultural evolution of Europe from the Stone Age to the present day, only to be put on trial for his misdeeds and invited to defend himself. This he does from the safety of a purpose-built, specially reinforced glass tank, in a manner recalling the trials of anarchists that took place in the 1970s. Obsessions reminiscent of *Don Quixote* and *Moby Dick* are treated with an exuberance that serves, in the end, to highlight the authors' biting castigation of human folly. Franz is a plaything of forces he cannot understand, equipped as he is with no more than a flimsy set of opinions cobbled together from news articles and dimly remembered precepts. His desire for respectability is woefully inadequate in a world that is very far from any notion of decency. The game of the glass beads is a pathetic misdirection of human talent, and can in no sense serve as the basis for a utopian society, but only to expose the ills of the present. Adrian's devotion to Esmeralda and his imaginary dialogue with the devil are, for all the sinister fascination they may exert on the observer, mere aberrations on the part of a hypersensitive and increasingly deranged mind, presented in such a way that their laughable qualities are never very far from the surface. The trial of a supposedly supernatural flatfish by a group of disgruntled, confused and badly organised feminists of doubtful morality is another instance of arrogance and folly at their most conspicuously futile.

Playfully unreliable narrators are an inseparable part of this satirical approach. Those who would dismiss them as tedious or pedantic intrusions run the risk of misreading an important stratum of the text. The narrators of *The Glass Bead Game* and *Doctor Faustus* have to appear pedantic because they themselves are the vehicles of their authors' critique: they represent an over-rigid mentality, and seem unequal to the task of accounting for the events they describe. Theirs is the impotence of the individual, however well-intentioned and well-motivated, when it comes to exerting influence on any sphere of public life. Hesse's chronicler and Mann's Zeitblom must capitulate before the magnitude of their labours. Theirs is no wilful rambling evasiveness, but a carefully controlled exercise in which men of great intellect dissipate their energies in situations highly unfavourable to personal self-expression. These two apologetic and confused writers tell us as much as we need to know about the position of the intellectual in a world which regards him as uncomfortable, embarrassing and ultimately redundant. Their cautious, oblique style, their digressions and defensive irony are no less illuminating than the material content of their stories.

The narratives themselves are both simple and complex. They are biographies of four men who combine ordinary human attributes with a towering representativeness. Their origins are always humble: Franz was a cement worker and furniture remover, Knecht may have been an orphan or a cobbler's son, Adrian is of peasant stock, and Grass's author is of Cassubian extraction, related 'via the gooseberry bush' to all the townsfolk and peasants of the area (F 591). Their careers could be summed up in a few sentences. Yet each novelist has gone to surprisingly similar lengths in attempting to portray these men against a background comprising as much of the recorded history of the world as could be accommodated within the text. Döblin's sources range from Genesis to the popular song; Adam and Eve, Abraham and Isaac, Job and Jeremiah, folk wisdom, the medieval religious lyric, the nursery rhyme and the Kellogg Pact all play a part in accompanying Franz on his journey through Berlin. The narrating voice is conscious that his world is the end product of countless centuries of human endeavour.

Hesse, too, goes back to the dawn of history in his 'Rainmaker' biography, and shows us what Knecht might have been had he lived during several remote historical epochs. Only the increasingly unwieldy format of the novel appears to have deterred him from incorporating more material of this type into it. The past is again a vital ingredient of the present. Castalia houses a timeless, futuristic and yet medieval culture. Elements from distant eras mingle with sinister practices from the present in her corridors and quadrangles. Time does not move forward on the linear model, but in 'gyres', looping backwards and repeating itself. As Döblin had intimated when he equated Berlin with Babylon, the deepest recesses of time may merge with an apocalyptic future. Knecht's poems tell of the ruination of Castalia and its hallowed Game. The kaleidoscope of enmeshed cultures is investigated further in *Doctor Faustus*. The city of Kaisersaschern may be noted for its thriving light industry and its importance as a junction of railway lines, but it also preserves some of Germany's oldest manuscripts, early medieval rain-charms of great antiquity. For this reason, it is a cradle of German culture – and also a warning that this culture will end in tragedy. It takes its name from the mortal remains of an Emperor who lived 1,000 years ago and was believed by his contemporaries to be the last head of the Holy Roman Empire. Children's crusades, ominous fanatical sermonising and St Vitus's dances can be imagined in this setting. Adrian's music makes use of medieval subject-matter and strictly impersonal compositional methods, but many of his works point forward to an apocalypse and hint at the ruination of mankind. Like Knecht and Biberkopf, he relives the destinies of many figures from the past: Faustus, Nietzsche and a host of authentic musicians and composers.

It remains difficult to disentangle fact from fantasy in *The Flounder*, where Grass's Author again projects himself into the prehistoric past, from which he moves forward through time in eleven re-enactments of history as it was or as it might have occurred. Human development in the literary, artistic, culinary and sexual spheres is appraised over a period of five millennia. And again there is a hint of Armageddon in the bleak denunciation, by the Flounder, of our insane accumulation of weapons, our unslakable thirst for violent self-assertion. That the prosperous world we have created for ourselves will soon collapse and leave us worse off than ever before is a threat that looms large at many points in the book, not least in the first poem (F 11f.).

This is not the time to reiterate the implications of the interdependent utopian and apocalyptic threads that run through each
of the four novels. It is beyond question that each author has
adopted a historian's perspective, surveying not just his own
epoch, but many others as well. Modern Germany is discerned
against backgrounds as diverse as the Old Testament, the Stone
Age, early Christendom, ancient India, medieval Europe, Impe-
rial China, the Reformation and many others. In these settings, it
becomes easy to lose sight of the individual, a diminutive atom in
a vast cosmos that stretches the creative imagination of the novelist to its limits. But put more positively, the hero emerges from the
chaos of history as a tiny link within the unending chain of existence, as an 'example' drawn from an infinite repertoire: a unique
case and also a reflection of wider issues affecting his country. It is
worth recalling that, from Roman times onwards, Germany was
often viewed by her neighbours as an example of what is best and,
simultaneously, worst in human nature.[6]

The pervasive tendency towards satire and parody in these
novels is not at variance with their authors' documentary concerns. Irony and parody signal a beneficial awareness of the ambivalence of experience and the multiplicity of interpretations that
can be placed on any single event once it has occurred and become
history. Each novelist juggles with quotations and reminiscences
while constructing his narrative. Döblin employs subtly modified
phrases from Goethe, Schiller and Lessing, along with stock exchange reports, to plot the dimensions of Franz's life in Berlin.[7]
His narrator asks teasing questions and offers advice which goes
unheeded. Hesse indulges in light-hearted parody when he sum-
marises a facetious essay on the perils of Feuilletonism and gives a
mock-serious history of the evolution of his Game. The entire
compilation may be seen as a parody of the methodical biography
of some long-deceased celebrity. Hesse is clearly no less sceptical
than Grass about our ability to fill in the gaps in the information
that reaches us from the past. The restrictive circumstances under
which his chronicler is working reveal some of the problems:
personal bias, censorship, adherence to current conventions, inadequate access to the right sources. Mann borrows proper names,
words, syntax and situations from the sixteenth century and
mounts them onto the present: Luther's letters and table-talk
provide the vocabulary for Adrian's confessions about the brothel
experience and other dubious events in his life. The lengths to
which Grass goes in his linguistic experimentation are considerable: he chooses an appropriate style for each era. Dorothea's

devotional lyrics are in a pastiche of Middle High German, Gret takes over the mannerisms of a sixteenth-century Grobianus, the Baroque poets commune via the *jammertalig* ('doom-laden') idiom of the seventeenth century, and in later times the Enlightenment, Romanticism, Naturalism and even the modern film ('Father's Day') yield compositional techniques appropriate to each successive period of history.

There are many other novels which provide insights into the pressures to which Germany was exposed during the tortuous evolution of her cultural identity. From the writings of the authors chosen, it would have been tempting to investigate Döblin's *November 1918* and Grass's Danzig Trilogy as histories of particular epochs.[8] But in terms of the periods covered, the present selection seemed to offer the widest range of subject-matter and the broadest historical perspective. Each of these four novels offers a sustained inspection of the state of the nation and its place within history, and each came from the pen of an author already well established and at the height of his career. Döblin was a man of fifty when he began *Berlin Alexanderplatz*; he never achieved a comparable success with any of his later novels. *The Glass Bead Game* was Hesse's last work, and Mann could speak of *Doctor Faustus* as 'the book of the end',[9] although he went on to complete several shorter works of distinction before his death. The appearance of *The Flounder* coincided with Grass's fiftieth birthday and bears, in common with the other 'fictions' which I have discussed, all the hallmarks of an author determined to take stock at a crucial point in his personal and professional life. To speak of these novels as valedictory would be a simplification – and, in one instance, premature – but it is beyond doubt that they all communicate not merely a private set of opinions or philosophy of life, but a decisive, final warning about the social and political situation as they see it developing in their own time. When Franz Biberkopf refuses, in the end, to march with the crowds who are on their way to some ill-defined partisan gathering, the reader is privy to a display of Döblin's cautionary intentions. It is not so much a question of man's dualism as a straightforward political choice. Here, at any rate, an unambiguous solution is imposed on the novel: a man who, for a long time, was a fellow-traveller of the National Socialists, now changes his mind and opts for a sober detachment from politics. Franz is typical of those people who were attracted to radical doctrines which offered a promise of fixed wages and renewed self-respect; he sees the error of his ways when he realises the folly of aligning oneself with any cause that advocates intolerance and brutality. Any association with men of violent means, he concludes, could cost him his head.

Fourteen years later, Hesse must be more circumspect. But he covertly equates Feuilletonism with Fascism and decries the evil present as 'the warlike century' (GB 386). The example of Josef Knecht shows how easily a man of talent and integrity can find himself dragged into the service of a totalitarian organisation without any viable alternative – and without a chance of surviving, should he refuse to identify himself with its ambitions. Castalia is a model of a state which, while claiming to act in the best interests of the individual, is run on autocratic lines and peopled by petty tyrants and stubborn, hidebound bureaucrats. Unable to condemn the carnage directly, Hesse pinpoints the crucial constituents (high-handed paternalism, feelings of cultural superiority, and the blind following of rules) with great perspicacity, exposing many of the factors which played their part in shaping Germany during the years from 1933 to 1945.

Writing during his exile in America, Thomas Mann enjoyed greater freedom of expression, but also ran the risk of producing something closer to a political pamphlet than an artifact. This danger is in part overcome by the device of the uncomprehending, desperately sincere narrator who adopts the role of the average citizen. The very immediate, physical experience of fear and anger which he evinces while writing his book and simultaneously witnessing the collapse of Germany from his study makes Serenus into no less memorable an indictment of current events than the equation of National Socialism with the temptations of the devil. This juxtaposition was, incidentally, first used by the author's son, Klaus Mann, in his novel *Mephisto* of 1936.[10]

Folding his hands after delivering his report, Serenus prays that peace and sanity may return to his country. Grass indicates that these prayers remain, for the present, unanswered. The nation has rearmed itself to the teeth, and is now equipped for battle with military hardware far in excess of anything deployed in the holocausts of the past. Even in not obviously martial contexts, violence lurks close to the surface, at many outwardly harmless public gatherings and festivities. Marginal figures and outsiders are as vulnerable as ever. The eighth and ninth months of the novel show, in different settings, the short run from the fuse to the powder keg. The wise Flounder finally shakes off his role as chief instigator of all misfortunes, as wished upon him by all those who search for scapegoats behind events to which they were a party, and delivers a desperate plea for peace to his largely indifferent audience. In it, he invites them to adopt a new attitude to history. Instead of searching for culprits and chewing over events that happened in the distant past, they should take account of what is going on right now, in their own world, where women enjoy far greater political influence than they ever knew in the past, at least since the days of prehistoric matriarchy. But they seem frustratingly unable to return the world to its senses by following the example set by their more pacific ancestors. The pursuit of the ideal dishwasher blinds Ilsebill to her responsibilities as a peacemaker; the rape of Billy exposes the female sex to greater exploitation and humiliation than hitherto, and the female politicians merely vie with their male colleagues in a blinkered dedication to warmongering strategies.

It is worth adding that, until recently, the message of fraternal tolerance and pacifism proclaimed in their different ways by each novelist has remained misunderstood. All the literary skills which they display have been marshalled in vain, with the professional literary critics showing themselves to be not much more receptive than the policy-makers. Döblin has been viewed as a cataloguer of meaningless ephemera, Hesse as an innocuous daydreamer who would have us all playing with glass beads in the cloisters of some supposedly utopian Castalia. Mann was vilified with equal vehemence for ignoring the 'other', better Germany and for not speaking out sufficiently strongly or directly against Nazism in particular. Grass has long found himself the target for insults ranging from the label of a gratuitous pornographer to that of an ineffective has-been. For many, he remains no more than the self-indulgent libertine that he appeared to be in 1959. The present volume, written during the years that saw Germany emerge from the unfavourable position which she has occupied among European nations during the twentieth century, will have served its purpose if it succeeds in dispelling premature judgements and fostering a deeper understanding of her novelists as champions of peace, individual freedom and the primacy of personal integrity.

NOTES

1. `Kafka 1954, p. 206; Koch-Hillebrecht, 1977, p. 23ff.
2. Mann, 'Der autobiographische Roman', GW vol. 11, p. 703.
3. It would be futile to attempt a summary of the arguments for and against the division of the country; among many others, see Grass, 1990, and Westphalen, 1990.
4. Kracauer, 1947, and Prawer, 1980.
5. See Chapter 4, n. 10, above.
6. Koch-Hillebrecht, 1977, 157ff; Kolboom, 1991, p. 207.

Select Bibliography

Arnim, Achim von, and Brentano, Clemens, *Des Knaben Wunderhorn. Alte deutsche Lieder*. Munich: Winkler, 1957.

Arnold, Heinz Ludwig, *Alfred Döblin*. Munich: text+kritik, 1972.

——, *Günter Grass*. Munich: text+kritik, 1978.

Arnold, Heinz Ludwig, and Görtz, Franz Josef (eds), *Günter Grass – Dokumente zur politischen Wirkung*. Munich: Boorberg, 1971.

Assmann, Dietrich, *Thomas Manns Roman 'Doktor Faustus' und seine Beziehung zur Faust-Tradition*. Helsinki: Suomaleinen Tiedeakatemia, 1975.

Bebel, August, *Die Frau und der Sozialismus*. Zurich: Volksbuchhandlung, 1879 (numerous reprints).

Becker, Helmut, *Untersuchungen zum epischen Werk Alfred Döblins am Beispiel seines Romans 'Berlin Alexanderplatz'*. Dissertation, Marburg, 1962.

Bergsten, Gunilla, *Thomas Manns Doktor Faustus. Untersuchungen zu den Quellen und zur Struktur des Romans*. Tübingen: Niemeyer, 1974.

Best, Otto F., '"Epischer Roman" und "Dramatischer Roman". Einige Überlegungen zum Frühwerk von Alfred Döblin und Bert Brecht'. *Germanisch-Romanische Monatsschrift* 22 (1972), 281–309.

Bolte, Johannes, and Polívka, Georg, *Anmerkungen zu den Kinder- und Hausmärchen der Brüder Grimm* (1912), reprinted Hildesheim: Olms, 1963.

Boulby, Mark, '"Der vierte Lebenslauf" as a key to "Das Glasperlenspiel"'. *Modern Language Review* 61 (1966), 635–46.

——, *Hermann Hesse. His Mind and Art*. Ithaca, NY: Cornell University Press, 1967.

Brady, Philip, McFarland, Timothy, and White, J. J. (eds), *Günter Grass's Der Butt. Sexual Politics and the Male Myth of History*. Oxford: Clarendon Press, 1990.

Brann, Henry Walter, *Nietzsche und die Frauen*. 1st edn 1933, 2nd edn Bonn: Bouvier, 1978.

Brecht, Bertolt, *The Other Germany*. In: *Schriften zur Politik und Gesellschaft 1919–1956*. Frankfurt: Suhrkamp, 1968, pp. 283–9.

Brode, Hanspeter, 'Musikgeschichte im Roman. Thomas Manns "Doktor Faustus"'. *Jahrbuch der deutschen Schillergesellschaft* 17 (1973), 455–72.

——, *Günter Grass*. Munich: Beck, 1979.

Brown, Calvin S., 'The entomological source of Mann's poisonous butterfly'. *Germanic Review* 37 (1962), 116–20.

Busch, Arnold, *Faust und Faschismus. Th. Manns* Doktor Faustus *und A. Döblins* November 1918 *als exilliterarische Auseinandersetzung mit Deutschland*. Frankfurt: Lang, 1984.

Butler, G. P., 'Grass skirts the issue. A reaction to *Der Butt'*. *Quinquereme* 2 (1979), 23–33.

Cepl-Kaufmann, Gertrude, *Günter Grass. Eine Analyse des Gesamtwerkes unter dem Aspekt von Literatur und Politik*. Kronberg: Scriptor, 1975.

Durrani, Osman, '"Here comes everybody": an appraisal of narrative technique in Günter Grass's *Der Butt'*. *Modern Language Review* 75, (1980), 810–22. Reprinted in: O'Neill, 1987, pp. 175–89.

——, '"Cosmic Laughter", or the importance of being ironical. Reflections on the Narrator of Hermann Hesse's Glasperlenspiel'. *German Life and Letters* 34 (1980/1), 398–408.

——, 'Shen Te, Shui Ta, and *Die drei Sprünge des Wang-lun'*. *Oxford German Studies* 12 (1981), 111–21.

——, 'Hermann Hesse's Castalia: republic of scholars or police state?' *Modern Language Review* 77 (1982), 655–69.

——, 'The tearful teacher. The role of Serenus Zeitblom in Thomas Mann's Doktor Faustus'. *Modern Language Review* 80 (1985), 652–58.

Duytschaever, J., 'Eine Hebbelsatire in Döblins Buch *Berlin Alexanderplatz'*. *Etudes Germaniques* 24 (1969), 536–52.

Eggert, Hartmut, Profitlich, Ulrich, and Scherpe, Klaus R. (eds), *Geschichte als Literatur. Formen und Grenzen der Repräsentation von Vergangenheit*. Stuttgart: Metzler, 1990.

Enright, D. J., 'Aimez-vous Goethe? An enquiry into English attitudes of non-liking towards German literature'. *Encounter*, April 1964, 93–8.

——, 'Casting out demons'. *New York Review of Books*, 3 June 1965, p. 8.

Falk, Walter, 'Der erste moderne deutsche Roman: *Die drei Sprünge des Wang-lun* von Alfred Döblin'. *Zeitschrift für deutsche Philologie* 89 (1970), 510–31.

Fassbinder, Rainer Werner, and Baer, Harry, *Der Film* BERLIN ALEXANDERPLATZ. Frankfurt: Zweitausendeins, 1980.

Fischer, Ernst, 'Doktor Faustus und die deutsche Katastrophe. Eine Auseinandersetzung mit Thomas Mann'. In: Fischer, *Kunst und Menschheit; Essays*. Vienna: Globus, 1949, pp. 37–97.

Flemming, Willi, *Andreas Gryphius. Eine Monographie*. Stuttgart: Kohlhammer, 1965.

Forster, Leonard, 'An unsystematic approach to *Der Butt'*. In: August Obermayer (ed.), *Festschrift for E. W. Herd*. Dunedin: University of Otago, 1980, pp. 55–77.

Freedman, Ralph, *Hermann Hesse. Pilgrim of Crisis. A Biography*. London: Cape, 1979.

Friedrichsmeyer, Erhard, 'The Bertram episode in Hesse's *Glass Bead Game'*. *Germanic Review* 49 (1974), 284–97.

——, 'Hagiography and humour in Hesse's Glasperlenspiel'. In: Adrian Hsia, 1980, pp. 259–67.

Glass, Derek, Rösler, Dietmar, and White, John J. (eds), *Berlin. Literary Images of a City. Eine Großstadt im Spiegel der Literatur*. Berlin: Erich Schmidt, 1989.

Grass, Günter, *The Flounder*, tr. Ralph Manheim. London: Secker and Warburg, 1978.

——, *Deutscher Lastenausgleich. Wider das dumpfe Einheitsgebot. Reden und Aufsätze*. Frankfurt: Luchterhand, 1990.

Greenblatt, Stephen, *Shakespearean Negotiations. The Circulation of Social Energy in Renaissance England*. Berkeley, CA: University of California Press, 1988.

Gruner, Wolf D., 'L'Image de l'Autre: Das Deutschlandbild als zentrales Element der europäischen Dimension der deutschen Frage in Geschichte und Gegenwart'. In: Trautmann, 1991, pp. 29–59.

Haberkamm, Klaus, '"Verspäteter Grimmelshausen aus der Kaschubei. Verspätete Utopie?" Simplicianisches in Grass' *Der Butt'. Simpliciana* 6/7 (1985), 123–38.

Härle, Gerhard, *Männerweiblichkeit. Zur Homosexualität bei Klaus und Thomas Mann*. Frankfurt: Athenäum, 1988.

Harscheidt, M., *Wort, Zahl und Gott bei Günter Grass*. Dissertation, Bonn, 1975.

Hasselbach, Karlheinz, *Thomas Mann. Doktor Faustus. Interpretation*. Munich: Oldenbourg, 1978.

Hatfield, J. T., 'The Faust-books and the synoptic gospels'. *The Open Court* 39 (1925), 464–72.

Henning, Hans (ed.), *Historia von D. Johann Fausten*. Halle/Saale: Verlag Sprache und Literatur, 1953.

Henning, Margit, *Die Ich-Form und ihre Funktion in Thomas Manns 'Doktor Faustus' und in der deutschen Literatur der Gegenwart*. Tübingen: Niemeyer, 1966.

Hollis, Andrew, 'Political ambivalence in Hermann Hesse's "Steppenwolf"'. *Modern Language Review* 73 (1978), 110–18.

Hsia, Adrian, *Hermann Hesse heute*. Bonn: Bouvier, 1980.

Hunt, Irmgard Elsner, *Mütter und Muttermythos in Günter Grass' Roman Der Butt*. Frankfurt: Lang, 1983.

Jacobs, Jürgen, and Krause, Markus, *Der deutsche Bildungsroman. Gattungsgeschichte vom 18. bis zum 20. Jahrhundert*. Munich: Beck, 1989.

Jennings, Anne Liard, *Alfred Döblin's Quest for Spiritual Orientation, with Special Reference to the Novels 'Die drei Sprünge des Wang-lun', 'Berlin Alexanderplatz', and 'Babylonische Wanderung'*. Dissertation, Illinois, 1959.

Kafka, Franz, *Tagebücher 1910–1923*, ed. Max Brod. Frankfurt: Suhrkamp, 1954.

Karasek, Hellmuth, 'Nora – ein Suppenheim'. *Der Spiegel* 38/1977, p. 103f.

Keller, Otto, *Brecht und der moderne Roman. Auseinandersetzungen Brechts mit den Strukturen der Romane Döblins und Kafkas*. Berne: Francke, 1975.

Kerényi, Karl (ed.), *Thomas Mann – Karl Kerényi 'Gespräch in Briefen'*. Zurich: Rhein Verlag, 1960.

Keyser, Erich, *Danzigs Geschichte*. Danzig: Kasemann, 1921.

Klotz, Volker, *Die erzählte Stadt. Ein Sujet als Herausforderung des Romans von Lesage bis Döblin*. Munich: Hanser, 1969.

Koch-Hillebrecht, Manfred, *Das Deutschlandbild. Gegenwart, Geschichte, Psychologie*. Munich: Beck, 1977.

Koester, Rudolf, *Hermann Hesse*. Stuttgart: Metzler, 1975.

Kolboom, Ingo, 'Deutschlandbilder der Franzosen: Der Tod des "Dauerdeutschen"'. In: Trautmann, 1991, pp. 212–43.

Köpke, Wulf, 'Abschied vom Mythos Berlin in *November 1918*'. In: Werner Stauffacher, (ed.), *Internationale Alfred Döblin-Kolloquien 1984–1985*. Berne: Lang, 1988, pp. 247–55.

Kort, Wolfgang, *Alfred Döblin. Das Bild des Menschen in seinen Romanen*. Bonn: Bouvier, 1970.

Koselleck, Reinhart, Lutz, Heinrich, and Rüsen, Jörn (eds), *Formen der Geschichtsschreibung*. Munich: dtv, 1982.

Kracauer, Siegfried, *From Caligari to Hitler. A Psychological History of the German Film*. Princeton, NJ: University Press, 1947.

Kreutzer, Leo, *Alfred Döblin. Sein Werk bis 1933*. Stuttgart: Kohlhammer, 1970.

Kurzke, Hermann, *Thomas Mann. Epoche – Werk – Wirkung*. Munich: Beck, 2nd edn 1991.

Lämmert, Eberhard (ed.), *Erzählforschung: Ein Symposion*. Stuttgart: Metzler, 1982.

Lämmert, Eberhard, Eggert, Hartmut, Hartmann, Karl-Heinz, Hinzmann, Gerhard, Scheunemann, Dietrich, and Wahrenburg, Fritz, *Romantheorie: Dokumentation ihrer Geschichte in Deutschland seit 1880*. Frankfurt: Athenäum, 2nd edn 1984.

Lehnert, H., and Pfeiffer, Peter C., *Thomas Mann's Doctor Faustus. A Novel at the Margin of Modernism*. Columbia, SC: Camden House, 1991.

Leonard, Irène, *Günter Grass*. Edinburgh: Oliver and Boyd, 1974.

Leonhardt, Hans Leo, *Nazi Conquest of Danzig*. Chicago, IL: Chicago University Press, 1942.

Links, Roland, *Alfred Döblin. Leben und Werk*. Berlin: Volk und Wissen, 1965.

——, *Alfred Döblin*. Munich: Beck, 1981.

Loschütz, Gerd (ed.), *Von Buch zu Buch. Günter Grass in der Kritik*. Neuwied: Luchterhand, 1968.

Lukács, Georg, *Deutsche Literatur im Zeitalter des Imperialismus; eine Übersicht ihrer Hauptströmungen*. Berlin: Aufbau, 1947.

McFarland, Timothy, 'The transformation of historical material: The case of Dorothea von Montau'. In: Brady, McFarland and White, 1990, pp. 69–96.

Marienwerder, Johannes, '*Das Leben der seligen Dorothea von Preußen*' (ed. Franz Hipler), *Zeitschrift für die Geschichte und Alterthumskunde Ermlands* 10 (1892), 297–511.

Martini, Fritz, 'Der Bildungsroman. Zur Geschichte des Wortes und der Theorie'. *Deutsche Vierteljahrsschrift für Literaturwissenschaft und Geistesgeschichte* 35 (1961), 44–63.

Mews, Siegfried (ed.), 'The Fisherman and His Wife'. Günter Grass's The Flounder in Critical Perspective. New York: AMS, 1983.
——, 'The 'professorial' Flounder: reflections on Grass's use of literary history'. In: Mews, 1983, pp. 163–78.
Michaelis, Rolf, 'Mit dem Kopf auch den Gaumen aufklären'. Die Zeit, 12 August 1977, p. 30.
Michels, Volker (ed.), Materialien zu Hermann Hesses Das Glasperlenspiel. Erster Band: Texte von Hermann Hesse. Frankfurt: Suhrkamp, 1973.
——, Materialien zu Hermann Hesses Das Glasperlenspiel. Zweiter Band: Texte über Das Glasperlenspiel. Frankfurt: Suhrkamp, 1974.
Mileck, Joseph, Hermann Hesse and his Critics. The Criticism and Bibliography of Half a Century. Chapel Hill, NC: University of North Carolina Press, 1958.
——, Hermann Hesse. Life and Art. Berkeley CA: University of California Press 1978.
——, 'Trends in literary reception: the Hesse boom'. The German Quarterly 15 (1978), 346–54.
Müller-Salget, Klaus, Alfred Döblin. Werk und Entwicklung. Bonn: Bouvier, 2nd edn 1987.
Negus, Kenneth, 'On the death of Joseph Knecht in Hermann Hesse's "Glasperlenspiel"'. Monatshefte 53 (1961), 181–9.
Neuhaus, Volker, Günter Grass. Stuttgart: Metzler, 1st edn 1979, 2nd edn 1993.
Nielsen, Birgit S., 'Adrian Leverkühns Leben als bewußte Imitatio des Dr Faustus'. Orbis Litterarum 20 (1965), 128–58.
Nietzsche, Friedrich, Werke in drei Bänden. Munich: Hanser, 1955.
Norton, Roger C., Hermann Hesse's Futuristic Idealism. 'The Glass Bead Game' and its Predecessors. Berne: Lang, 1973.
O'Neill, Patrick (ed.), Critical Essays on Günter Grass. Boston, MA: Hall, 1987.
Oswald, Victor O., 'Thomas Mann's Doctor Faustus: the enigma of Frau von Tolna'. Germanic Review 23 (1948), 249–53.
Pfeifer, Martin (ed.), Hermann Hesses weltweite Wirkung. Frankfurt: Suhrkamp, 1977.
Phelan, Anthony, 'Rabelais's sister: food, writing, and power'. In: Brady, McFarland and White ,1990, 133–52.
Pickar, Gertrud Bauer, Adventures of a Flounder: Critical Essays on Günter Grass' Der Butt. Munich: Fink, 1982.
Prangel, Matthias, (ed.), Materialien zu Alfred Döblin: Berlin Alexanderplatz. Frankfurt: Suhrkamp, 1975.
——, Alfred Döblin. Stuttgart: Metzler, 1st edn 1973, 2nd edn 1987.
Prawer, Siegbert S., Caligari's Children. The Film as Tale of Terror. Oxford: Oxford University Press, 1980.
Pütz, Peter, Kunst und Künstlerexistenz bei Nietzsche und Thomas Mann. Bonn: Bouvier, 1963.
——, Friedrich Nietzsche. Stuttgart: Metzler, 1975.
Raddatz, Fritz J., '"Wirklicher bin ich in meinen Geschichten": "Der Butt" des Günter Grass – Erste Annäherung'. Merkur 31 (1977), 892–901.

Reddick, John, *The 'Danzig Trilogy' of Günter Grass*. London: Secker and Warburg, 1975.
——, 'Günter Grass's *Der Butt* and the "Vatertag" chapter'. *Oxford German Studies* 14 (1983), 143–58.
Reed, T. J., *Thomas Mann. The Uses of Tradition*. Oxford: Clarendon Press, 1974.
Reid, James H., *'Berlin Alexanderplatz* – a political novel.' *German Life and Letters* 21 (1967/8), 214–23.
Roberts, David, and Thomson, Philip (eds), *The Modern German Historical Novel. Paradigms, Problems, Perspectives*. New York: Berg, 1991.
Röllecke, Heinz, *Der wahre Butt. Die wundersamen Wandlungen des Märchens vom Fischer und seiner Frau*. Düsseldorf: Diederichs, 1978.
Rüsen, Jörn, 'Rhetorik und Ästhetik der Geschichtsschreibung: Leopold von Ranke'. In: Eggert, Profitlich and Scherpe, 1990, p. 1–11.
Schöne, Albrecht, 'Alfred Döblin: *Berlin Alexanderplatz*'. In: Benno von Wiese (ed.), *Der Deutsche Roman vom Barock bis zur Gegenwart. Struktur und Geschichte*, vol. 2. Düsseldorf: Bagel, 1973, pp. 291–325.
Schwimmer, Helmut, *Alfred Döblin. Berlin Alexanderplatz. Interpretation*. Munich: Oldenbourg, 1973.
Seidlin, Oskar, '*Doctor Faustus*: the Hungarian connection'. *The German Quarterly* 56 (1983), 594–607.
Smeed, J. W., *Faust in Literature*. London: Oxford University Press, 1975.
Stenzel, Jürgen, 'Mit Kleister und Schere – Zur Handschrift von "Berlin Alexanderplatz".' In: Arnold, 1972, pp. 39–44.
Stern, J. P., 'A game of utopia'. *German Life and Letters* 34 (1980/1), 94–107.
Suhl, Abraham, 'Anglizismen in Thomas Manns "Doktor Faustus"'. *Monatshefte* 40 (1948), 391–5.
Swales, Martin, *The German Bildungsroman from Wieland to Hesse*. Princeton, NJ: University Press, 1978.
Thomas, Noel L., 'Günter Grass's *Der Butt*: history and the significance of the eighth chapter ('Vatertag')'. *German Life and Letters* 33 (1979/80), 75–86.
Trautmann, Günter (ed.), *Die häßlichen Deutschen? Deutschland im Spiegel der westlichen und östlichen Nachbarn*. Darmstadt: Wissenschaftliche Buchgesellschaft, 1991.
Tudor, J. M., 'Soups and snails and political tales ... Günter Grass and the revisionist debate in "Was Erfurt außerdem bedeutet" and *Der Butt'*. *Oxford German Studies* 17 (1988), 132–50.
Tusken, Lewis W., 'A mixing of metaphors: masculine-feminine interplay in the novels of Hermann Hesse'. *Modern Language Review* 87 (1992), 626–35.
Vaget, Hans Rudolf, 'Kaisersaschern als geistige Lebensform. Zur Konzeption der deutschen Geschichte in Thomas Manns Doktor Faustus'. In: Wolfgang Paulsen (ed.), *Der deutsche Roman und seine historischen und politischen Bedingungen*. Berne: Francke, 1977, pp. 200–35.
Voss, Lieselotte, *Die Entstehung von Thomas Manns Roman 'Doktor Faustus'. Dargestellt anhand von unveröffentlichten Vorarbeiten*. Tübingen: Niemeyer, 1975.

Westphalen, Joseph von, *Von deutscher Bulimie: Diagnose einer Freßgier. Vergebliche Streitschrift gegen die deutsche Einheit.* Munich: Knesebeck und Schuler, 1990.

Weymbergh-Boussart, Monique, *Alfred Döblin. Seine Religiosität in Persönlichkeit und Werk.* Bonn: Bouvier, 1970.

White, J. J., '"Wir hängen nicht vom Gehänge ab": the body as battleground in *Der Butt'*. In: Brady, McFarland and White, 1990, pp. 109–31.

White, I. A. and White, J. J., 'The place of Josef Knecht's *Lebensläufe* within Hermann Hesse's *Das Glasperlenspiel'. Modern Language Review* 81 (1986), 930–43.

Witte, William, 'The literary uses of obscenity'. *German Life and Letters* 28 (1974/5), 360–73.

Ziolkowski, Theodore, *The Novels of Hermann Hesse. A Study in Theme and Structure.* Princeton, NJ: Princeton University Press, 1965.

——, Foreword to: Hermann Hesse, *The Glass Bead Game.* New York: Holt, Rinehart and Winston, 1969.

Index